THE SECURITIES MARKETS

Sidney Robbins

THE SECURITIES MARKETS

OPERATIONS AND ISSUES

The Free Press, New York
Collier-Macmillan Limited, London

To the Special Study,
an adventure in securities planning

Foreword

Professor Robbins' excellent book is most welcome to lawyers, economists, or indeed anyone interested in finance and the securities markets—whether as practitioner or student. Most books in this area provide either a description of the stock market or an analysis of the institutions which affect or regulate it. No one, to my knowledge, has attempted to cover both, and bring out their interrelationships, and finally to provide his personal evaluation. To phrase it another way, most works tend to be either legalistic or economic without recognizing the necessity of tying law and economics together. This is the job he has undertaken so well here.

For this undertaking, Professor Robbins is uniquely equipped. While a Professor of Finance at the Graduate School of Business, Columbia University, he has written widely in economics and corporate finance, including most recently a book on The Financial Manager, of which he is a co-author. At the same time he has acted as a consultant in financial matters and has a firm grasp of practical as well as theoretical implications. All this background was put to use during 1962–63 when he served as Chief Economist of the Special Study of Securities Markets, a massive report submitted to Congress by the Securities and Exchange Commission in 1963. A study of some three thousand pages, its breadth may perhaps be appreciated by a notation of the range of its subject matter: from qualification standards in the securities industry and selling and investment advisory practices, to the distribution of securities, and thence, to a study of the operation of the securities markets (viz. the New York Stock Exchange, the regional exchanges, the "third market," and the over-the-counter market) and the interrelationship of these markets. Professor Robbins' participation in this study was of crucial importance, and the result can perhaps best be illustrated in the comment of the *London Economist*: "Americans who have long admired the quality of investigations conducted by the British Royal Commission may take heart. It can happen here."

It is rare that one university colleague can totally agree with the views and recommendations of another in the same field, particularly when they are fresh and imaginative rather than conventional. As a lawyer and law teacher, I am probably sensitive about Professor Robbins' view that lawyers tend to have occupational limitations in the formulation of long-term programs (see pp. 78–80). Yet I agree wholeheartedly with his opinion that there has been too much dominance of lawyers and legal thinking in the work of the Securities and Exchange Commission. It was for this very reason that while I was chairman in 1961–64, we felt the need for the advice of an experienced economist such as Professor Robbins. The Commission can never afford to be without economic as well as legal counsel. Nor can it limit itself to the flood of ad hoc decisions with which it is faced; long-range planning is essential to its vitality.

At the same time, as a former administrator of an agency— commonly referred to as an ex-bureaucrat—I see difficulties in putting into effect some of the suggestions in Chapter 5 ("Criteria in the Securities Markets"). Perhaps I may be too inhibited by experience with Congressional attitudes and political pressures to accept suggestions which warrant favorable reception. For example, can the SEC be staffed to identify a market decline and to take measures soon enough to check it? Should it share a seat with the Federal Reserve Board and the Treasury, whose economic powers are much broader though by no means omnipotent? Even today (in mid-December, 1965) *The New York Times* reports that "those who have the responsibility for policing the securities markets . . . confess privately to a considerable degree of concern over the recent surge in stock trading and prices, especially in the lower quality stocks. . . . Both are afraid that any public warning might touch off a decline in stock prices that would upset investors, scare businessmen and . . . enrage President Johnson." In the event of a market break the President, groping for "the solution" and believing strongly in action, may be raising the same questions posed by Professor Robbins. For this reason I urge the reader to ponder the suggestions in this provocative and refreshing study.

The securities markets are changing swiftly; it is only recently that the Special Study described the trading of listed securities over the counter as the third market, and there has now developed a so-called fourth market. Furthermore, the question of competition and the application of the antitrust laws, the role of the regional exchanges, and of the institutional investor are all coming to public attention. This book is an ideal base for anyone concerned over their implications for the securities markets of the next decade.

WILLIAM L. CARY

DWIGHT PROFESSOR OF LAW,
COLUMBIA UNIVERSITY

Preface

For some two years, I served as chief economist of the Special Study of Securities Markets of the Securities and Exchange Commission. Whatever other responsibilities were involved, the job entailed certain diplomatic overtones. It required convincing a group of talented but skeptical lawyers that the methods of the economist could make a contribution toward a better understanding of the securities markets and convincing a group of able but equally doubtful economists, statisticians, and financial analysts that the lawyer could be so persuaded. Occupying this unexpected role of diplomat *pro tem*, I learned to appreciate better the need for combining the skills of both professions toward the development of more effective securities markets. Yet, writers in this area, reflecting the bias of training and background, have tended to view their subject through a single rather than a double lens. Accordingly, one of the purposes of this book has been to provide an integrated approach in assessing the problems of the securities markets—although, admittedly, somewhat greater stress has been given to the role of the economist because on this stage he has been kept more consistently in the wings.

In the hurly burly of gathering and verifying new information, evaluating its implications, drawing conclusions, and framing the Special Study's Report which attained gargantuan proportions— a number of ideas were not included because of lack of time to develop them sufficiently, while others were omitted from the published work because they did not receive the support of enough members of the staff. These circumstances seem eminently reasonable to me now, as then, since it is desirable for a public document to reflect a diversified viewpoint in order to provide greater assurance that the proposals submitted are couched in sound terms. On the other hand, a book issued under private aegis does not possess the same implicit suggestion of later governmental action and so its author can afford a more relaxed attitude. What may be considered an error of commission in the public sector could be construed as an error of omission in the private sector. For the reasons mentioned above, some of my ideas regarding the securities markets had fallen by the wayside during the course of the Report's preparation. Another purpose of this book, therefore, was to revive those notions that appeared to justify exposure.

These are crucial and controversial times for the securities markets. Legal challenges have been hurled against the dominance of the New York Stock Exchange in certain areas; special forms of trading have become sufficiently important to be described as the "third" market and, with less justification, the "fourth" market; institutional transactions are causing significant changes in trading procedures; automation is casting long shadows over the various segments of the markets; and the concept of self-regulation is assuming new meanings. Perhaps it was some left-over zeal from my prior association with the Special Study but I also felt the urge to express my views on these critical issues.

The book has one further objective. The recommendations of the Special Study, the Securities Acts Amendments of 1964, the rules of the SEC issued over recent years, and the manifold changes adopted by the self-regulatory agencies have all exerted a major impact on the character of the securities markets. To provide the required analyses and expressions of opinion, it was necessary to describe the operations of the markets in the light of these developments. With this in mind, enough background and introductory material have been furnished to gear the book for possible use as a text for courses in the securities markets.

It has been frequently said that busy men give most generously of their time. Mr. Walter Werner, formerly director, Office of Policy Research, Securities and Exchange Commission, provided ample evidence of this oddity of human relations. His reading and penetrating observations of the manuscript were done with a meticulousness far beyond that customary for this type of review. Dr. Rolf Kaltenborn, then director of research for the American Stock Exchange, also gave generously of his time in commenting on my efforts. Professor J. Fred Weston, of the University of California, Los Angeles, provided warmly appreciated support in encouraging the project and afforded useful critical suggestions. Professor Eugene M. Lerner of New York University and Professor Robert Bartell, Jr. of the University of California, Los Angeles, made numerous helpful comments. My research assistants, Allan Young and Amos Sapir, both doctoral candidates at the Graduate School of Business of Columbia University, performed the various basic research assignments involved in a work of this sort with alacrity and understanding. These acknowledgments reflect my gratitude for and appreciation of the assistance provided but, of course, the usual caveat applies that mine alone is the responsibility for the ideas expressed and whatever errors may exist. I should also like to thank my secretary, Miss Gail Dreier, for her diligence in performing the chores of typing and retyping the manuscript.

Finally, it seems fitting to take this occasion to express my debt to Mr. Milton Cohen, formerly director of the Special Study, and my colleagues on the staff for the incalculable benefits I received from my association with them. The hours of lively discussion and debate with the members of this unusual group and the rare opportunity to acquire information and insights not generally available have helped to formulate the ideas expressed in this book. These memories and associations are not easily forgotten.

SIDNEY ROBBINS

Contents

CHAPTER 1

An Overview of the
Financial Markets

On August 20, 1964, President Johnson put his signature to the Securities Acts Amendments of 1964. This was the first major legislation affecting the capital market since the heyday of the New Deal, three decades previously, when a series of new measures was passed that drastically altered the character of this market. Several weeks later, the First National Bank of Boston, which ranks among the twenty largest banks in the country, performed a bit of financial derring-do by announcing that it had arranged to borrow money through issuance of its own unsecured notes. These notes were patterned after the negotiable commercial paper that the nation's major finance companies issue regularly in the money market. Together, the capital market, concerned primarily with the transfer of longer-term funds, and the money market, where shorter-term funds are traded, constitute the nation's financial markets.

The enactment of a law or the creation of a new type of instrument represents only two of the numerous legal and institutional changes that, over the years, have been grafted into the financial markets to enable them to meet the shifting economic needs of the country. In this process of development, a complex system has been constructed to guide the flow of funds from economic units whose savings exceed their investment requirements to those units that have investment needs beyond their own resources. If there is a flaw in the system so that the costs of operations are excessive or the movement of funds misdirected, the economy of the country is likely to suffer. Accordingly, it is important to identify those problems of the financial markets that could become flaws in the system if they are not adequately resolved beforehand. In view of the intricacies of the financial markets and the peculiarities of the issues underlying the major segments, it is desirable to concentrate on each component separately, but this segregation for purposes of understanding should not obscure the close interrelationships of the various participants.

Essentially, the participants in the financial markets do not change; only their focus of activity changes as they concentrate on, tap the services of, or veer their interests towards either the capital- or money-market segments. The demand for funds may come from individuals, firms or governments for a multiplicity of purposes; and the supply, from other individuals, firms or governments. The transfer may be effected through any one or several financial intermediaries, including commercial banks, insurance companies, securities dealers and brokers, savings institutions, finance companies, and investment companies. As a result of these differences, the money flow may take devious paths. Thus an individual, impressed by the prospects of IBM, may desire to buy shares of the company's stock but have insufficient funds to pay the purchase price in full. He makes up this difference by buying on margin, that is, by borrowing from his broker, who obtains the stock for him through the facilities of the New York Stock Exchange. In this transaction, the individual provides the bulk of the funds transferred; the broker, in the capacity of a commercial banker, furnishes another portion, which he in turn had obtained previously as credit balances left with him by customers. Also, in the capacity of an agent, the broker discovers, through the mechanics of the NYSE, an owner of IBM shares who was willing to sell his shares— possibly because he required the funds. This is the typical involvement of the capital market in the purchase and sale of common stock on the NYSE, with the flow of funds from customers to

broker (by means of credit balances)—to the buying individual—
to the owner of IBM stock through another broker.

Or a large business firm, desiring to expand its plant, may
obtain the funds for this purpose by selling securities through an
investment banker to a number of different institutions, such as
insurance companies and pension funds, as well as individuals.
In order to pay the issuing firm for the securities prior to disposing
of them to the eventual buyers, the investment banker may have
to borrow on short term from a commercial banker, who in turn
had previously obtained funds from a large number of different
depositors. In this case, the flow of funds is from the depositors
to the bank—to the investment banker—to the issuing corporation;
another flow is from the buying individuals and institutions to the
investment banker and back to the bank once more as the loan is
repaid. The magnitude of the flows are not the same, of course,
as portions are absorbed in such forms as compensation to the
investment banker and interest to the bank. In this transaction,
both the capital and money markets are involved, with the corporation seeking long-term funds; and the investment bankers, a
short-term loan to finance the purchase from the corporation.

Then again, a corporation may have gathered together a large
sum of money in anticipation of a dividend payment three weeks
later. In order that the funds should not remain fallow for the
three-week period, it buys commercial paper directly from a finance
company which "tailors" the instruments to meet the maturity
requirements of the corporation. In this typical money-market
transaction, no intermediary is involved and the flow is directly
from the corporation to the finance company, which employs the
funds in its own lending operations.

There are no geographic boundaries to the financial markets.
The money flows may be local, national, or even international.
The markets exist wherever there is trading in the financial instruments employed for the transfer of funds—and that means in the
offices and exchanges, not only in New York, where the markets
are centered, but also throughout the country. Nor can neat lines
be drawn between the money and capital market segments of the
financial markets. Money is fungible, and a corporation that borrows in the capital market may use the funds for short-term pur-

poses while, as we have seen, short-term loans sometimes provide the basis for long-term transactions. Moreover, even though an intermediary may be characteristically associated with one segment more than with the other, it is likely at some time to participate in the movement of both long- and short-term money flows. Nevertheless, in a loose way, the distinction between the two segments of the financial markets exists. Our principal interest is in the major issues currently affecting the capital or securities markets, but as a prelude to this discussion, we will consider briefly the major aspects and activities of the money market.

The Money Market

In Europe, great financial centers historically emerged to meet the requirements of trade. The United States too rose to prominence as an international money market only after it had attained commercial ascendancy. Over the years, the country's money market, highlighted by the clustering of leading institutions in New York, developed its own operating mechanisms, achieved tradition, and learned to adapt to changing circumstances. Thus, prior to the Civil War, the nation's foreign trade was largely conducted through British banks in sterling rather than in dollars. But as the foreign trade of the United States grew and as the commercial banks increased in strength and sophistication, they began to lend their names to bankers' acceptances and to buy these instruments as investments. As a result, the basis was laid for transactions in acceptances as an aspect of money-market operations.

Other phases of the money market declined, however, as the forces that gave rise to their growth faded away. This was the history of the call market, which was once of major importance as substantial funds were shipped into New York to be loaned *on call* for the purpose of financing a rapidly growing volume of securities. Then came the reaction as trading in securities dwindled, as restrictions on loans for the purchase of securities were imposed, and as banks were prohibited from making call loans on the behalf of others. After the New York Stock Exchange discontinued the call-money desk on the floor of the Exchange, what was left of this business was returned to the commercial banks; there it has become a minor portion of their ordinary activities.

Through this ability to withstand the loss of former functions, exploit new situations, and to develop instruments as the need has arisen, the institutions of the money market have remained active and viable; they are, as a result, capable of moving huge volumes of short-term funds over brief periods of time to match the shifting demand-supply needs of corporate and individual participants. Different instruments move through varying channels that are overlapping in scope but distinguishable in character. These instruments and their market mechanisms, representing various segments of the money market, are now described briefly.

TREASURY SECURITIES

For purposes of the money market, treasury securities cover maturities up to one year. They include bonds and notes that fall within this maturity range. The major security of this type is the Treasury bill, which is sold weekly by the Treasury at a discount by means of competitive bidding. Through such bills, the Treasury may borrow at relatively low rates of interest, adjust its operations to current conditions, and influence the reserve position of member banks of the Federal Reserve System by means of open-market operations.

The Treasury has used bills with maturities of three months, six months, and one year; including tax anticipation series with maturities up to about nine months. The Treasury has also employed certificates of indebtedness, with or without coupons, and bearing maturities of not more than one year. At the close of 1964, there were $56.5 billion worth of Treasury bills, but no certificates were outstanding at that time.

Although Treasury bonds are listed on the New York Stock Exchange, virtually all trading in Treasury securities takes place over the counter. The focal point of trading is a group including seven dealer bankers, which trade in all maturities of Government securities, and some fourteen dealer firms, which may also participate in other sectors of the money and capital markets. Because of these overlapping activities, a common thread runs through all segments of the money markets.

COMMERCIAL PAPER

Originating in the early 1800s, commercial paper forms the oldest segment of the money market, although its modern development occurred in the beginning of the twentieth century. In general, the term *commercial paper* refers to the short-term unsecured promissory notes issued by industrial and financial companies, principally as a supplement to bank loans for the purpose of meeting seasonal requirements.

The commercial paper market is not an homogeneous one. Historically it was dominated by leading industrial firms that market their paper through dealers in these instruments. This phase of the market still exists, although the number of industrial firms using it has shrunk considerably. At the same time, their size has grown and therefore the amount of outstanding paper has risen, particularly since the close of World War II. Normally, prime industrial paper is sold today at a discount through a small number of commercial-paper dealers. These dealers also make available the notes of some finance companies. Although there is no secondary market for dealer-marketed paper, buy-back arrangements for finance paper ordinarily may be negotiated through the dealer. At the close of 1964, $2.2 billion worth of commercial- and finance-company paper placed through dealers was outstanding.

The most striking development in this market has been the extraordinary growth in the use of commercial paper issued directly to investors by a small group of giant sales finance companies. Like industrial paper, these unsecured promissory notes generally are issued in bearer form and are sold on a discount basis, although some interest-bearing paper has been used. No secondary market exists, but most companies will repurchase outstanding paper if requested by the buyer. At the end of December, 1964, $6.1 billion worth of directly placed paper was outstanding, almost three times the amount of dealer-placed paper.

BANKERS' ACCEPTANCES

Bankers' acceptances are time drafts drawn on and accepted by a bank. The market in these instruments had its origin in the Federal Reserve Act of 1913, which authorized member banks to create acceptances for different purposes, principally for the import and export of goods. Once the instrument is accepted, the bank substitutes its own credit for that of the drawer, the draft becoming an acceptance, and representing a negotiable money-market instrument. The accepting bank may either elect to hold the instrument or discount it with a bankers' acceptance dealer for subsequent sale to investors. Accordingly there is an active secondary market in this instrument.

While the use of bankers' acceptances diminished rapidly in the depression years of the 1930s and during World War II, it has since had a rapid revival. At the close of 1964, there were $3.4 billion worth of acceptances outstanding, drawn principally to finance the import and export of goods and the foreign and domestic storage of goods prior to shipment. Acceptances drawn for the purpose of dollar exchange represented a much smaller portion of the total. The Federal Reserve System has from time to time participated in the acceptance market for its own account and for the accounts of foreign central banks; its holdings however have been characteristically small.

NEGOTIABLE TIME CERTIFICATES OF DEPOSIT

Negotiable time certificates of deposit, known as CDs, are interest-bearing, negotiable, marketable instruments offered by commercial banks. Their history represents a classic illustration of the role the money market may play in augmenting the financing potential of an enterprise through imparting liquidity to the instruments it issues. Prior to 1961, banks were limited in their ability to attract deposits from large businesses principally because they could not compete with other money-market media for the large volume of short-term corporate funds seeking investment. To the extent banks obtained such funds, they took the form of deposits arising out of loan agreements, and if an institution's service area was limited to a particular region, geographical considerations created further impediments.[1]

In an attempt to tap the national market for short-term funds, a New York City bank in early 1961 arranged for a Government securities dealer to provide a market for its certificates. As other

---

1. Federal Reserve Bank of Chicago, *Business Conditions*, "Trends in Banking and Finance—Negotiable Certificates of Deposit," February, 1963, pp. 6–7.

banks began to issue CDs and other dealers undertook to trade them, liquidity was imparted to the market, and corporations became interested in this form of short-term investment. Once an active secondary market appeared, banks were able to compete for corporate funds in any part of the country by means of CDs, which could be converted to cash at any time, although, of course, the issuing bank's liability remains until maturity.

The most active market occurs in the certificates of the major banks in the country's principal money-market centers. The instruments of the less-known institutions outside these centers also appear in the market but tend to sell at prices that afford higher yields. While the rate paid by the banks is regulated by law, there is no restriction on market prices. Once issued, the effective yield reflects money-market conditions. Since their original issuance in 1961, the volume of outstanding CDs has risen rapidly and by the close of 1964, the weekly reporting member banks in leading cities had $12.6 billion worth outstanding.

In the spring of 1965, there was comment in some quarters that banks may have pushed the CDs too far. The reasons for this reaction stemmed from several factors: the burden imposed by the high rate of interest, particularly in the case of those banks that paid an additional fee to money brokers for finding depositors willing to buy these instruments; the instability introduced into bank finance because there is no assurance that the CDs will be renewed or replaced when they expire; the fact that several of the some thirteen relatively small banks that had been closed in the prior two years had large amounts of CDs outstanding at the time of failure; and the possibility that funds received from CDs might represent money shifted from checking accounts, on which the bank pays no interest. Also, Federal banking regulators began to look more sternly at CDs. The Comptroller of Currency announced that bank examiners would check a bank's over-all operations if 10 per cent or more of its deposits consisted of CDs; the Federal Home Loan Bank Board placed some technical limitations on the ability of savings and loan associations to purchase CDs; and the Federal Deposit Insurance Corporation questioned the applicability of its insurance coverage under circumstances that permitted fees paid to brokers for the placement of CDs to be counted as interest (thereby bringing the total charge above the then prevailing maximum legal limit).

Despite these difficulties, it is probable that the banks will continue to sell CDs aggressively so long as they find it necessary to compete for new money. To help in this effort, they have designed a number of different forms that meet the needs of various groups. Rates and maturities on the CDs issued to corporations, particularly by the big institutions, are often "tailored" to particular requirements while savings and other time certificates may be issued to individuals typically in relatively small denominations and frequently in nonnegotiable form, or even if negotiable, not readily marketable.[2]

BANK COMMERCIAL PAPER

The experience in bank commercial paper is indicative of the receptivity of the money market to new approaches. The First National Bank of Boston, in the fall of 1964, as mentioned previously, announced its intention to issue negotiable promissory notes in order to compete further for the large amount of available corporate funds. As other banks, all located outside New York State, followed suit and several dealers began to trade the instrument, the basis was laid for a full-blown market in commercial-bank negotiable promissory notes. Hampering this development was the reluctance of most banks in New York State to participate because of legal conflicts that had Gilbert and Sullivan overtones.

The basic uncertainty stemmed from a hoary section of the New York State Penal Law declaring it a misdemeanor for a bank to issue any evidence of debt as money. While the proscription hardly seemed applicable to large denomination notes of the type under consideration, the state banking department apparently considered it a barrier on the ground that the notes might be construed to be currency. Regardless of this possibility, the Comptroller of Currency, who regulates the national banks, published a ruling explicitly authorizing these institutions to issue the notes. Without questioning the authority of the Comptroller, the New York State Superintendent of Banks, in turn, raised another legal specter. He cautioned that investors buying the notes might not be able to enforce payment and that the Supreme Court had not yet resolved the question of whether a state could prohibit the issuance of notes

2. Federal Reserve Bank of Chicago, *Business Conditions,* "The Rise of CDs at District Banks," October, 1965, pp. 11–15.

by a national bank through a penal-law provision uniformly applicable to all banks in the state. To eliminate these difficulties, he indicated, however, that the state banking department would sponsor legislation to repeal the restrictive section of the code.[3]

These views restrained the New York institutions from issuing negotiable notes of this type. But in August, 1965, the state banking department made public an opinion to the effect that nonnegotiable, short-term notes are permissible as "acknowledgment of advances." This decision paved the way for the issuance of such notes by the New York banks. But the nonnegotiable limitation did not make the sailing entirely smooth since the president of the Federal Reserve Bank of New York indicated his skepticism regarding the usefulness of bank promissory notes, whether negotiable or nonnegotiable in form. Apparently concerned about the possibility of their widespread adoption, he issued the warning, not so veiled, that, while the Board of Governors for the present considered the notes to be deposits, it may possess the statutory power to redefine deposits to include notes.

Like CDs, short-term unsecured negotiable notes of commercial banks are intended to attract funds but, unlike the certificates, the notes represent borrowings rather than deposits. As such, the notes are not subject to the interest ceilings imposed by the Board of Governors of the Federal Reserve System under Regulation Q; do not fall under reserve requirements; and are not covered by deposit insurance, making them exempt from the assessment of insurance premiums. In view of these advantages, should the New York State Legislature eliminate the legal uncertainty clouding the use of the notes, the banks might rely upon them much more extensively, particularly when tight credit conditions make it difficult to meet customers' borrowing demands. Anticipating such a possibility, the NewYork Federal Reserve Bank obtained permission from the institutions concerned to publish weekly data as soon as the amount outstanding is sufficiently large not to reveal competitive secrets. Some members of the Board of Governors, however, are uneasy about the instrument, and if such an extension of

3. *The Wall Street Journal*, September 3, 1965; *The New York Times*, October 28, 1965.

the market occurs, the Board might reexamine the character of the notes to determine the advisability of applying restrictions against them.

There are still other factors countering any wide expansion of the market in unsecured promissory notes. National banks are limited to issuing an amount equal to capital stock plus 50 per cent of surplus, and even this limit may be overstated in fact, since some banks may want to reserve borrowing capacity for future issuance of long-term subordinated debentures. Also, the Internal Revenue Service has ruled that if funds obtained by means of borrowing are invested in tax-exempt obligations of state or local governments, the interest income of such securities might be subject to the corporate income tax. Therefore, it is believed likely that the banks will employ the notes principally as defensive instruments, using them, for example, when they cannot compete for funds through CDs because of interest ceilings under Regulation Q.[4]

FEDERAL FUNDS

The Federal-funds segment of the money market arose in response to the desires of commercial banks to gain more flexibility in adjusting their reserve positions and to hold excess reserves, a non-earning asset, to a minimum. Originating in New York City during the early twenties, the market dwindled during the subsequent depression years and in the period during and immediately following World War II. After the Federal Reserve–Treasury Accord and the abandonment of pegged rates, the banks became more dependent upon borrowing rather than upon the sale of securities to obtain reserves. For this reason, and because of several technical factors, a revival of the Federal funds market occurred and interest has continued high since that time.[5]

Banks dominate the Federal funds market, although Government securities dealers, corporations, and agencies of foreign banks also participate. There are no dealers maintaining positions;

4. Federal Reserve Bank of Boston, *New England Business Review,* "Short-Term Notes and Banking Competition," December, 1964, pp. 2–7.

5. Board of Governors of the Federal Reserve System, "The Federal Funds Market: A Study by a Federal Reserve Committee," 1959, pp. 1–12; Parker B. Willis, "The Federal Funds Market, Its Origin and Development," The Federal Reserve Bank of Boston, 1964.

the participants either make arrangements directly with each other, are brought together through several Federal-funds brokers, or deal with various banks that perform an *accommodating business* for correspondents. Transactions may take various forms: in a *straight* overnight, unsecured loan, the lender may give a check on its reserve balance in exchange for the borrowing bank's own check payable through the clearing house the next day, as occurs in several cities; or, increasingly, settlement may be arranged by direct debits and credits to the reserve accounts. The loan also may be secured by Government securities maturing within eighteen months and placed in a custody account for the one day until the funds are repaid. In a different type of transaction, securities may be transferred as repurchase agreements or buy-backs. In a re-purchase agreement, the lender makes two simultaneous contracts: one to buy securities for delivery and payment the same day, and the other to sell the same issue for delivery and payment usually the following day. The difference in the price or discount (in the case of Treasury Bills, the usual security in this transaction) repre-sents the interest cost to the borrower of Federal funds.

SHORT-TERM TAX-EXEMPT SECURITIES

Included in the category of short-term tax-exempt securities are principally the temporary and preliminary loan notes of local public housing agencies, tax and bond anticipation notes of states and municipalities, and early maturities of serial bond issues. Obligors have become aware of the advantages of tailoring maturi-ties to the requirements of investors; therefore there is a tendency to hold such issues to maturity. Moreover, while there is a reason-ably good secondary market, it is not big, consisting at full strength of about five large banks and the same number of large dealers.

A SUMMARY VIEW

Principally, the money market consists of these various seg-ments in which short-term instruments are traded to provide the rapid shifts of vast sums of money between lenders and borrowers, buyers and sellers. It also includes the direct, short-term loans made by financial institutions to borrowers to finance current oper-ations, such as carrying inventories and accounts receivable. The desire to use and the willingness to provide funds for brief periods of time reflect current urgencies, and the resulting money flows are not limited by geographic boundaries. Therefore the money market is particularly sensitive to economic and political events throughout the world, and its rate changes may be harbingers of developments in the capital market.

The swiftness with which the influence of passing events is felt in the money market aggravates the need for knowledge in a hurry—for rapid and frequent communications both in negotiating transactions and in keeping abreast of circumstances affecting the markets. Therefore, the locus of the market is a small group of financial intermediaries, serving as dealers and brokers, who endeavor to bring the participants together and to balance the demand and supply of funds. Through their knowledge of the play of forces affecting money-flows, they provide a steadying influence that permits a greater continuity in prices and rates than would otherwise be the case.

Also playing an important role in the money market is the Federal Reserve System. Through its powers to change (within designated limits) the legal reserve requirements of member banks, to adjust rediscount rates, and to effect open-market operations, the Federal Reserve exerts a major influence on the volume of bank reserves and therefore on money-market rates. Indicative of this influence, the system kept interest rates low during the war period of the 1940s by accepting Government bonds offered to it at par; in the decade of the 1950s, the system adopted an active monetary policy, supplying reserves to the member banks through open-market operations in the recessions of 1953–1954 and 1957–1958, thereby driving interest rates to low levels, and reversing this policy during the years of high business activity; in the early 1960s, a new program was adopted, designed to hold up short-term rates because of an unfavorable balance of international payments but to nudge down long-term rates to encourage economic growth. Through its debt-management policies, the Treasury also plays a part in controlling the level and, more particularly, the structure of interest rates.

The money market is the handmaiden of trade; as different regions of the United States have grown, local money-market centers have developed. Nevertheless, the primary market is in New York, where the confrontation of experts reduces risks, the external economies of size permit the rendering of special services, an unusually efficient market mechanism facilitates the easy movement of paper, and tradition creates a strong protective barrier. These are powerful influences that appear likely to permit the New York money market to maintain its ascendancy in channeling the flow of short-term funds throughout the country and world.

The Capital Market

Like the precise moment when a plain woman becomes pretty, the precise point at which the money market blends into the capital market is difficult to determine. Nevertheless a distinction can be made. By and large, the capital market is the market where bonds, stocks, and mortgages—instruments that stay outstanding for relatively long periods of time—are issued and often traded. The capital market has its own operating mechanism, in which a highly specialized organization such as the New York Stock Exchange occupies a pivotal role, and the market is subject to the regulation of specialized agencies such as the Securities and Exchange Commission. At the same time, as has been mentioned previously, the flow of money cannot be fenced in, and considerable overlaps occur. Thus the same dealer that makes a market in short-term, money-market instruments may also handle long-term bonds and stocks, while the major intermediary in the Federal-funds market may also be a member of the New York Stock Exchange. Our concern now, however, is not with the coincidences but with the distinctive features of the capital market. For this purpose, the discussion will be divided into two parts: the new-issue market and the trading market.

THE NEW-ISSUE MARKET

In the new-issue segment of the capital market, those who require funds obtain them directly or indirectly from investors who have savings that they are willing to commit for long periods of time. The seekers of funds include the Federal government, local governments, Federal agencies, foreign governments, and business firms. Among the investors are banks, insurance companies, investment companies, pension funds, corporations, and individuals. The flow of funds may be arranged through investment bankers or may be effected directly.

Investment Bankers—On February 1, 1963, the Communications Satellite Corporation (Comsat) was incorporated under the laws of the District of Columbia as authorized by the Communications Satellite Act of 1962. According to its prospectus, the Corporation plans to establish and operate a global communications satellite system in cooperation with telecommunications entities in other countries. Because of the national interests at stake and the necessary involvement of terminal stations in foreign countries, the Corporation functions under a statute that provides a comprehensive plan for the conduct of its business. Not only was it created under Federal supervision, but the principle underlying the distribution of its shares, as set forth in the Act, required among other things that up to half the number of shares of common stock would be owned by United States communications carriers. The other half was sold to the public through an intricate network of underwriters who agreed to a purchase contract under which they were required to use their best efforts to offer the common stock so as to encourage the widest distribution of shares to the American public.

Unique in conception, Comsat provides a model example of a major underwriting distribution. In June, 1964, some 400 investment bankers bought 5,000,000 shares of stock from the Corporation at a price of $19.20 per share and offered them to the public at a price of $20.00 per share, keeping the 80-cents differential as payment for their services. The Corporation thus received $96,000,000 less $650,000 of expenses that it incurred; the underwriting discount of $4,000,000 was the price required to free the Corporation from any responsibility of distributing the shares and to make certain that it would receive the sum desired regardless of the vicissitudes of the market.[6] Of the underwriters, eleven purchased 100,000 shares each and served in the capacity of representatives for the entire group. The amounts acquired thereafter ranged downward to 3,500 shares, an amount that was bought by some ninety underwriters.

---

6. The Corporation also sold 5,000,000 shares, Series II, at $20 per share to 163 communications "common-carrier" companies.

The fee, set at 4 per cent of the offering price, was relatively modest, reflecting the mild risks borne by the underwriters. Indeed, interest in the offering was so keen that the allotments were restricted to not more than fifty shares for each individual, and many buyers found that they could not even obtain this amount. Further to insure a wide distribution, the underwriters were permitted to make sales to certain dealers at a concession of not more than 50 cents per share.

The offering was quickly sold out, and the stock rose to a sharp premium. The method of distribution illustrates the traditional use of investment bankers to underwrite the risks of an offering, to arrange for a huge financing with great efficiency, and to effect swiftly a wide distribution of shares. At the same time, the offering brought to light the nucleus of a problem that is causing some disaffection in the investment-banking fraternity. At least six of the firms in the original underwriting dropped out because of dissatisfaction with the amounts of shares assigned to them; included in this group were two major organizations. The dispute highlighted the growing desire of securities firms with national-branch systems to play an enlarged underwriting role in which they would have more direct dealings with corporate issuers, rather than serving only as members of a distribution system and receiving their shares from other underwriting specialists.[7]

Negotiation vs. Competition—The traditional method of financing non-government issues is through negotiation. The corporation interested in raising funds "shops around" among investment bankers in order to find the one that he believes will provide the best advice, handle the offering most efficiently, and charge the smallest fee. The route travelled is not the same in each case. Over its full course, however, the investment banker will serve the issuer in many different ways. At the very outset, he may advise on the need for funds, the amount that can be raised, and the desirability of obtaining a wide distribution of securities or of catering to any special group. Once the type of transaction is decided, the investment banker may offer help in determining the securities to be employed; for debt issues, he will provide recommendations on such factors as sinking fund, coupon, call price, collateral, conversion

---

7. *The Wall Street Journal,* September 14, 1964.

terms, and restrictive covenants; for common stock, he will make suggestions regarding par value, degree of underpricing, and number of shares to be issued. Also the investment banker may evaluate the costs of the different types of securities and their effect on the issuer's capital structure. He may help prepare the prospectus, the registration statement, and supporting documents, and insure compliance with the numerous rules of the applicable regulatory authorities. Finally he will gauge the market's receptivity to the offering and endeavor to time the actual issuance to obtain a swift sale at the best possible price. Expert advice on this phase could make considerable difference in the costs of the financing to the issuer. Thus, had the Ford Foundation delayed its original distribution of Ford Motor stock by only a few weeks, it might have obtained $10 a share less. When Tidewater Oil discovered that it would have to pay ¼ of 1 per cent more than was expected for a contemplated issue of $50 million in bonds, it called off the sale and substituted a five-year term bank loan.

It is the hope of the investment banker that the issuer will travel the full route and make use of all his services. The corporate management may already have made up its mind about some part, however, and rely upon the investment banker for only certain aspects of the transaction. The investment banker will obtain whatever business is available and in the end may assume the role of manager, co-manager, or participant in the underwriting group with or without a selling position. He may earn a fee for assistance rendered on certain phases. Or he may find that a competitor has obtained the entire deal.

Over the years, issuers have found that certain investment bankers serve their interests effectively and therefore they tend to direct their business to the same bankers. In the early 1950s, the Government used this *traditional banker* concept as a major point in its contention that a small group of investment bankers had entered into a conspiracy to monopolize the securities business of the United States. But the Court's decision held otherwise. Judge Harold Medina pointed out that it would be a waste of time for one banker to go through the elaborate preparation and studies incident to competing for the business of an issuer who already had long, continuous, and satisfactory relations with another banker. As a result, it is not uncommon to find comparatively close relationships in the field. Thus Morgan Stanley ordinarily handles the financings of U.S. Steel and General Motors, and Lehman Brothers is associated with Allied Stores and Federated Department Stores.

The issuer may feel that he is sufficiently knowledgeable in the ways of the capital market to undertake much of the preliminary work by himself. Accordingly he may prefer to open his financing to public bidding. For this purpose, he invites interested groups to submit sealed bids, which are opened at an appointed time, with the award going to the highest bidder, unless the issuer believes that none of the prices is adequate. The bidding may be keen for large attractive issues, rival managers forming competing syndicates. The prices submitted may be determined on the morning the bids are opened in order to evaluate fully prevailing market conditions, and the differences in offers may amount to only a few cents per unit.

From the point of view of corporate management, the major advantage of competitive bidding is the higher price that is likely to be received for the securities. Against this important benefit must be weighed the inability of obtaining the continuing counsel of a competent investment banker, whose experience and background could be of inestimable value in planning and bringing to fruition a major financing. Also, the competitive bidding process creates rigidities that are not suited to handling special situations, the junior securities of established corporations, and the senior obligations of enterprises with slim earnings. Difficulty also may be experienced in marketing very large or very small issues by means of competitive bidding. As a result, the practice has received its greatest acceptance in the sale of prime bonds, which can be regarded as a standard commodity where quality does not influence price variations and where both the advance preparation and marketing processes are likely to be less difficult. Thus for a number of years competitive bidding has been widely used for the distribution of state and local bonds, and a growing number of state public service commissions require competitive bidding in the sale of securities under their jurisdiction.

In early 1963, the Treasury extended competitive bidding to the field of Federal financing by offering two different issues of bonds at auction, but it is still questionable how much continuing use will be made of this method. The Securities and Exchange

Commission with respect to securities of corporations subject to the Public Utility Holding Company Act, and the Interstate Commerce Commission with respect to equipment trust obligations at first and later all bonds issued under Section 20a of the Interstate Commerce Act, require competitive bidding. While this form of bidding probably will continue to grow in importance in the distribution of high-grade bonds, the practice is not likely to be extended to the marketing of stocks and of secondary issues in the capital markets, where flexibility is important and the judgment of the investment banker particularly valuable. Neither has it proved very popular for the offerings of industrial companies.

Other Forms of Financing—A corporation seeking long-term funds has many alternative paths other than that to a negotiated or competitive bid offering. The corporation may undertake a direct placement with a buyer or group of buyers; it may make a direct offering to its present security holders; it may seek a term loan from a bank, enter into a leasing arrangement, or obtain a loan from a mortgage company.

Recognizing the scope of opportunities available to the corporation and the need for adapting its own arrangements to this broadened and more amorphous capital-market structure, the investment banker engages in different types of transactions. For a fee, he will provide advice or serve as middleman in effecting a private placement of securities, generally to a single institutional purchaser or a small group of such purchasers. In the case of a rights offering to existing stockholders, the investment banker agrees to stand by and assume whatever part of the issue that remains unsold after the rights expire. When serving in this role, he charges a fee which may, at a minimum, assume that the entire issue is subscribed, or at a maximum that nothing will be subscribed. Also, the investment banker may seek to broaden his activities both in the buying and selling fields, and to find special avenues for investment by the firm. He may serve in other areas of the capital market, for example as a dealer making a continuing market in securities, or as a broker buying and selling securities on a commission basis.

The discussion of the investment banker, principally associated with the primary markets for securities, has led us to the trading markets, where the securities that have already been issued are bought and sold. This transition highlights once more the difficulty of drawing fences around any one segment of the financial markets. Whatever distinctions are made, it is likely that participants will overlap in their activities. Rules designed to cope with one phase of the market will have to be amended because of their implications to another. For example, investment bankers, because of their important advisory functions, are not uncommonly given seats on the boards of directors of the companies with which they have some affiliation. As a member of a board, the investment banker is subject to the insider provisions of the Securities Exchange Act of 1934 with respect to issuers whose securities are listed on a national securities exchange. Formerly he was exempt from these requirements if the securities were not registered for listing. The Securities Acts Amendments of 1964 eliminated this distinction for unlisted securities of corporations whose size brought them within the jurisdiction of the 1964 act. Many bankers, however, made continuing markets in these securities and the insider provisions governing recapture of short-term profits and the proscription against short selling would have interfered with their market-making activities. Therefore, the 1964 act incorporated an exemption from these insider trading restrictions for transactions in stocks by an over-the-counter dealer in the ordinary course of business and incident to the establishment or maintenance of a continuing market in the stock. It is clear that a major problem in developing regulations governing one phase of the financial markets is the difficulty of anticipating their eventual repercussions upon other phases; truly they are integrated rather than separated markets.

THE TRADING MARKETS

Once a security has been issued, it is bought and sold in the trading markets. From the broadest and perhaps the most direct point of view, these may be divided into the organized markets and the over-the-counter market. The organized markets consist of stock exchanges. Each of these exchanges has specific locations where trading takes place, a formal administrative structure, prescribed rules of procedure, a definite body of membership, and facilities for providing various related functions to its members, such as stock quotation services. There are fourteen stock exchanges registered with the Securities and Exchange Commission; three are exempt because of the local character of their trading. Of the fourteen exchanges, the dominant one is the New York Stock Exchange (NYSE), which in 1964 had $60.4 billion worth of transactions in stocks, representing 83.8 per cent of the total dollar volume on the exchanges.

Separated from the NYSE by a few city blocks and a churchyard is the American Stock Exchange (Amex), which in 1964 reported 8.2 per cent of all dollar volume, an amount that was small compared with the NYSE but large relative to the other exchanges. Of the remaining exchanges, three, the Midwest, Pacific Coast, and Philadelphia-Baltimore-Washington, accounted for 6.8 per cent of the dollar volume of all trading in 1964. The rest of the registered exchanges produced only 1.2 per cent.

All purchases and sales outside of the stock exchanges take place in the over-the-counter market, which is not defined by any geographic barriers or central marketplace. Here transactions are consummated through the facilities of a large number of broker-dealers interconnected by an intricate network of private wires and telephone lines. These broker-dealers may be members of an exchange, although most are not. Their o-t-c dealings are subject to the rules of the National Association of Securities Dealers, Inc. (NASD). Of some 5,000 active broker-dealers registered with the SEC, the great bulk are members of NASD, the only self-regulated national securities association registered under the 1938 Maloney Amendment (which added Section 15A to the Securities Exchange Act of 1934). Unlike the exchanges, membership in the NASD is open to all qualified persons and, to encourage joining, the Act provides that only members may receive discounts. This is a powerful inducement, since without a discount the broker-dealer would have to pay the same price as the public.

The primary purpose of the NASD is to regulate the over-the-counter market, a job that is complicated by the heterogeneous nature of this market. But in contrast to the exchanges, the NASD does not operate a marketplace nor provide any related facilities except for its role in the dissemination and sponsorship of retail quotations. The 1964 Amendments of the Securities Exchange Act require a registered securities association to provide appropriate standards with respect to the training, experience, and other qualifications of members. The SEC itself is authorized to provide such standards for registered brokers and dealers that are non-members of a national securities association.

Trading Methods in the Stock Exchanges—Because of the importance of the NYSE, the following description of trading methods is largely confined to that exchange, although these methods typify those on the other exchanges (except for the specialist doubling as odd-lot dealer and the differences in handling dually traded stocks). In a typical transaction, an individual gives an order to an employee in the branch or correspondent office of a member firm, from where it is transmitted by wire or telephone to the firm in New York and then by direct telephone or teletype to its receiving clerk on the floor of the NYSE. To speed transactions some firms have orders transmitted directly from the originating office to the floor of the NYSE.

The receiving clerk summons the firm's floor broker, who takes the order and goes to the post where the stock is traded. There are eighteen posts on the floor of the NYSE, each with about seventy-five stocks assigned to it, plus a nineteenth, known as *Post 30,* which has about 200 inactive stocks assigned to it. If the order is limited to a particular price, the floor broker will give it to the specialist for entry in his book and subsequent execution when the indicated price is reached. If it is a market order, the broker has the responsibility of obtaining the best possible price for his customer. He glances at a price indicator on the outside of the post, operated by a reporter who is an employee of the Exchange, and notes whether the price is above, below, or at the same level as the last sale.[8] This information provides him with the basis to start bidding.

The crux of the method of trading stock on the Exchange is the bidding, which is generally referred to as a *continuous auction.* This means that securities are sold to the broker bidding the highest price, bought from the broker offering the lowest price, and that this two-way auctioning process is regularly taking place. Thus sellers are continuously competing with each other to sell their customers' securities (thereby creating pressure towards lowering the asking price) and bidders are constantly competing

---

8. It is expected that the form and arrangement of the posts will be changed when the NYSE moves into its new building.

.nares. In order to permit the continuous auction market to function efficiently, there must be a minimum of delays and uncertainties. Therefore the Exchange has developed a number of technical operating rules including those that govern the assignment of transactions when bids or offers are submitted at the same levels. Moreover, to reduce uncertainties regarding the character of the companies whose shares are traded and to help insure the existence of trading interest, listing requirements are established that provide standards of company size, earnings, and shares distribution.

In stock exchanges where activity is insufficient to support continuous auction trading, a call market has existed. Such a market, for example, prevailed during the early years of the New York Stock Exchange and exists today in countries such as Israel, where trading markets are still in the developmental stage. In a call market, the name of each security is *called* at a particular time, and the prices are established through auction bidding and offering that will match existing orders. In this manner successive calls are made, and trading in each stock occurs at that time.

The floor broker, having competed in the auction market, either obtains or sells the security for his customer, as the case may be, exchanges identities with the broker on the other side of the transaction, reports the information to his clerk, who in turn notifies the central office, possibly by means of automatic equipment that relays duplicate reports to the originating office. At each of the posts, reporters are stationed. In accordance with the traditional method, conducted for a number of years, the transaction was recorded on a slip of paper and given to a carrier page who forwarded it via pneumatic tubes to the stock exchange ticker room, where it was transmitted to tickers throughout the country by means of mechanical equipment. Quotations, in turn, were phoned by a clerk at each trading post to the Exchange's Telephone Quotations Service, where member inquiries were handled by private telephone lines.

Indicative of the impact of automation on the Exchange's operations, these methods, efficient though they were in precomputer years, are being replaced by more modern techniques that make use of the computer. The new system operates as follows: The reporter at the trading post has special cards on which he can record the details of each transaction by merely drawing lines through boxes designating stock symbol, number of shares, price, and bid-ask quotation. The marked cards are placed into an electronic *data reader* that scans the pencil marks optically and transmits the information to the data-processing center in the Exchange building. At the center, the information is checked automatically for validity and processed through an IBM receiving and transmitting unit, a processor, and a drum storage unit. Duplicate computers insure continuous operation in the event of technical failure in one unit.

Quotations are also handled by such electronic data-processing equipment. In the latest development, subscribers to the Exchange's Telephone Quotation Service can interrogate the computer center over their private wires by dialing four-digit codes for any of the 1,600 listed stocks. Within a few seconds, the computer identifies the stock, locates the latest information, assembles the response from a recording drum vocabulary of 126 words, and transmits the required information to the inquirers. When the basic four-digit code is dialed, the subscriber obtains the stock's current bid, ask, and the price of the last sale; by adding three to the first letter of the code, he can also obtain the opening price, high, low, last price, and the volume.

Special high-speed access equipment links the computing center with 1,000 direct private telephone lines capable of handling calls from 300 member subscribers at one time, and provides voice responses to 400,000 phone inquiries a day. According to the program, computer-assembled announcements and all round-lot prices for stocks traded there are broadcast at each post over loudspeakers to odd-lot dealers and are recorded on special printers. Floor inquiry stations are also stationed at each post to provide printed responses to requests for information on volume, prices, quotations, and ranges. Finally, transactions are transmitted in the form of telegraphic signals to activate the tickers. The new tickers operate at variable speeds (to keep pace with the trading) up to 900 characters a minute compared with a single speed of 500 characters for the former unit and are designed to handle, depending on trading patterns, up to 10 million shares a day.

..ice movements cur-
..ue delays in executing
orders were eliminated. The prevalence of a calmer atmosphere
is likely to modify the disturbance to investor psychology that
confusion in handling transactions tends to breed during days of
high activity and rapid price changes.

Reflecting the fact that it operates one of the largest computer
service centers in the world, the NYSE announced, in November
1965, the formation of an Electronic Systems Center. Included
within the scope of its operations are the Market Data System
described above, the Central Certificate System which is expected
to eliminate as much as 75 per cent of the physical delivery and
processing of stock certificates between clearing members, and
the Central Computer Accounting Corporation to provide a
comprehensive brokerage accounting service to all member organizations desiring to employ its services. Additionally, the new
department also provides systems design, programming and related data systems services to the various Exchange departments
and member firms. These computerized processes and arrangements have been described in some detail because the introduction
of automation into the Exchange's operations represents a major
breakthrough and, as will be discussed later, has important implications to the trading markets that go beyond the efficient recording and transmission of information.

There follows a discussion of classes of Exchange members
that play different roles in the consummation of transactions:

THE SPECIALIST.   Of principal importance is the specialist, who
is assigned a number of stocks traded at the post where he is
stationed and who conducts business both as a broker and a
dealer. The specialist is registered with the exchange of which he
is a member, and stock assignments are made by the exchange.
As a broker, the specialist receives orders that the floor broker
is not in a position to execute at the moment, either because he is
busy at other posts or because the order was placed at a limit

away from the prevailing price. The specialist records the limit orders in his book for subsequent execution when the market reaches the price specified in the order. As a dealer, the specialist is responsible for buying and selling for his own account in order to maintain a "fair and orderly market." In September, 1961, out of 1,366 members, there were 351 specialists registered on the NYSE, organized into 114 units or firms of between one and nine specialists each; on the Amex, out of 597 members, there were 160 specialists organized into fifty-six units.

Because of their importance and the potential conflict inherent in their dual functions as brokers and dealers, the specialists have been under the close scrutiny of the exchanges to insure that they properly fulfill their responsibilities. In 1964, the SEC adopted a new rule, discussed later, designed to provide a framework of regulation for specialists, under which the exchanges perform the maximum degree of direct regulation and the Commission serves as active overseer. The rule is applicable to the NYSE and the Amex, both of which modified, expanded, and adopted new rules governing the activity of specialists.

THE TWO-DOLLAR BROKER.   These are independent brokers or firms that serve commission houses having no members on the Exchange floor, or provide assistance to commission houses in handling orders when their own floor brokers have more business than they can handle. For his services, the two-dollar broker receives a minimum fee which is part of the total commission paid by the investor. The two-dollar broker is not limited to trading at any particular post, may serve as agent for commission firms with no floor partners, and in recent years has in some instances specialized in the handling of larger orders that might engage an undue amount of time by the floor broker of the commission house.

THE FLOOR TRADER.   The floor trader, also an independent participant, buys and sells for his own benefit. He does not execute orders for the public nor does he have any responsibility for maintaining fair and orderly markets. Floor traders may engage in this activity on a full-time basis or they may be floor members, who buy and sell for their own accounts when their other activities do not engage their full time. In order to ascertain that a floor trader does not take undue advantage of his position on the floor

THE ODD-LOT BROKER AND DEALER.   To facilitate its functioning, the major exchanges have provided standard quantities of trading, known as round lots. Except for certain inactive stocks, the unit
of trading on the NYSE is 100 shares, and transactions in smaller
amounts are termed odd lots. Two member firms of the Exchange,
Carlisle & Jacquelin and DeCoppet & Doremus, handle about
99 per cent of the odd-lot volume of trading. These two firms
retain the services of a large number of associate brokers who
execute odd-lot orders and also trade round lots to offset the
long- or short-positions acquired in the course of their odd-lot
trading. For their services the odd-lot dealers do not receive any
portion of the commission paid to the brokers with whom the
odd-lot customers do business. Instead, the odd-lot dealers receive
a premium, expressed as a differential added (in the case of a
purchase) or subtracted (in the case of a sale) from the price of
the next round-lot transaction. The differential for 100-share-unit
stocks is ⅛ of a point for stocks priced at less than 40, and ¼
of a point for issues selling at 40 or more.

THE BOND BROKER.   Bond trading occurs in a separate section
of the trading floor. This room is small compared with the large
area where stock trading occurs because of the relatively modest
volume of bond transactions on the Exchange. In the bond room,
there is an active section where securities are traded by auction
bidding, and an inactive post where trading is done by the *cabinet*
method (as in the case of inactive stocks). In this method, bids
and offers are filed in cabinets on the basis of their levels, and
sales are consummated as these bids and offers are matched by
incoming orders to sell or buy.

Trading in the Over-the-Counter Market—There is no specific
center to the over-the-counter market. Trading takes place throughout the country wherever participants can communicate with each
other. Buying and selling revolve around the wholesale dealer,

who *makes a market* by advertising his willingness to buy or sell securities for his own account. Unlike the stock exchanges, where one specialist generally makes a market for a stock, in the over-the-counter market a score of wholesale dealers may compete with each other in a particular stock, or there may be no wholesaler interested in the issue.

A wholesaler ordinarily is closely connected only dealing in transacting with a public buyer or seller; in effect he serves as a conduit through which orders flow between broker-dealers whose customers are on one side of a transaction and those whose customers are on the other side. Without having any legal responsibilities to do so, the wholesale dealer also may add marketability to a security by assuming the risk of taking long or short positions. It is commonplace to call the over-the-counter market negotiated. In many instances a retailer receiving an order will shop among various firms to get the best possible price for his customer. Indeed some commission houses require their traders to check at least several sources. Yet retailers generally execute standard-size transactions at the bid or offer of the wholesale dealer, who adjusts his quotations to attract trades and ordinarily does not initiate transactions at another dealer's quotations.

An integrated firm engages in both wholesale and retail activities. The accumulation or disposal of inventories in such a firm is likely to flow from the activities of its retail department. Also, in so-called *riskless* transactions, broker-dealers who are neither primary market-makers nor have inventory positions, execute customers' orders through buying or selling, as the case may be, from other broker-dealers, and conducting reverse transactions with their customers on a net basis. Since there is no central marketplace nor auction trading, interdealer quotations in the over-the-counter market, ordinarily recorded in sheets operated by private organizations, do not necessarily reflect firm commitments to buy or sell.

Between 1935 and 1961, it is estimated that over-the-counter sales of corporate stocks rose from $2.1 billion to $38.9 billion representing 14 per cent and 61 per cent respectively of sales on all exchanges. The Securities Acts Amendments of 1964 extended to over-the-counter corporations, meeting minimum standards of size, the periodic-reporting, proxy-solicitation, and insider-trading may be retarded compared with that of the stock exchanges.

The Economic Basis
of the
Securities Markets

In a running dialogue on the securities markets that occurred among academic writers in 1964 and early 1965, the assertion was made that "the paramount goal of the regulations in the securities markets is to protect the innocent . . . investor."[1] Without doubt, such legislation is concerned with the protection of the investor, but the preoccupation with this objective obscures the other major purposes of the regulatory mechanism and in this instance is probably reflected in the skeptical views expressed by one of the participants regarding the value of regulation. These other aims, as discussed later, are at least in part contained in the coordinate

1. George J. Stigler, "Public Regulation of the Securities Markets," *The Journal of Business of the University of Chicago,* April, 1964, pp. 117–142. This article stimulated a series of responses, including: Irwin Friend and Edward F. Herman, "The SEC Through a Glass Darkly," and Sidney M. Robbins and Walter Werner, "Professor Stigler Revisited," *The Journal of Business of the University of Chicago,* October, 1964, pp. 382–403 and 406–413. There was also a "Comment" by Stigler, October, 1964, and "A Further Comment" by Friend, January, 1965. See also Richard C. Henshaw, Jr., Alden C. Olson, and John L. O'Donnell, "The Case for Public Regulation of the Securities Markets," *Business Topics,* Autumn 1964, Michigan State University, pp. 69–77.

objective of public interest and encompass the major contribution of the securities markets to a national economy.

To a large extent, these contributions reflect prevailing economic conditions in a country. During the early stages of economic development, the large majority of industrial and business units in a country are small in size. Their capital needs are small; the use of the corporate form is not widespread, and there is no substantial and widely scattered class of persons with surplus savings.[2] In these circumstances, trading in securities is likely to be restricted, and the principal function of the securities markets is directed towards permitting the government and corporations to raise funds that otherwise might not be available. Disclosure may be less important at that time for the following reasons: government securities tend to dominate the market, virtually all the companies embody the risks of new enterprises, there is little background information available, and adequate financial techniques of analysis have not yet been developed. Also, in the initial vigor of its growth, a country such as the United States may better sustain the pressures of isolated financial difficulties, the impact of which in a mature system would be more quickly felt throughout the economy. Another important function of the securities markets during this early period is to afford the mechanism for public distributions of family-owned enterprises. In the United States, many of our present-day corporate giants, with widely dispersed stock ownership, had their beginnings as small and humble enterprises, which sought public distribution during the early years of the new issue market.[3]

As the economy progresses, national income grows and becomes more widely spread, individuals obtain savings which are increasingly placed in the shares of new corporations and of established enterprises that were once family owned but now seek a public distribution. Also, the rise of major financial institutions, such as insurance companies and investment companies, results in a large number of persons having indirect interests in equities, as the institutions place the funds entrusted to them in stock.

2. Opinion of Harold R. Medina, C.J., In the District Court of the United States for the Southern District of New York, Civil Action No. 43–757, *United States of America* v. *Henry S. Morgan, et al.*, n.d., p. 17.

3. Ibid., p. 21.

The growth of a geographically scattered investor class, in turn, pushes into the forefront the role of trading markets which provide stockholdings with liquidity, which can be defined as the ability of investors to dispose of their stock promptly at a price reasonably related to the preceding one. Liquidity also endows stock with a unique advantage as a form of collateral, provides the means for determining the amount of loans that may be granted through this collateral, and facilitates the establishment of valuation bases for taxation and the handling of trust funds.

At this stage of economic development, corporations, as in the United States at present, tend to raise less of their equity needs through direct sales to the markets and a larger percentage through reinvested earnings.[4] In these circumstances, the securities markets reflect more closely the attitudes of the investor class to the company. If its prospects are promising and the price of its shares are bid up, investors are willing to defer receipt of dividends in favor of long-term capital gains achieved through internal growth. The judgment of the market, revealed in this price movement, then indirectly permits the company to finance by reinvested earnings, and to grow through the process of exchanging its shares for purposes of corporate acquisitions. For an efficient process, it is important that the pricing mechanism permits the maintenance of a logical relationship between a company's financial position and the price of its shares.

Determining the Price of Stocks

Like any commodity, the price of a stock is determined by the interaction of the demand and supply schedules. Indeed a call market, such as prevails in many nations, may be used as a laboratory illustration of how this relationship occurs. A stock

---

4. For some statistics since 1900 on the increased reliance by corporations on internal financing and the declining share of equity financing, see Joint Economic Committee of the United States, Part I, *Investment and Its Financing,* "Variability of Private Investment in Plant and Equipment," 87th Cong., 1st sess., 1962, pp. 40–41; Simon Kuznets, *Capital in the American Economy,* National Bureau of Economic Research, Princeton University Press, 1961, pp. 410–419.

is *called* at a particular price, say the previous day's close. Demand and supply orders are filled at this level. If there is an excess demand, the price is raised until a sufficient supply is forthcoming to absorb the excess, and the converse occurs if the supply exceeds the demand. In one technique of market forecasting, the demand and supply of stock is predicted, and the market direction is determined by where the excess lies. This approach however is used primarily to provide some rough approximations because of the complexity of attempting to gauge demand and supply.

THE DEMAND FOR STOCK

Many factors affect the demand for stock. The amount of national income represents the basic source from which funds must be drawn. Individual savings patterns influence the flow of these funds to the stock market or to competing savings outlets. Credit availability may add to this flow. Because of the importance of credit availability, the Securities Exchange Act of 1934 gives the Board of Governors of the Federal Reserve System authority to regulate the amount of security credit that may be granted by broker-dealers and by banks. The SEC Special Study indicated the significance of the large volume of still unregulated credit potential in adding to the demand for stocks during boom periods. The public interest in the stock market, which may be stimulated through the uses of modern advertising practices, as illustrated by the campaigns of the New York Stock Exchange, may divert funds from other sources, thereby augmenting demand. Similarly public confidence in the integrity of the securities markets is a powerful factor in creating willingness to buy stocks. Much of the apathy toward securities in countries like Turkey and Iran, which have little history of financial markets but are eager to develop them, arises from public reluctance to trust funds to this source. In order to overcome this reluctance, efforts to develop securities markets in these countries place considerable reliance upon the commercial banks, which are held in high regard by the general public.

While all these circumstances play on the demand for stock, demand emanates more fundamentally from a desire to satisfy certain wants. This desire creates the demand for all commodities, but in most cases its satisfaction comes directly—bread for food, a coat for warmth, a movie for entertainment, and so forth. The individual knows that the consumption of bread will satisfy his hunger, wearing the coat will keep him warm, and seeing the movie will provide some degree of entertainment.

The desire motivating the purchase of a stock is more complex. In the case of a proxy battle, the desire may be for power and to obtain control of the business. Or a corporation may desire to repurchase its own stock in the open market to raise its book value, to procure shares for subsequent use in option and savings programs, or to effect corporate acquisitions. More fundamentally in most cases, stocks are bought for two principal reasons: income or capital gains. Both reasons may, and indeed probably will, be present at the same time, but depending upon the period involved and the nature of the investor, one is likely to be more prominent than the other. Thus during an economic boom, as the stock market rapidly swings upward, the capital gains motive may be in the ascendancy, while during periods of greater uncertainty, the interest may veer towards stocks that afford high current income, even though their profit opportunities may not be as great. As an illustration, during the great market boom of the late 1950s and early 1960s, the decreasing importance of dividend income was reflected in the shrinkage of the median yield in NYSE dividend-paying common stocks from 6.1 per cent in 1957 to 3.3 per cent in 1964,[5] when the return was actually below that available from long-term Government bonds. Clearly at that time, the predominant interest motivating demand for stock was capital gains rather than dividend income. Similarly, certain investors, such as conservative income funds, may prefer issues that afford good returns, while more aggressive investors and growth funds move towards speculative stocks. Or investors may seek to satisfy both motives by purchasing a diversified group of stocks, but even here the portfolio composition will probably reflect the bias towards conservatism or aggressiveness.

Unlike the consumer who knows that eating the bread he has purchased will satisfy his want for food, the investor does not necessarily know that the purchase will satisfy his want for income or profits. In most instances this will depend upon the economic

---

5. The New York Stock Exchange, *The Exchange,* March, 1965, p. 1.

fortunes and financial policies of the firm whose stock he has bought. In guiding his purchases by attempting to anticipate these conditions, the investor influences the prices of the stock and therefore the company's direct and indirect financing potential. If, through lack of information or other reasons, the investor is not in a position to gauge the condition of the company, he is simply buying a piece of paper as an end item, rather than the paper as representative of a company. In this case, the efficacy of the pricing system of the securities markets in reflecting the economic status of the company is largely destroyed.

THE SUPPLY OF STOCK

As has been indicated, corporations in the United States, over the long term, have tended to raise a decreasing proportion of their financing requirements by new issues of common stock. As the demand for securities has grown, coincident with rising income and an expanding investing community, upward pressure on stocks has been exerted. This relationship probably has contributed to the long-term rising tendency of common-stock prices in this country. In the trading markets, however, supply is determined not only by the amount of new issues but also by the amount of currently held shares that may be offered by existing holders. At any one time, this potential volume represents a more significant consideration than the new offerings that may appear and if abruptly dumped on the market could disrupt the price structure.

Like the demand for stock, similar forces affect the supply in the trading markets but in an obverse manner. During an economic boom, investors are more likely to hold their shares, and therefore supply characteristically lags behind demand, driving prices upward. As the cycle turns, and profits shrink while unemployment rises, both individual and institutional investors find it necessary to sell stock to protect profits or to raise funds not forthcoming from other sources. Supply moves ahead of demand, and prices recede.

Securities markets that are firmly established, carefully administered,[6] and responsive to the public interest tend to reduce the danger of sudden large supplies flooding the market. Similarly,

---

6. It should be made clear that the prices are not being administered but only the mechanism that sets the prices.

when the capital requirements of a country historically have been met in large part through use of securities, confidence in the role of stock is buoyed, and there is less possibility that extraordinary events will lead to selling onslaughts. The relative infrequency with which the New York Stock Exchange has suspended trading, in the face of a number of national and worldwide crises that have occurred during the twentieth century, is indicative of investor resistance to panic.

More fundamentally, the sale of a stock is the concluding phase of the originating purchase, and therefore simply represents the other side of the coin that was first turned up by the forces of demand. And just as the existence of pools of credit may augment demand, so may credit sources add to supply. Only in this case credit operates through the short sale. That is, the investor borrows stock in order to effectuate a sale, and therefore the credit process leads to an enlargement of the supply of stock.

Margin requirements govern credit availability for demand, and both margin and short-selling requirements regulate the availability of credit for supply. These latter requirements are in the form of rules of the exchanges and the SEC. The principal thrust of the current Commission rule is to prohibit short sales unless made above the last different sale price, usually by ⅛ or more. The rule's objective is to permit the expansion of supply through short selling as the market advances but to prevent short selling at successively lower prices, a device that otherwise could be used to engineer a bear raid. The rule is also intended to prevent short selling from exhausting all remaining bids at one price level, thereby accelerating a declining market as "long" sellers dispose of their shares at successively lower prices. As a more extreme restriction the suggestion has been made that all short selling should be prohibited during rapidly declining markets.

Supply has an aspect, however, that sets it apart from demand. The purchase of a stock is a voluntary act. It may be stimulated by advertising, induced by hard-driving salesmen and motivated by greed—or it may fill a genuine economic need and follow the careful evaluation of a company's outlook. In either case, the final decision must be made by the investor. Supply on the other hand may also be created without any voluntary concurrence on the part of the seller. He may have purchased his stock on margin or may have used stock as the collateral for a *nonpurpose loan* (not for the purpose of purchasing or carrying securities). Both brokers who grant loans to buy securities and banks who grant nonpurpose loans collateralized by stocks have rules that govern the levels at which calls will be issued to add to the collateral during declining markets. If additional cash or stock is not deposited, the collateralized securities may be sold. The issuance of a call may lead to the liquidation of the collateral by the borrower, or the liquidation eventually may be done by the broker or bank. The resulting addition to the supply of stock overhanging the market may further depress prices. This leads to further calls and more liquidation which again adds to supply, thereby depressing prices, and so the vicious cycle unfolds. The important thing is that the increase of supply in this case is an automatic phenomenon that results when declining stock prices trigger rules governing the carrying of loans secured by collateral.

CREATING AN ARTIFICIAL MARKET

In our discussion, a distinction has been drawn between demand and supply created in two principal ways. First, these forces may come about because of an economic process that is geared to the financial outlook of business firms; second, the demand and supply may revolve around pieces of paper with little concern about the position of the related company. In the latter instance, artificial markets are created that are outside of the economic stream of the country. Let us examine the demand and supply forces under these conditions.

In pre-SEC days, it was common practice to manipulate prices without any regard to the worth of the company concerned. Those who participated in this process were literally trading pieces of paper whose prices were the outcome of a contrived demand and supply. The history of that period provides a classic illustration of the degree to which manipulation may flourish when restraints are reduced to a minimum. Without the pressure of adequate internal or external regulatory control, there is little incentive for an issuer to provide the disclosure of information or for a market to evolve the structure and operating rules necessary to encourage public efforts to achieve economic profits. If the data necessary to make informed investment decisions about a company are absent, the gambling motivation becomes more important, and professionals in the field are in a position to take advantage of this desire by creating artificial demand and supply forces. To a large degree, prices in turn become the playthings of such induced buying and selling.

From January, 1933, to July, 1934, Ferdinand Pecora served as counsel for the Senate Committee on Banking and Currency in investigating practices in the securities markets. During the course of his examination, Arthur H. Wiggin, then head of the Chase National Bank, described these markets as "God-given." In commenting on this statement, with its inference that the actions of the markets were free from any human criticism or supervision, Pecora noted that to the contrary, they were "man-made." He later elaborated this point by saying:

Far from being an impartial forum for the free play of supply and demand, as pictured by its authorities, the Exchange was in reality neither more nor less than a glorified gambling casino where the odds were heavily weighted against the eager outsiders. On this 'free and unrestricted market' there were operating in 1929 pools, syndicates, joint accounts and the like—however one terms them—in not less than 105 public stocks listed on the New York Stock Exchange. The public who bought these stocks at dizzily mounting prices did not do so merely because of impersonal economic forces; they were the victims of a determined, organized group of market-wise operators, armed with special information and special facilities, and backed generously with bankers' credits.[7]

As described by Pecora, a typical pool was designed to stimulate public demand and push prices upward. For example in early 1933, American Commercial Alcohol had outstanding 194,748 shares of common stock. In order to issue new shares without the need of first offering them to existing stockholders, Russell R. Brown, Chairman of the Board of American Commercial Alcohol, had two associates form two dummy corporations. In exchange for their promissory notes, these associates received all the stock of the dummy corporations, which they promptly submitted to the American Commercial Alcohol Corporation for 25,000 shares of its common stock. Thus Brown now controlled 25,000 newly

7. Ferdinand Pecora, *Wall Street Under Oath,* New York, Simon & Schuster, 1939, p. 263.

issued shares of American Commercial Alcohol, while the dummy corporations owned two promissory notes of questionable worth. Brown then gave a professional trader an option to buy the 25,000 shares at $18 per share, thereby providing him with both a reliable source of stock to use as a base for trading and with a convenient means of incurring substantial profit. The stage was now set for the operation of the pool. As finally formed, it consisted of eight individuals, of whom two represented Brown and his associates and certain other directors of American Commercial Alcohol. Its purpose was to stimulate interest in the stock and to draw the public into a maelstrom of activity.

Operations of the pool began on May 2, 1933, and by July 24 it had purchased 54,894 shares and sold about the same amount. Reflecting this frenetic buying and selling, the price of the stock was catapulted upward from a starting level of about $20 per share on May 2 to an all-time high of 89⅞ on July 18. How successful the pool was in attracting the public may be gauged by the fact that the total number of shares of stock traded on the Exchange between May 15 and July 22 was 1,145,100, compared with the company's total original capitalization of some 194,000 shares. How successful the pool was in manipulating the price of the stock is indicated by the fact that after its termination on about July 18, the price promptly skidded downward to about 30 by July 22. Member firms of the NYSE with public accounts as well as specialists participated in the process. Whatever may have been the intrinsic worth of the stock as gauged by the economic condition of American Commercial Alcohol was forgotten in the market illusions created by the tactics of the pool. In such circumstances it is difficult to find a difference between the public market for securities and a private gambling club; in both instances the odds are likely to be loaded in favor of the professional participants.

In addition to pool operations, other means, limited only by the ingenuity of the manipulators, were devised to generate interest in an issue and to guide its price movements. In a *wash sale,* an individual would place a buy and sell order for the same stock at the same time. In *matched orders,* similar operations were conducted by two individuals buying and selling the same stock at the same time. In all these transactions, the participants simply took the necessary means of pushing prices to the desired levels and then unloaded on the unsuspecting public their accumulations of stock, at least part of which might have been originally acquired through options. After their artificial prop was removed, the prices would skid downward and the public would absorb the losses that inevitably had to be incurred. When manipulation was under way, the names of the stocks meant little; they might just as well have been letters or numbers, except when the name created a basis of interest that could be whipped up by false rumor and concocted stories into a storm of trading activity.

Artificiality was also created through limiting the supply of a security available for trading. The historical method of achieving this objective was through *cornering* a stock. This might be the result of a battle over a corporate empire, as in the notorious Hill-Harriman struggle for domination of the Northern Pacific Railway Company in 1901. James J. Hill controlled the Great Northern; and E. H. Harriman, the Union Pacific Railroad Company. Both were interested in the Northern Pacific in order to absorb the Chicago, Burlington & Quincy Railroad Company, in which the Northern Pacific had large holdings. As a result of their buying efforts, Northern Pacific stock climbed at great speed from a price of 149 to 1,000. With the two battling colossuses in possession of most of the shares, a corner resulted in which smaller traders could not get possession of the stock in order to cover their own contracts. As reported by the Interstate Commerce Commission, "the sacrifices necessary to secure funds for covering contracts precipitated a panic of widespread proportions."[8] Thus, not only did the Northern Pacific corner destroy any thread of reality between the price of the stock and any value that might have been reasonably represented by the road's outlook and financial condition, but also it had detrimental repercussions on the recovery of the country.

Of less national significance than the Northern Pacific corner but both picturesque and representative of the corner pattern of that period was the Piggly Wiggly case. As a typical procedure the corner of those years represented a battle where few financial

8. Quoted in Gustavus Myers, *History of the Great American Fortunes,* New York, Modern Library, 1936, p. 589, citing Interstate Commerce Commission, Report No. 943 (1907), p. 333.

holds were barred. On one side were the *bears* who executed selling raids supported by rumor and engineered by *short* transactions, involving the sale of borrowed stock which was expected to be purchased in the market and returned to the lender at a later date when prices had been forced lower. On the other side were the *bulls* whose strategic counter was to corner the stock's floating supply so that the short seller, who was forced to return the borrowed shares, would have to obtain them from the architect of the corner at whatever level he established. The resulting whipsaw price movements of the stock of course had no relationship to those that might have been determined through buyers and sellers freely vying for the issue of a company that represented a measurable bundle of economic values.

In June, 1922, there were listed on the New York Stock Exchange the shares of the Piggly Wiggly Stores, a chain of retail self-service markets located primarily in the South and West.[9] In November, several small grocery stores operating in the East under the Piggly Wiggly name failed. Although these companies had virtually no financial connection with the parent firm, merely having the right to use its name, the opportunity was exploited by speculators to attempt a bear raid. Through use of the standard tools of rumor and short sales, the price of the stock was quickly lowered from about 50 to 40. At this point the Company's president, an imaginative and free-wheeling promoter named Clarence Saunders, entered the picture. Supplementing his own funds with a loan of $10 million from a group of southern banks, he briskly embarked upon a buying campaign and within a week obtained 105,000 shares, more than half of the 200,000 outstanding. Reflecting his activity, the price of the stock reversed its downward course and by late January, 1923, had been driven to over 60, higher than ever before. The subsequent tactics of Saunders, including a wild-eyed advertising campaign to sell stock on an installment basis so that its shares would have a wide distribution but could not be dumped on the market, made it clear that he was trying for a corner. On Tuesday, March 20, Saunders sought to

9. See John Brooks, "Annals of Finance—A Corner in Piggly Wiggly," *The New Yorker,* June, 1959, pp. 128–150; Robert Sobel, *The Big Board: A History of the New York Stock Market,* New York, The Free Press, 1965, pp. 263–265.

spring his trap by calling for delivery of the stock. Pandemonium burst loose around the post where Piggly Wiggly was traded, as desperate short sellers tried to obtain shares but found that the floating supply had vanished into the hands of Saunders.

As the price of Piggly Wiggly leaped upward, short sellers sought to buy the stock in the face of a dwindling supply, and by noon it was selling at 124. Apprehensive of the effects of the corner, the Governing Committee of the New York Stock Exchange announced both suspension of trading in the stock and the extension of the delivery deadline. This double-barrelled reprieve gave the short sellers the opportunity to seek out shares held by small investors throughout the country and to settle directly with Saunders, who realized that his corner had been broken by the action of the Exchange. Except for its final sale at $1 per share at auction, the price of Piggly Wiggly, as it fell from 50 to 40, zoomed to over 100, and then collapsed once more, never was tied to the company's intrinsic financial position, nor was the need for this relationship ever injected into the campaign. Under current regulatory practices, the ability of a control group to influence unduly the price of a stock through the historic corner has been virtually outlawed. In its constitution, the NYSE for example has spelled out a procedure to govern situations where securities cannot be obtained for delivery on existing contracts except at prices and on terms arbitrarily dictated by an interest group. If need be, the last step in this procedure is the determination of a fair settlement price by the Board of Governors of the Exchange.[10]

Finally, artificial markets could be created through the issuance of false information. It was not uncommon during the great bull market of the 1920s for a market manipulator to have as his Man Friday a commentator on financial news that could use the public press or radio as a vehicle for generating the desired attitude towards a stock. In this camp, for example, were Raleigh T. Curtis, who wrote a column entitled "The Trader" for the *New York Daily News* and William J. McMahon, president of the McMahon Institute of Economic Research, and for a while a widely followed radio commentator on stock market affairs. Through appropriately timed optimistic or gloomy reports concerning particular com-

---

10. For a description of this procedure, see the Constitution of the New York Stock Exchange, Article III, Section 8.

panies, stocks could be moved through price gyrations that had nothing to do with financial reality but which could be exploited for the immense personal gain of the manipulator.[11] On a different level of market influence, but with overtones reminiscent of the old-fashioned, deliberate misuse of information were the revelations by the Special Study, which became the basis for a general lifting of standards in this area, of the publication of irresponsible or reckless investment advice.

THE BEHAVIOR OF STOCK PRICES

In theory, the prices of stocks in the securities markets are the outcome of the buying and selling decisions of large numbers of independently competing investors, whose actions in turn are determined by their judgments concerning the effects of an endless parade of rapidly changing events, both real and imaginary. In fact, as we have seen in the history of the organized stock exchanges, this theory has been only partially true. While there probably always have been stocks whose prices were determined in this impersonal way, in a number of significant instances prices have been affected by external monopolistic practices—of the pool operator, the designer of corners, the insider with special facts at his disposal, the purveyor of misleading information, and other practitioners of the not so mystic art of market manipulation.

Any attempt to evaluate the full impact of these practices through study of the over-all market movements of prior periods is obscured by the smoothing effect of averages. The price moulders generally were too wily to pay much attention to the averages; they gained their economic training in the hard school and soon learned the powerful influence of the margin—of concentrating their attention on the individual security. To Jesse Livermore, king of the speculative twenties, is attributed the remark, since become a cliché, that it is a market of stocks, not a stock market.[12] And skilled traders were selected to manage specific pools; or commentators, to mould opinion concerning individual stocks, and the rest of the market was largely left to find its own level. As a result, two types of price movements would occur, one controlled and the other free, except that the activity of the manipulator at

11. Robert Sobel, op. cit., pp. 248–249.
12. Robert Sobel, op. cit., pp. 246–247.

the margin, operating on selected issues, undoubtedly had a spreading influence, depending upon various other factors, such as the importance of the issues and the basic character of the economy at the time. It seems reasonable to believe, therefore, that any explanation of market behavior of earlier periods must take into account the main external forces at work as evidenced by the activity of the manipulator and the vacuum of financial ignorance that surrounded the typical individual investor.

The lawyer has changed this picture significantly. His concern with "public interest" and the "protection of the investor" has led to the passage of the securities acts, the creation of a theory of regulation uniquely "tailored" to the securities field and the considerably elevated standards of conduct that now characterize its operations. The thrust of this regulatory scheme is to permit a fair and orderly market where prices are truly responsive to the expected influence of past and future events. In these circumstances, the economist or statistician is better able to examine and explain the underlying currents in the stream of changing stock prices.

To this end, he defines the securities markets as "efficient." By this he means that there are a great many rational investors who desire to increase their profits and therefore vigorously compete with each other to predict the prices of securities on the basis of information freely available to all participants.[13] Since these investors act by means of logical evaluations of current knowledge regarding the past and future, they tend to force prices of stocks to levels that reflect these conditions. If a large number of investors think the market in an issue is too high, they sell, thereby forcing its price down, while if they believe the market too low, they buy, driving the price upward. In an uncertain world, this basic level, representing the intrinsic value of a stock, cannot be ascertained with precision, but if there were any systematic explanations of the variations from it, they would be recognized by intelligent investors, who would then initiate their price-adjusting buying and selling policies. As a result, the investors' best expectations of the intrinsic value of a stock is its present price, which presumably will change only when new information comes along. Such addi-

13. Eugene F. Fama, "Random Walks in Stock-Market Prices," Graduate School of Business, University of Chicago, *Selected Papers No. 16*, pp. 3–4.

tional information is not likely to appear in any organized fashion, and the associated price changes may either follow or anticipate the new events. Accordingly, from period to period, the successive price changes will be independent of each other, following what the statistician terms *a random walk* and what the physicist calls *Brownian motion.*

Various tests of this hypothesis have been devised. Through statistical measures of a number of different series representing speculative prices, it has been found that during long time spans the price change of one component period was not significantly correlated with that of the preceding period nor with the change of any earlier period. In these studies, it seemed "almost as if once a week the Demon of Chance drew a random number from a symmetrical population of fixed dispersion and added it to the current price to determine the next week's price."[14] Runs of consecutive price changes of the same sign have not differed materially from the expected number.[15] The plotted changes of security prices have behaved very much as if they had been generated by a suitably designed roulette wheel.[16] In addition, the investigations have led to suggestions of refinements to the basic theory. It has been pointed out, for example, that the logarithms of price changes are independent of each other rather than the absolute price changes because investors are more interested in proportionate changes in stock values rather than in absolute dollar values.[17] Or that there are certain limitations on the degree to which stock prices may wander under the notion of a pure random walk.[18]

Even with the major regulatory advances that have been achieved to obtain "fairness" and "freedom," it is difficult to accept fully the notion that the securities markets at present are truly "efficient" in the technical sense described above. Too many mo-

---

14. M. G. Kendall, "The Analysis of Economic Time-Series—Part 1: Prices" in Paul H. Cootner, ed., *The Random Character of Stock Market Prices,* Cambridge, Massachusetts, The M.I.T. Press, 1964, p. 87.

15. Harry V. Roberts, "Stock-Market 'Patterns' and Financial Analysis: Methodological Suggestions" in Paul H. Cootner, ed., op. cit., pp. 14–15.

16. Ibid., 7–12.

17. M. F. M. Osborne, "Brownian Motion in the Stock Market" in Paul H. Cootner, op. cit., pp. 100–127.

18. Paul H. Cootner, "Stock Prices: Random vs. Systematic Changes" in Paul H. Cootner, op. cit., pp. 231–251.

nopolistic barriers still exist. Investors are not uniformly logical or rational; information is not equally available to all participants; serious maldistributions between demand and supply elements may develop for purely technical reasons. Accordingly, despite the intriguing aspects of the random-walk theory, there appear to be limitations on the mobility of price movements, as have been suggested by some analysts, and in many instances the current level probably is not an accurate representation of an issue's intrinsic worth.

In the stock market of the future these obstructions to the randomness of price fluctuations may be substantially eliminated. Regulatory pressures are further likely to squeeze out manipulation; antifraud rules against insiders plus the tendency for expanded disclosure will move in the direction of making information more broadly available at the same time; the increased importance of institutions and the greater stress on entry qualifications in the securities field will raise analytic standards. The existence of a large number of skilled analysts, with considerable resources at their disposal, including the computer, actively competing for profit realization, will help narrow statistical discrepancies and cause present prices more truly to reflect intrinsic values. In these circumstances, the opportunities for achieving gains will become more subtle. They may occur in those instances when prices wander temporarily from intrinsic values; when an analyst can anticipate future developments more accurately than his competitors and can interpret more efficiently the impact of a new event; or when fresh insights indicate the logic of a change in the intrinsic value itself. If this price-determining accuracy materializes, the "efficient" market of the future is also likely to mean one that can better serve to allocate the nation's limited capital resources to the needs of individual corporations, inasmuch as prevailing price levels that largely influence financing ability will also realistically reflect financial prospects.

THE SECURITIES MARKETS AS AN ALLOCATOR OF FUNDS

Whether the demand for a stock is motivated by income or profits, so long as it is related to a corporation, the prices of the securities markets will play a realistic part in determining the corporation's ability to raise funds. For those enterprises that must finance externally, the receptivity of the market to their offerings establishes both the volume and cost of the capital raised. For those companies that finance the bulk of their requirements through reinvested earnings, the willingness of stockholders to defer dividends in the expectation of a higher return through capital gains, establishes both the volume and cost of the capital raised. If a company's outlook is very promising and buyers bid up the security's market value, new financing becomes easier—whether through external or internal sources—the earnings/price ratio is reduced, and the cost of capital becomes correspondingly low.

Essentially therefore, the price of a company's securities in the primary and secondary markets is the beacon providing the signals that suggest the amount of capital it may obtain and the cost that it will pay. The securities markets thus serve the major function of allocating the scarce resource of capital to the nation's business firms. Since capital is the lifeblood of a capitalistic society, this guiding function represents a major economic responsibility.

In this context, the securities markets have a deep-rooted meaning that is both compatible with the principles of a capitalistic society and contributes to the maintenance of these principles. That is, the markets provide the means for substituting the judgment of the many for the judgment of the few in charting the growth of the economy. Yet it is easy to overlook the fact that only in this context can the markets effectively perform their allocative functions. If investors, who buy and sell securities, have insufficient information on which to base their opinions, they are in no position to distinguish between potentially successful and unsuccessful businesses. Similarly, if the information is available, and investors make no use of it through ignorance or the difficulty of obtaining such information, the economic role of the markets will be based upon probability tables rather than judgment decisions. Furthermore, if information is available and can be used, but professional insiders are free to manipulate prices, the economic role of the markets is not even subject to the restraints of the probability table, but becomes a pawn of gambling motivations. And finally, if data are available and manipulation is reduced to a minimum, the economic role of the markets can still be destroyed if the judgments of investors are too easily blinded by hysteria and emotion rather than by analysis.

If the administrative structure that provides the conditions described above to keep the relationship between prices and corporate conditions is absent, it is not probable that the tie will exist. Accordingly, the requirement is for the creation of a structure that will regulate the markets so as to permit the prices of securities freely to respond to the genuinely shifting economic status and prospects of business firms. Admittedly this is a difficult and sensitive problem because of the wisdom required to develop regulation in a limited area in order to maximize freedom in a larger sense. The very problems that are inherent in the undertaking reflect the slow progress of securities regulation; they do not however minimize the need of such regulation to permit the markets to render their economic function and to guard against the much greater controls that might otherwise be necessary if the Government rather than the market place served as the allocator of capital in the United States.

The Conditions Implicit in the Administrative Structure

Four major conditions have been mentioned that insure the existence of an effective administrative framework within which the price changes of securities are likely to reflect demand and supply forces based on the financial outlook of the issuing corporations. Other conditions may also apply, but these four, now briefly reviewed and subsequently discussed in connection with other problems, may be considered the minimum.

THE INFORMATION ON WHICH TO BASE DECISIONS

Left to their own devices, corporations have been traditionally reluctant to keep the public informed regarding their financial status. The inhibiting reasons are obvious. Management is fearful of revealing information that might be of help to competitors, and at least some corporate insiders prefer the secrecy that affords them an advantage in trading their corporations' securities. Other factors that have discouraged the issuance of reports are the expenses involved, a reluctance to expose the effectiveness of management's performance in public view, and a belief that such information is private and therefore not properly subject to public issuance.

These reasons have not proved valid. The considerable expansion of information provided to the public as a result of the efforts of the major stock exchanges and the requirements of the securities acts has not by and large created new competitive threats in industry. Even for small companies, the additional expense of publicly distributing data is not likely to prove onerous, particularly since a large portion of this information is required for internal purposes. It has been estimated that the costs of preparing the financial information, legal documents, and other material that must be filed with the SEC is between 5 and 8 per cent of the principal value of a $300,000 issue and that the percentage is much lower for bigger issues.[19] Moreover, the SEC may grant exemptions to the disclosure requirement when an undue hardship is created or there is little trading interest in the stock. At the present time it is not likely that the justification of secrecy would have many proponents. Clearly, accurate information is necessary to afford some protection against fraud and manipulation, to minimize the danger of insider abuses, to provide a basis for investment decisions, and to represent a minimum degree of corporate democracy.

Thus disclosure is an imperative for securities markets to meet their acknowledged economic function. Without information, investors must resort to indirection to acquire the knowledge necessary to buy or sell securities based upon the financial performances of corporations. For example, the senior partner of a large brokerage firm has described how, in the twenties, he had to go to the plant gate of companies at stated intervals and count the number of employees reporting for work to obtain some idea of the trend of their business as reflected in employment. Or since most investors probably would not have the ingenuity or time to resort to such devices, they would buy and sell on the basis of rumor, guesswork, and the "hidden persuaders" of the market manipulators.

Disclosure does not infer that buyers have a guaranty as to the correctness of their buy-or-sell decisions. It simply places upon the issuers the burden of "telling the truth" about their financial

---

19. Salomon J. Flink, *Equity Financing for Small Business*, New York, Simmons-Boardman Publishing Corporation, 1962, p. 158.

status so that investors may be in a position to make reasonable judgments as to their prospects. As stated by President Roosevelt, in his message to Congress of March 29, 1933, the philosophy of the Securities Act is implied in the addition "to the ancient rule of caveat emptor, the further doctrine 'let the seller also beware.' It puts the burden of telling the whole truth on the seller. It should give impetus to honest dealing in securities and thereby bring back public confidence."[20]

Even with the general acceptance of the principles of disclosure, management on its own initiative has shown little evidence of a desire to provide full and comprehensive information to their stockholders. In repeated examinations of over-the-counter companies not subject to the requirement of filing financial reports (prior to the enactment of the Securities Acts Amendments of 1964) the Securities and Exchange Commission ascertained that about half of the published statements did not meet its minimum standards. In a further analysis made in 1961, the Special Study of the Commission discovered that more than 25 per cent of the 1,965 issuers covered in a survey did not disseminate any financial information at all to shareholders. It was also found that almost half of the approximately 300 public complaint letters received by the principal office of the Commission in an average month in 1961 were from investors whose complaints were that they either could not obtain information about a company in which they had invested or that the information sent them was inadequate.[21]

It has not been unusual for corporations to file more accurate information with the Commission than they issue publicly—a distinction that has sometimes led even professional analysts to base their conclusions on public information that proved misleading. This problem has led to an SEC requirement, in line with a Special Study recommendation, that financial statements included in reports to stockholders should be prepared and presented on substantially the same basis as the financial statements in officially

20. S. Rept. 47, pp. 6–7; and H. Rept. 85, pp. 1–2, 73rd Cong. 1st sess., 1933.

21. Report of Special Study of Securities Markets of the Securities and Exchange Commission, 88th Cong., 1st sess., H. Doc. 95, 1963, Part 3, Chapter IX, pp. 10–12. For a description of the Special Study, see pp. 76–77.

filed reports; any material differences that exist must be reconciled and explained.[22]

Even with this pressure to fuller disclosure, serious inadequacies still exist that aggravate the difficulty of suitable evaluation. The spread of decentralization and the growth of big corporations, with largely autonomous divisions, have rendered information on a product basis of increasing importance. Yet relatively few companies have seen fit to disclose this information to their stockholders although there has been some trend in this direction. Similarly, to control internal operations, corporate management has found it mandatory to decompose cost data into their fixed and variable segments. Such information is imperative for useful forecasts of earnings that in turn are necessary for suitable judgments concerning the valuation of securities. Despite the obvious usefulness of the information, corporations generally keep it a carefully guarded secret from stockholders.

Disclosure is the keystone of the intelligent investing that makes it possible for securities markets to render a positive contribution to the economy of a nation. The evidence is clear that such disclosure can only be obtained through the constant pressure upon corporations by supervisory agencies. In the United States, both the self-regulatory agencies and the SEC have the continued responsibility of reviewing corporate practices in this respect and taking the necessary measures to insure that, as data reporting becomes more accurate and comprehensive, the benefits of this informed reporting are transmitted to the public. Additionally, if the accounting profession cannot standardize the reporting practices of its members, so as to produce the consistent profit reporting that more realistically reflects the results of operations, the self-regulatory agencies in the securities field and the SEC may have to step into the breach. It is not in the public interest for accounting permissiveness to create informational shadows that limit the effectiveness of securities prices to mirror true performance.

USING THE INFORMATION

It is important that the SEC take all reasonable measures to insure that the data filed by corporations are actually made avail-

22. See Securities and Exchange Commission, *General Rules and Regulations, Securities Exchange Act of 1934*, Rule 14a–3(b).

able to the investors. This may seem like an undue extension of functions because, once the data are filed, it might be argued that the burden is upon the investor to obtain and use them. Without minimizing the responsibility of the investor to seek available information on his own initiative, recognition must be taken of the lack of awareness of many investors, the difficulty of reaching filed sources, and the greater accessibility of digested information served to him by brokers, investment advisors, and financial publications. Also, it must be remembered that a major purpose of these efforts is to permit the securities markets appropriately to render their function of allocating the country's capital. To do this efficiently, investors must have available to them, and not in files located elsewhere, the data upon which to base investment decisions. While the Commission cannot substitute its own judgment for that of investors in evaluating securities, it can take the necessary steps to make more certain that the required information actually is reasonably accessible to investors.

Towards the objective that information be made more readily available, the Special Study recommended that in many instances dissemination rather than filing should be required. It pointed out that development of modern techniques of duplicating and communicating the printed word makes such dissemination feasible at present, whereas it would have been impracticable some years ago. For example, it suggested that officially filed information might be presented in form for inexpensive duplication and distribution. It also seemed possible to require that copies be filed in appropriate Commission or NASD offices and/or that broker-dealers making markets or recommending purchases have copies on file or actually distribute them to customers in stated circumstances.[23]

Even so, the facts of the matter are that in an industry geared to salesmanship, as the securities industry is and possibly must be, the point of contact between investor and securities firm often is the salesman. In these circumstances, regardless of the measures taken to provide dissemination of data, such information will be transmitted by the salesman. Accordingly, the claim has been made that "one of the most important contributions of the Special Study was the emphasis it placed on the importance of point of contact in the distribution of securities to the public. The Special Study

---

23. Report of Special Study of Securities Markets of the Securities and Exchange Commission, Chapter IX, op. cit., Part 3, p. 64.

underscored what many people knew: that individual investors frequently did not use the prospectus as a primary aid in determining whether to purchase a particular security. The key to the sale often was the salesman."[24]

Reflecting this awareness of providing suitable information at the point of contact, the Special Study recommended that officially filed disclosures by issuers—both reports and proxy statements—should have wider and more prominent use in selling activities. It was suggested that both the self-regulatory agencies and the Commission define the obligations of broker-dealers in this regard. Such obligations might include actually consulting available officially filed data prior to recommending or selling specific securities; furnishing copies to customers in appropriate cases; and advising customers whether officially filed information is available with respect to any security recommended for purchase.[25] In each of these instances, the decision that must be made is whether the implementing burden upon the broker-dealer firm and the supervisory burden upon the regulatory agencies are worth the benefit to the investor. As the science of communication is extended, the move constantly should be in the direction of raising the standards of reporting through the salesman.

THE QUESTION OF MANIPULATION

Manipulation as historically practiced through pools and corners has been largely eliminated by the securities acts. The ingredients leading to manipulation, as described previously, remain, however, and it would be naïve to assume that efforts to influence prices for personal gain have been eliminated. The difference is that, though reduced considerably in scope and size, such efforts still exist in new and sometimes more subtle forms.

Modern public relations represent a legitimate and important means of transmitting information and, when properly used in the securities industry, can provide a helpful supplement to disclosure of data concerning a company. Publicity however can also be a

---

24. Robert H. Mundheim, Foreword to issue on Securities Regulation, *Law and Contemporary Problems,* The Duke University School of Law, Summer, 1964, pp. 647–648.

25. Report of Special Study of Securities Markets of the Securities and Exchange Commission, op. cit., Part 1, Chapter III, p. 329. .

dangerous tool. It was once characteristically used to attract demand for a stock in pool operations, but various legal restraints have been enacted to prevent its more obvious abuses. Thus the Securities Act of 1933 sharply restricts the use of public relations immediately before a public offering; the Securities Exchange Act of 1934 controls the information that may appear in proxy statements; the securities laws contain antifraud and antimanipulative provisions that have proved of value against issuance of false and misleading publicity.

These restraints, however, are relatively mild and have not prevented the use of publicity to influence the prices of securities for the personal gain of company officials and of public-relations men who acquire the shares of their clientele. When employed in this manner, publicity has a snowballing effect that can augment existing interest in a security enormously and influence its price materially. In these circumstances, the level of transactions in the securities markets may bear only a remote relation to the financial status of the related company. To minimize the danger of inducing artificial demand of this type, the self-regulatory agencies have the responsibility of establishing high standards for the dissemination of corporate publicity. The Special Study went so far as to suggest the enactment of a statute providing criminal sanctions and civil liability for intentional or reckless dissemination of false and misleading statements by issuers or their agents and the adoption of Commission rules requiring disclosure of material facts concerning compensation paid to public-relations counselors.[26]

Demand may also be influenced through extensive pressure employed by salesmen to attract orders. Salesmen interest may be stimulated through public-relations campaigns, and the salesmen in turn may add their fuel to the simmering fire of investor interest. To obviate the dangers of creating artificial prices through hardsell efforts, the self-regulatory agencies have adopted extensive programs to obtain men for the securities field of suitable character and understanding of the markets and to raise supervisory practices. The Special Study not only applauded these efforts but suggested that greater emphasis be placed on the concept of suitability of particular securities for particular customers and that a review

---

26. Ibid., Part 3, Chapter IX, p. 102.

of compensation practices should be undertaken to ascertain if rules could be adopted to reduce the extreme form of bias towards selling created by relating compensation to volume of output.[27]

On the supply side, although the old-fashioned corner has been largely outlawed, other devices have been employed to control the supply of a stock and thereby affect its price, particularly in the case of a new issue. In reviewing the exaggerated premiums to which such issues were often driven during the hot-issue period of 1959–1961, the Special Study found that the artificial limitations of supply were often a contributory factor. Included among the devices used were the selection of customers who were expected to retain their allotments, the placing of allotments in discretionary accounts, the failure to notify customers that they had been alloted stock, the delaying of the delivery of certificates, and the withholding of stock from the market. Although some of these practices were legitimate, others were questionable; still others were outright manipulative. These restrictions on supply "when combined with stimulation of after-market demand, helped produce some of the exaggerated price movements of 'hot' issues."[28] Illustrative of these conditions, almost all the new offerings of companies in the automatic-vending-machine, scientific-instrument, research, printing-and-publishing, and aerospace industries went to immediate premiums during this period, regardless of the basic merits of the issuing companies, so long as their title was appropriately attractive. Subsequently many of the stocks experienced substantial reactions. Thus in 1961, some seventy-five unseasoned issues of such companies more than doubled in price immediately after offering, but almost two-thirds of them were selling below their offering price at the end of September, 1962.[29]

In order to reduce the possibility of artificially restricting the supply of stock, the Special Study recommended that the NASD or the Commission adopt various rules, such as requiring for first issues of common stock the prompt notification of allotments to purchasers resulting from solicitations or indications of interest prior to the effective date of the registration statement.[30] While

27. Ibid., Part 1, Chapter III, pp. 237–330.
28. Ibid., Part 1, Chapter IV, p. 523.
29. Ibid., pp. 516–518.
30. Ibid., p. 558.

considerable progress has been made in eliminating some of the more obvious practices of inducing demand for or limiting the supply of stock, the continued attention of the regulatory authorities to this problem is required because of its importance in permitting the markets to render their economic function.

THE IMPLICATIONS OF AN EMOTIONAL ENVIRONMENT

The three prior conditions—adequate disclosure, appropriate use of information, and suitable controls to minimize the creation of artificial forces of demand and supply—are the basis for the normal economic functioning of the securities markets. The danger still exists that outside events may temporarily paralyze the judgment of investors and distort these normal operations. Such a danger is aggravated by the very efficiency of modern price-dissemination facilities, which enable investors throughout the country to know promptly the reactions of others, as reflected in price changes, to any major event. The speed with which these changes are communicated sets the pace for the investing public to act quickly, often before an opportunity has been afforded for adequate evaluation of the precipitating event. This tendency for price movements to influence sympathetic responses may exaggerate the sharpness of the swings and upset the orderly functioning of the markets. The combination of these circumstances could interfere with the ability of investors to exercise reasonable judgments in their decisions and lead to price fluctuations that unrealistically portray the status of the corporations involved.

When temporary conditions create an imbalance in supply and demand, leading to sharp price changes, specialist intervention to maintain orderliness becomes important. To test the effectiveness of the specialists' contribution towards preventing temporary imbalances in supply and demand, the notion of *price continuity* is introduced. With respect to this criterion, in turn, the organized exchanges have formulated surveillance procedures and tests to assess the effectiveness of the specialists' role. Under extraordinary conditions, when price movements have become so frantic and disorderly that the limits of the specialists are breached, extreme measures by the self-regulating agencies or the SEC may be called for, as is discussed later.

Summary

The primary functions of the securities markets tend to shift in reflection of prevailing economic conditions in a country. In an advanced economy, individuals directly and indirectly employ the markets to an increasing degree as an outlet for savings. Also, publicly held corporations tend to meet a larger percentage of their financing requirements by means of reinvested earnings, a process that requires the willingness of their stockholders to defer the receipt of dividends in anticipation of future capital gains. Under these conditions the trading markets assume an important role in the economy, and the price movements of securities, reflecting the attitudes of investors throughout the country, serve as a guide to the allocation of capital.

An examination of the history of securities markets reveals the steps that have been taken to manipulate demand and supply of securities in order to produce desired price changes. Such movements, unrelated to the financial condition and outlook of corporations, tend to destroy the capacity of the markets to fulfill their economic functions. In order to minimize the possibility of creating artificial fluctuations and provide greater assurance that price changes of securities will be reasonably related to the prospects of the issuing corporations, effective regulations are required. For this purpose, there must be created a framework that provides for the disclosure of information, permits the appropriate use of this information, reduces manipulation, and maintains orderly trading conditions. These principles, important to permit the securities markets to contribute positively to the nation's economy, arise out of the statutes and rules that have been enacted over the past three decades. In few areas has it been more important for the lawyer and the economist to cooperate to the betterment of the public interest. In the following two chapters, the long-term legal structure of the securities markets is considered.

CHAPTER 3

The Securities
and Exchange
Commission

There are seven laws in which the Securities and Exchange Commission is given administrative responsibilities of varying importance. An eighth, the Securities Acts Amendments of 1964, is of major significance, but is not actually a new piece of legislation, although it does provide extensive revisions to the Securities Exchange Act of 1934 and amends the Securities Act of 1933 in one respect.

Of the seven laws, the Public Utility Holding Company Act of 1935 was passed following a Federal Trade Commission investigation that was considered one of the most comprehensive ever made of an American industry. The investigation revealed a number of abuses that had crept into the vast utility holding-company systems that stretched across the country at that time. While the measure embodied complex and far-reaching provisions to eliminate these abuses, its principal thrusts were aimed at creating integrated systems capable of economic operations within a single region in one or several contiguous states, and the simplification of corporate structures. During the twenty-four-year period between 1938 and 1962, some 2,419 companies have been subject to the Act as registered holding companies or subsidiaries. Through extensive reorganizations, mergers, distributions, and exchanges of properties and securities, the bulk of utility companies no longer falls within the scope of the Act. As a result, by mid-1964, there remained only sixteen active, registered holding-company systems totaling 155 companies, the aggregate assets of which accounted for no more than 20 per cent of those of the entire privately-owned industry.[1] Thus, the role of the Holding Company Act, which produced a monumental rehabilitation of the entire industry, has waned substantially and the SEC's responsibilities in this area of activity are no longer of major consequence.

After its establishment, the SEC undertook a study of protective and reorganization committees. This study revealed numerous instances where the indenture trustee, presumably responsible for protecting the interests of holders of indenture securities, failed to do so because of loyalties that were divided between the debtor and public investors. To remedy this condition, the Trust Indenture Act of 1939 was adopted, which among other things requires the indenture to specify the rights of the holders of securities, imposes high standards of conduct and responsibility upon the trustee, provides for the submission of reports by the trustee to security holders, and prohibits impairment of the individual security holder's right to sue for principal and interest except under certain circumstances. In examining trust indentures for compliance with these principles, the Commission has integrated this activity closely with its responsibility for administering the registration provisions of the Securities Act of 1933.

The SEC study also showed striking shortcomings in the part played by protective committees in corporate reorganization proceedings. Much of these deficiencies have been eliminated by Chapter X of the Bankruptcy Act, which, for reorganizations beyond a stipulated minimum size, provides for the appointment of a disinterested trustee to assume charge of the debtor's operations and to arrange for the issuance of a reorganization plan. The SEC has only limited responsibilities in this area because it can neither initiate nor determine any of the issues in Chapter X proceedings.

---

1. Securities and Exchange Commission, 30th Annual Report, Fiscal Year Ended June 30, 1964, p. 88; "The Work of the Securities and Exchange Commission," December, 1962, p. 17.

Where the indebtedness of the debtor exceeds $3 million, the court must, and if less may, submit plans of reorganization to the Commission, which then may prepare an advisory report analyzing the fairness and feasibility of the terms.

The Public Utility Holding Company Act of 1935 authorized the SEC to undertake an investigation of investment companies. Following five years of study, the Commission proposed legislation that was vigorously opposed by the industry on account of the extent of the suggested regulations, but finally a compromise statute was achieved in the Investment Company Act of 1940. Among other things, it requires investment companies to register with the Commission and to disclose information on financial conditions and investment policies, prohibits the companies from changing such policies without stockholder approval, prevents persons guilty of security frauds from serving as officers and directors, provides for outside directors with stipulated responsibilities, bars unfriendly transactions between companies and affiliated persons, permits issuance of senior securities only on certain conditions, and necessitates shareholder approval of management contracts. Because of the rapid growth of the investment-company industry, this is an important law. As of June 30, 1964, there were 731 investment companies registered under the act, including seventy-two small-business investment companies, with an estimated aggregate market value of assets of some $41.6 billion. The substantial size and continued rapid progress made by the industry have induced the Commission to press intensive examinations into this area. There is one investigation by the Wharton School of the University of Pennsylvania, undertaken for the Commission and submitted by it to the Congress in August 1962, another by the Special Study in its comprehensive survey of the entire securities industry, and still another by the Commission's own staff. These studies have led to the considerable extension of the reporting requirements of investment companies and eventually may result in both legislative proposals as well as issuance of new rules under the act.

Also adopted in 1940 was the Investment Advisers Act, which, with its amendments, is patterned after the broker-dealer registration provisions of the Securities Exchange Act of 1934. In general, it requires the registration of persons or firms engaged in the business of furnishing securities advice for compensation and for their observance of statutory standards of behavior designed to protect the interests of investors. As of June 30, 1964, there were 1,613 investment advisers registered with the Commission.

In particular instances, the application of the provisions of any of these statutes may become important. In general, as has been indicated, the Public Utility Holding Company Act of 1935 now entails primarily a reviewing function by the SEC, and the Commission's role in bankruptcy proceedings is primarily advisory, whereas the Investment Advisers Act of 1940 calls for the registration of advisers and a check to observe compliance with statutes. Although these laws have eliminated major abuses, none of them at present has significant implications for the over-all operations of the securities business. The Investment Company Act of 1940 is much more demanding, but its application is specialized as is that of the Trust Indenture Act and therefore both measures are largely outside the scope of this book, which is concerned with principles affecting the entire securities industry. Primary attention, therefore, is given to the initial two statutes that were enacted—the Securities Act of 1933 and the Securities Exchange Act of 1934, as well as the later amendments—and to the role of the Securities Exchange Commission in the administration of these statutes.

Character of the Securities and Exchange Commission

It is a truism that the character of the SEC, like that of any administrative body, depends upon the people who compose it. But a distinction may be drawn between the commissioners, the Chairman, and the staff.

THE COMMISSIONERS

Created by the Securities Exchange Act of 1934, the Securities and Exchange Commission is composed of five commissioners appointed by the President with the advice and consent of the Senate. They have five-year terms, staggered so that one expires each year. An effort is made in the act to obtain diversity of viewpoints by minimizing the danger of political domination. It is provided that not more than three of the commissioners shall be members of the same party and that members of different political parties shall be appointed alternately as nearly as is practicable.

In practice, the provision for alternate appointment of members of different political parties has been difficult to implement because characteristically, the majority of commissioners, as in the case of most other regulatory agencies, have been members of the Administration party. Moreover, party affiliation may be an inadequate gauge of the policies a commissioner will favor because lines of demarcation are more likely to be drawn on the basis of social judgments. Thus a liberal-minded Republican commissioner may more often find himself siding with a Democrat of a similar philosophic bent than with his fellow-commissioners of the same political party but of different social viewpoints.

Finally, the effort to obtain a bipartisan balance may be destroyed if an appointee has little interest in fulfilling his responsibilities or is thwarted in his efforts to do so by a lack of knowledge of the complex apparatus of the industry. Conversely, the view of a strong-willed, vigorous commissioner may color the activities of the entire Commission, even though these views are held by a numerical minority. Also, the relationship of the Commission to the industry, reflected in the degree to which the Commission is a passive observer of industry action or is willing to assert itself when necessary, depends as much on the dynamic character of the individual commissioners as on their philosophic attitudes. Unfortunately, while the opinions of prospective appointees may be gauged reasonably well in advance, their manner of conduct in office is more difficult to anticipate.

THE CHAIRMAN OF THE COMMISSION

The Securities Exchange Act states that the Chairman should receive a very modest additional salary, presumably to provide for his expenses of office, but says nothing about his method of appointment or additional responsibilities. Until 1950, the Chairman was elected annually by the members, although at least until 1945, he was in substance designated by the President. The Hoover Commission, which in 1949 submitted a Report on the Organization of the Independent Regulatory Commissions, recommended the designation of the Chairman by the President and the centralization of administrative authority in his hands. This recommendation was substantially followed in the President's reorganization plan for the SEC pursuant to the Reorganization Act of 1949. In accordance with this plan, the Chairman is now designated by the President and is given special administrative responsibilities with respect to personnel, internal organization, and budgets.[2]

The question of concentration of power in the hands of the Chairman and the corollary possibility that his designation by the President will tend to subordinate the operations of an independent regulatory agency to the desires of the Executive Office of the President have been raised. Although issues involving the direct interest of the Chief Executive in the policies of the SEC have not frequently occurred, there is little doubt but that the power to designate the Chairman is important because the prestige of the office enables a strong-minded individual to exert an influence over the entire Commission that is greater than that suggested by the additional authority that he possesses. As some offset to this condition, the recommendation has been made that the chairmen of independent regulatory agencies should be selected by the members, as was the procedure during the early years of the SEC, and that the powers of the chairmen should be reduced in relation to those of the members of the agencies acting as a body.[3]

It is true that there is some risk of concentration of power in the hands of a strong Chairman, but because of the respect given to the office, he is also in a position to be a constructive force. As an illustration, the recognition of the SEC as one of the most firmly consolidated and influential of New Deal reform agencies may largely be attributable to the nature of its early leadership.[4] A glance at the roster of chairmen during the Commission's formative period highlights the distinctive quality of this leadership.

2. Louis Loss, *Securities Regulation,* Boston, Little, Brown, 1961, Vol. III, pp. 1878–1879.

3. See, for example, Report of Subcommittee No. 1 on Regulatory Agencies and Commissions to the Select Committee on Small Business House of Representatives, *The Organization and Procedures of the Federal Regulatory Commissions and Agencies and Their Effect on Small Business,* 84th Cong., 2d sess., H. Rept. 2967, December, 1956.

4. Ralph F. de Bedts, *The New Deal's SEC,* New York, Columbia University Press, 1964, p. 203.

Combining great wealth with a sense of public responsibility, Joseph P. Kennedy, the first Chairman, set the pragmatic tone for creation of SEC policies and acceptance by the financial community. Once the groundwork had been dug, the legal foundations for an expansion of these policies was laid by the careful studies of the next Chairman, James M. Landis, a brilliant professor of law and political philosopher. Following him came William C. Douglas, subsequently elevated to the United States Supreme Court, who took up the reform battle with the Old Guard of the New York Stock Exchange, leading to a major reorganization of that institution in March, 1938, and who importantly helped in fashioning the principles of self-regulation that govern the relationship of the SEC to the industry. In May 1939, he was succeeded by Jerome Frank, the third star in the intellectual constellation of Landis-Douglas-Frank, a grouping that would be difficult to match in the history of administrative agencies.

Men of this caliber were able to attract dynamic and gifted assistants. Although the social turmoil of the period, reflected in dramatic reforms on many fronts, created pressure for changes in the securities field, there can be little doubt that the outstanding character of these early chairmen and their associates contributed vitally to the legislative transformation that occurred. Between 1933 and 1940, the seven major acts that constitute the basis for regulating the industry were adopted. From that time until 1964, there was a legislative hiatus. And it is no accident that the important amendments of that year occurred during the administration of William L. Cary, another strong Chairman, whose judicious firmness and negotiating skills paved the way for their adoption. There have been other chairmen and commissioners of talent during the intervening years but, for one reason or another, the results of their periods in office have made a less enduring impact on the securities markets. It is clear that effective administrative leadership alone may not be sufficient to engineer progress, but the absence of such talent makes the possibility of achievement much less likely.

THE COMMISSION'S STAFF

The Commission has characteristically operated with a small staff, the bulk of which is engaged in work of a professional nature;

on June 30, 1963, 65 per cent of the positions were in the professional category.[5] At the close of its first fiscal year, there were 696 persons in the Commission. Its personnel strength grew rapidly thereafter, reaching a prewar peak of 1,678 at the end of the 1941 fiscal year.[6] The staff then decreased sharply as special studies were completed; as work under the Holding Company Act was reduced; and as budgets were cut, reflecting the decreased emphasis given to the Commission's activities during the war and postwar years of economic readjustment. More recently, interest in the securities markets has grown and both the budgets and the staff of the Commission have increased. Between fiscal 1960 and fiscal 1965, its budget rose from $8.1 million to $15.4 million, and its staff from 1,000 to 1,462.[7]

From its inception, the Commission's staff has included a general counsel, as the chief legal officer; a secretary responsible for administrative affairs; and, starting in the second fiscal year, a chief accountant to supervise the development of accounting practices. Various divisions, the names and functions of which have changed from time to time, have also been provided to carry out the responsibilities given to the Commission under the acts that it administers. To perform the investigatory and enforcement aspects of its operations, there were nine regional offices as of June, 1964.

During the course of its history, the SEC's staff has included outstanding persons. A number of career employees have risen to Commission status while others, after spending some time with the SEC, have left for major posts in industry and education. By and large, the quality of its personnel has reflected the caliber and interests of the commissioners and particularly of the chairmen. Thus, in commenting on the fact that upon his installation to office, he had been warned about the difficulty in attracting outstanding personnel, Chairman Cary, after his resignation stated, "We strove to demonstrate the error of the first point—to bring again to the Commission the reputation it enjoyed in the 1930s, when almost

5. Securities and Exchange Commission, 29th Annual Report, Fiscal Year Ended June 30, 1963, p. 149.

6. Securities and Exchange Commission, 1st Annual Report, Fiscal Year Ended June 30, 1935, p. 38; 7th Annual Report, Fiscal Year Ended June 30, 1941, p. 242.

7. Securities and Exchange Commission, 30th Annual Report, Fiscal Year Ended June 30, 1964, p. 161.

every young lawyer in the government wanted to be associated with the SEC or the Solicitor General's Office—as the two best law offices in Washington."[8] Over the long run, the quality of SEC performance appears to flow from top down, rather than from bottom up. That is, the caliber, reputation, interest, and drive of the Chairman and the other commissioners are reflected in the appointment of able division heads, who in turn attract personnel of high quality to perform the functions of the Commission. Without appropriate backing at the top, it is questionable whether the SEC, which is generally not ranked among the so-called glamor agencies of the Government, could maintain a staff of top quality.

The Vitality of the Commission

To a large extent, as it has been contended above, the ability of the SEC to fulfill its responsibilities in overseeing the effective performance of the securities markets depends upon the vigor displayed by the Commission, in the pursuit of its activities. Various factors tend to dissipate this drive. It is therefore important to assess these factors in order to determine how the vitality of the Commission can be sustained.

THE PREOCCUPATION WITH CURRENT LEGISLATIVE, JUDICIAL, AND ADMINISTRATIVE ACTIVITIES

The seminal authority for creation of independent regulatory agencies lies in the power of Congress to regulate commerce. As American society grew more complex, Congress found itself unable to devote the time required for the continuous fulfillment of this responsibility and adopted the independent regulatory agency as the solution to the problem. The first such agency, the Interstate Commerce Commission, was established in 1887 and was thereafter followed by a number of other agencies, including the SEC in 1934. The enactments creating these agencies carry considerable authority and power that are legislative in character,

---

8. William L. Cary, "Administrative Agencies and the Securities and Exchange Commission," Duke University School of Law, *Law and Contemporary Problems*, Summer, 1964, p. 661.

while the process of deciding controversies through hearings that afford the contesting parties opportunities for briefs and oral arguments is quasi-judicial. Because of the potential conflicts and difficulties inherent in such embracive responsibilities, there was eventually passed, in 1946, the Administrative Procedure Act, which requires the agencies to establish detailed sets of rules of practice to govern their activities.[9]

In carrying out the requirements of the seven acts under which it functions, the Securities and Exchange Commission has a full quota of administrative, legislative, judicial, and enforcement chores. The burden of this work, particularly with regard to the pressure of routine duties and the concentration on individual cases, is suggested in the reports that the Commission submits annually to Congress. The large volume of registration statistics on securities and broker-dealers, as well as the information called for by the various acts, indicate the considerable effort required to review and handle this vast amount of paper work. The lists of indictments returned for violation of securities acts, injunctive proceedings brought, and court cases and reorganization proceedings in which the Commission participates provide a gauge of its extensive enforcement and judicial responsibilities. Legislative aspects of its work are reflected in the summaries of its rule-making functions, while other phases are covered in its investigatory activities and relations with the exchanges and the NASD. Invariably the reports recite the specific cases bearing upon issues of particular interest. When consideration is given to its relatively small staff, this wide range of Commission concern points to its inevitable absorption with the problems that rise in the ordinary course of its activities. Its preoccupation with such everyday matters has tended to place long-range planning for policy into limbo. As a result, there has been a tendency to relax critical review, to let well enough alone, and to be reluctant to devote time and personnel to study new theoretical areas, the benefits of which might only come at a much later date. After all, prescribed duties must be done; those of uncertain or of long-term values can be postponed.

----

9. Report of Subcommittee No. 1 on Regulatory Agencies and Commissions to the Select Committee on Small Business, H. Rept. 2967, op. cit., pp. 7–20.

The history of commission rates illustrates the slippage that can occur in the exercise of critical review and the development of basic principles applicable to the solution of individual problems. The various exchanges have established rules governing both the structure and level of these rates. Under Section 19(b)(9) of the Securities Exchange Act, the Commission, after formal request for a change and opportunity for hearing, may modify such rules if considered necessary for the protection of investors or to insure fair dealings in securities.

Since the enactment of the Exchange Act in 1934 until the time of the present writing in late 1965, the New York Stock Exchange has amended its nonmember commission rates five times, each amendment involving an increase in the general level of rates and in some instances a structural modification. The Exchange characteristically justified its action on the grounds that cost-volume relationships were such that the increases were necessary in order to provide the fair return required in order for the Exchange community to serve the public interests. The Commission never even went this far in publicly articulating standards, although on several occasions it indicated that it was not in a position to evaluate the appropriateness of the request and invariably pointed to the need for further study. Following the 1938 increase, the NYSE engaged the engineering firm of Stevenson, Jordan & Harrison to study the cost structure of the industry, the first of a number of similar studies that were to be made. In connection with the 1953 increase, the Exchange prepared a form for an Income and Expense Report, which it then employed as a basis for annual surveys of the income, costs, and profits of the participating members. Pursuant to a recommendation of the Commission in February, 1959, the Exchange engaged the accounting firm of Price, Waterhouse & Co. to conduct a cost study for the purpose of establishing objective methods of allocating expenses among a firm's operations and therefore obtaining more realistic financial data. This study lead to the introduction of several basic changes into the Income and Expense Report.

Thus, during a period of some thirty years of Commission interest in the rates charged by the member firms, the most tangible progress has been the development by the Exchange of some statistics dealing with costs and profits, which have been used principally to justify rate increases.[10] No real effort has been made by either the Exchange or the Commission to formulate a theory of rate determination in the securities business, although some modest whispers on this subject have been heard. This void is surprising because any immunity from antitrust action in the securities field that may be brought on the grounds of price fixing by member firms presumably rests heavily upon the Commission's jurisdiction in this area.[11] It is to be expected, therefore, that the Commission would have translated the statute's general reference to "reasonableness" and the Exchange's vague references to such notions as "fair return" into more meaningful guidelines of action. This need is all the greater because the securities business is different from that of the typical public utility. Absent, for example, are the monopoly franchises, stable demand, heavy capital investment, and costs and rates applicable to individual firms that are characteristic of the utility field. In view of the acknowledged inability of the Commission to evaluate rates without some theoretical framework upon which to base its decision, the long emancipation of the securities field from price-fixing charges because of Commission jurisdiction, the special difficulties inherent in formulating a theory of commission rates, and the need for obtaining uniform and accurate data, it would have appeared logical to expect a thorough study of the problem to have been made and some conclusions reached.[12] At least in part, this absence may be explained by the Commission's preoccupation with handling the burdens of its everyday legal, enforcement, and judicial responsibilities.

THE NEED FOR LONG-TERM PLANNING

Apprehension that adjudicatory, administrative, and investigative duties might interfere with planning and policy-making

---

10. In late 1965, the Chairman of the SEC indicated that the Commission was studying the question of commission rates, and that it planned to obtain broader financial reporting from securities firms.

11. See Chapter 8 for a discussion of antitrust action in this area.

12. For a discussion of the commission-rate problem, see Report of Special Study of Securities Markets of the Securities and Exchange Commission, 88th Cong., 1st sess., H. Doc. 95, 1963, Part 2, Chapter V, pp. 294–351.

functions has led to proposals to separate these responsibilities. Thus, when Louis Hector resigned from the Civil Aeronautics Board in 1959, he submitted a memorandum to the President in which he contended that combining functions was inefficient. He proposed turning over an agency's planning and policy-making role to new executive branch agencies, its adjudicatory duties to an administrative court, and the enforcement responsibilities to an executive department or agency already performing in this capacity. General agreement with these views was indicated by Newton Minow, four years later, in a letter to the President, when he resigned as Chairman of the Federal Communications Commission. But Minow proposed splitting the activities of the FCC, the agency to which he addressed his remarks, only between a single administrator and an administrative court.

Despite the convincing nature of these suggestions, it is hard in practice to separate the legislative, judicial, and policy-making functions of a regulatory agency. As former Chairman Cary has stated, "I start from the premise that authority and responsibility should be centralized. If not, differences of opinion may develop, and policy directives set by the administrator may be frustrated by the court."[13] Moreover, insights gleaned from judicial determinations may lead to and bulwark the need for policy formulations that result in legislative measures through issuance of rules or recommendations to Congress. Manuel F. Cohen, who followed Mr. Cary as Chairman of the SEC, and his legislative assistant have described the interrelationship of this process in developing broker-dealer selling-practice standards.[14] They point to the importance of interlocking formal rules, administrative decision, and statements of policy in the formulation of such standards.

1. From its inception to the summer of 1964, the Commission adopted twenty-two rules generally concerned with selling practices.

---

13. William L. Cary, "A Review of the Work of the Securities and Exchange Commission," *The Record of The Association of the Bar of the City of New York,* November, 1964, p. 467.

14. Manuel F. Cohen and Joel J. Rabin, "Broker-Dealer Selling Practice Standards: The Importance of Administrative Adjudication in their Development," Duke University School of Law, *Law and Contemporary Problems,* Summer, 1964, pp. 694–710.

These cover prescriptions for a general standard of conduct, prohibitions against certain fraudulent representations, establishment of requirements for use of representations that would otherwise be misleading, and the utilization of the disclosure principle.

2. In decisions arising out of administrative proceedings, the Commission has articulated the so-called *shingle* theory, which holds that merely by doing business with the public, the broker-dealer implies that he will conduct his affairs in accordance with standards of the profession. Under this theory, as well as the closely related *fiduciary* or *trust and confidence* theory, the Commission has developed case rules on specific practices directed towards the maintenance of high standards of conduct in the business as well as rules concerned with such areas as representation, disclosure, and manipulation. In some instances, a case rule may be closely related to a formal rule as that extending the ban against excessive trading in discretionary accounts (Rule 15cl–7) to accounts controlled by broker-dealers because of a customer's reliance on his recommendations.

3. Through statements of policy, the Commission has elaborated upon the implications of new rules and has set out more specific guidelines on selling practices.[15]

Each of these elements relates to the others. Together they have contributed to establishment of policies with respect to selling practices. To break the chain that link these parts in the functioning processes of the SEC would be a mistake. It is equally important to remember, however, that these links do not constitute the entire chain; there is also long-term planning. In the ordinary course of events, both formal and case rules stem from problems that have been brought to the Commission's attention. In effect, Commission action tends to chase industry needs, and in this context, there is a lag between what the Commission is doing and the developments in the industry. It is equally important for the Commission to sit back and view the long picture in order both to anticipate changes and to examine in greater depth those issues that are disturbing the industry. To be effective, this examination must be freed from the intricacies and perplexing trials of everyday affairs.

In part, the tendency for the Commission to slough off its long-term planning responsibilities may be offset by freeing the commissioners from much of the extensive routine functions. Additionally, however, the commissioners themselves must be motivated

15. Ibid.

by a willingness to tackle the kind of problems that require long-term planning for resolution and the kind of investigations that will keep them abreast of industry changes and needs. To accomplish such long-range planning necessitates a constant search for data and facts that establish the basis for investigations and the development of studies that use this information in the eventual formulation of policy decisions. This type of activity does not produce immediate results and is more difficult to formulate into concrete action, but the recommendations that emanate from it are likely to be basic in character and therefore meet challenges from the industry. In addition to time and opportunity, the backing and interest of the commissioners are important requirements necessary to permit the introduction of long-term planning into the activities of the SEC.

THE EFFECTS OF AGE

The early years of any commission are likely to be filled with intellectual derring-do and the challenge of accomplishment, resulting in an emphasis on planning activities and legislative proposals. As the years advance, the tendency is to give more attention to the routine chores involved in implementing the policy decisions that have been adopted. A commission develops a working relationship with its industry that inhibits the close scrutiny of activities or any break with tradition. Accordingly, unless some strong outside force intervenes, the resulting euphoria may well breed a condition of status quo that overlooks the dynamism of industry activity and the accompanying need for change.

The life cycle of an independent commission has been described, perhaps a bit melodramatically but with considerable truth, as falling into four periods. Phase One is "Gestation" and climaxes a prolonged struggle for reform in which advocates of such change "demand some specific action to cure a specific evil."[16] In Phase Two, "Youth," the newly created agency begins its career in "an aggressive, crusading spirit."[17] It assumes a broad view of its responsibilities and defines its role in expansive terms. Phase Three is "The Process of Devitalization," where the spirit of con-

---

16. Marver H. Bernstein, "Regulating Business by Independent Commission," Princeton University Press, 1955, p. 75.

17. Ibid., p. 80.

troversy gradually disappears from the regulatory setting. Here "the approach of a mature commission is heavily judicialized. It routinely devotes most of its time to the adjudication of individual cases. Any latent ability to reconsider regulatory objectives and formulate programs of action is buried under a burden of cases awaiting decisions."[18] In Phase Four, "Debility and Decline," the creative force of the commission is gone and it plays for safety. "Splintered responsibility at the top level, the growth of passivity, acceptance of the judicial model as sacred, and inability to take the initiative required for planning its operations, reduce the commission to managerial ineptitude."[19] This period of old age "is unlikely to terminate until some scandal or emergency calls attention dramatically to the failure of regulation and the need to redefine regulatory objectives and public policies."[20]

This description magnifies the issues, and difficulty probably would be experienced in attempting to divide the life span of any particular commission into such neat categories. In the case of the SEC, the description can be considered as being applicable only in a general manner. Perhaps three broad stages might be more realistic. The first would embrace the initial half-dozen years following the Commission's creation—years marked by the drive for reform, the pursuit of major investigations, vigorous action, and the sponsorship of significant legislation. The next stage would bear the earmarks of "The Process of Devitalization," as the spirit of controversy faded, the approach of the Commission became increasingly judicialized, and it devoted the bulk of its time to the consideration of individual cases and the administration of routine responsibilities. The third stage might be labelled "Drive vs. Decline." With the passage of time, the SEC gave signs of heading towards the debility phase as the judicial model grew more sacred and the absence of planning made inroads into managerial efficiency. Reflecting this condition, the Commission remained passive while serious abuses crept into the operations of the American Stock Exchange, the nation's second largest stock market, just as they had affected the New York Stock Exchange some three decades previously. Then the Commission exhibited renewed buoy-

18. Ibid., p. 89.
19. Ibid., p. 94.
20. Ibid., p. 99.

ancy. In May, 1961, it revoked the broker-dealer registration of the leading specialist firm of the American Stock Exchange, Re, Re & Sagarese, and embarked upon a thorough investigation of that Exchange. This vigorous action, along with the efforts of the Amex, itself, led to an effective reorganization of the Exchange and considerable subsequent gains under a new, strong management. Following a major examination of the securities business, the Commission thereafter took the initiative in sponsoring important legislation and issuing a number of significant rules. These developments may foreshadow a basic change in Commission attitudes that could usher in a period of drive rather than a reversion to the sluggishness that has tended to characterize the old age of other commissions.

The danger of commission desuetude has not gone unobserved, particularly in view of the expanding importance of regulatory agencies as an arm of the Government, and there has been considerable interest in how to maintain their effectiveness. Thus, subsequent to the issuance of the Hoover Commission Report, there was enacted, in 1949, a law to reorganize these agencies. Thereafter other studies and plans of reorganizations followed, including an extensive program by James M. Landis, submitted to the Senate in December, 1960. Much of these efforts have been concerned with spending procedure; the delegation of commission responsibilities to staff members; the relationships of the agencies to Congress and the President; costs of operations; ethical conduct; and, in general, with the amendment of the Administrative Procedure Act and the possible establishment of a permanent administrative conference that would continuously review agency procedures.

Constant observation of regulatory agencies, reduction of the burden of routine chores, and the speeding of procedures will provide greater assurance that the agencies will fulfill their responsibilities. It is questionable, however, whether or not such measures are sufficient to reintroduce vitality into an agency's operations so that it effectively reviews industry developments and encourages or, if necessary, introduces programs that insure the continuing ability of the industry to meet the nation's economic needs. One way of doing so, however, is through the institution of special studies into major problem areas. It is of interest that such studies have preceded many of the major reforms adopted by the regulatory agencies, as indicated by James Landis in his analysis of these agencies.

Admittedly, many of the commissions have neglected their planning or creative functions. This is due in large part to the burden of the routine business thrust upon them and also to the caliber of appointments which have been made in recent years. Planning and policy making have, however, on occasion been carried on effectively by Commissions. The specialist study by the Securities and Exchange Commission, its unlisted trading study, its examination of corporate reorganizations, its investment company study, its examination of corporate trustees, the public utility holding company study of the Federal Trade Commission, its basing point study, the international route study of the Civil Aeronautics Board, are all examples of effective studies and planning undertaken by commissions, all of which have eventuated in basic national policies.[21]

The Special Study of Securities Markets authorized by Congress in 1961 and completed on August 8, 1963, is the most recent illustration of a major SEC investigation that has led to important legislation, a series of self-sponsored reforms by the exchanges and the NASD, and to a spate of new rules by the SEC. Various circumstances combined to induce Congress to authorize the study: the record number of companies that were going public; the "hot issue" phenomenon marked by the appearance of a number of newly formed, inadequately capitalized dealer-firms that marketed the issues of little known companies whose stocks had a rapid initial rise and subsequent collapse; the elevated price-earnings ratios of many companies; the high trading volume and high "fails" to deliver or receive stock certificates; and the spreading of interest in securities manifest by the rapid growth of the investment companies. In lieu of undertaking the job itself, which might have resulted in concentrating the study on an investigation of the Commission, responsibility was turned over by Congress to the SEC, which, recognizing that it did not have the personnel or time for an investigation of the magnitude indicated, called upon outside experts. Eventually, use was made of personnel from the Com-

---

21. Report on Regulatory Agencies to the President-Elect, Submitted by the Chairman of the Subcommittee on Administrative Practice and Procedure to the Committee on the Judiciary of the United States Senate, 86th Cong., 2d sess., December, 1960, p. 18.

mission, the securities business, universities, and the legal profession. Although the Commission worked closely with the staff of the Special Study, the final report was submitted as an independent document to the Commission, which was thus in a position to sift the recommendations into programs for immediate action, later adoption, and further investigation.

The usefulness of such special studies as devices to probe particular problems of major significance or to assess general areas of the field has been demonstrated. Such studies have preceded and sparked much of the major reforms adopted by the SEC. In a number of instances, the requirement for study has been written into legislation, such as Section 11(e) of the Securities Exchange Act, which directed the Commission to study the feasibility of separating the functions of dealer and broker, such study to be submitted by January 3, 1936; Section 19(c), which called for a study of membership rules of national securities exchanges, to end by January 3, 1935; Section 19(d), which created the Special Study and authorized an investigation of the rules and regulations of national securities exchanges for the protection of investors, to be submitted by April 3, 1936; Section 28 of the Securities Act, which called for a study of protective and reorganization committees, to be submitted by January 3, 1936; and Section 30 of the Public Utility Holding Company Act of 1935, which authorized the Commission to make a study of the functions and activities of investment companies, to be submitted by January 4, 1937. To prevent the laxness that might otherwise set in with age and the tendency for a Commission to learn to live in amiable comfort with the regulated industry, the Securities Exchange Act might be amended to require a special study periodically to serve as a soul-searching review of the effectiveness of regulations and the adequacy of existing standards.

The Composition of the SEC

A periodic grand effort at a self-analysis appears desirable to prevent the barnacles of age from growing and to preserve an appreciation of the over-all objectives of regulation divorced from the pressures of current problems or the needs of particular areas. Such studies would be undertaken only occasionally, say every ten years, and might entail outside direction so that the Commission itself may be included in the scope of the survey. But this is not enough. Policy planning must also occur regularly so that recurring needs for action can be disclosed and steps taken on the basis of effective evaluation. The Special Study recognized this requirement. It recommended:

To be able to see the forest instead of just the trees, to be able to evaluate current trends and future potentials as well as past results, the Commission should have a permanent staff group, small but expertly manned, that is free from routine administration and assigned the responsibility of observing and measuring important trends, identifying and evaluating new developments, and from time to time making special studies of particular subjects.[22]

The Commission has taken some steps in this direction. It is not visualized, however, that such a group would either have the personnel or time to conduct the periodic, over-all study of the field that might be undertaken each decade. Accordingly, the periodic study would be done by an outside group of experts, but the Commission's planning staff would be a focal unit within such a group.

THE NEED FOR CHANGE

The high role that the lawyer has played in American history is one of the hallmarks of our culture. In commenting on this characteristic, Henry Steele Commager has observed, "Surely in no other country have lawyers occupied a comparable position or played a comparable role."[23] And he proceeds to cite the extent to which high-ranking officials in different departments of the government have had legal training. The historical composition of the SEC has more than fulfilled the cultural criterion of legal dominance. Between its inception in 1934 and June 30, 1965, there have been 43 commissioners including 15 chairmen. Of the com-

22. Report of Special Study of Securities Markets of the Securities and Exchange Commission, op. cit., Part 1, Letter of Transmittal to the Chairman and Members of the Securities and Exchange Commission, p. XIV.

23. Henry Steele Commager, *The American Mind,* New Haven, Yale University Press, 1950, p. 364.

missioners, approximately two thirds were trained in the law; and of the chairmen, all but two.

In order that the broader view should not be lost in the welter of daily events, a basic change in the composition of the Commission seems desirable. The preoccupation of the Commission with the everyday currency of judicial decision-making and legislative rules is reflected in its legal composition. In view of the important judicial and legislative aspects of Commission responsibilities, it is logical that a large proportion of the commissioners should be lawyers, but this overwhelming bias appears unnecessary and even preventive of the kind of planning function that is imperative. It is to be expected that legally trained commissioners will show a proclivity towards the demanding judicial and legislative chores that must be undertaken and to avoid the equally demanding but perhaps more frustrating planning requirements that often have economic overtones. Accordingly, it seems logical, as a minimum requirement, to include a commissioner whose principal training and interests have been in economic or financial areas, or at least who will be designated as being primarily responsible for planning programs.

The attitudes and methods that an individual brings to a job reflect his background, and there is a sharp difference between those of the lawyer and the economist. The experience of the SEC Special Study highlighted this dichotomy. The lawyer tends to draw conclusions from the evidence of cases and from hearings that often probe into cases more deeply by amassing the testimony of participating individuals. The economist relies for his evidence more heavily on masses of data and attempts to ascertain the trends, relationships, characteristics, and probabilities embodied in large quantities of statistics. When revealed deficiencies call for a cure, the lawyer tends to seek his remedy by the issuance of a corrective rule; when the studies of the economist disclose deficiencies, he prefers to find his cure in the development of a theory which may lead to institutional changes. The lawyer is more concerned with standards of conduct of the participants in an industry; the economist with the economic impact of their actions. The lawyer may be more disposed to view the action of the securities business as it influences private property; the economist may see its role tied more closely to its function as an allocator of capital.

The important thing to recognize is that both these approaches are vital in order to understand the operations of the securities business and to insure its continued usefulness in the economy. Because the authority of the SEC is largely legislative and its functioning judicial, it is to be expected that the lawyer will predominate in its councils. Accordingly, in order to obtain adequate balance in the Commission's decision-making activities, it is important to take positive action to provide for the kind of thinking represented by the economist.

To attain this objective will require the sympathetic support of the commissioners and more particularly of the Chairman, who at least, at first, would have the primary responsibility for overseeing any group established for the conduct of planning studies. The Chairman would be concerned with nurturing its existence during its development period and for obtaining the appropriations necessary for its continued operations. One of the reasons for the restricted activity of the SEC during its hiatus years from World War II to 1964 was the lack of suitable appropriations and personnel. It is a grim truth that much of the efficiency of an independent regulatory agency depends upon the skills of its Chairman in obtaining from both the Bureau of the Budget and Congress the appropriations required for its operations, particularly during periods when public interest is centered on more dramatic areas such as defense and space development.

THE PLANNING STAFF

The SEC has recognized the need for establishing a planning staff within its organization. It has formed a new office for this purpose and created within its framework an economic unit to give greater attention to the economic aspects of the Commission's planning. As this office gains in experience and acquires suitable personnel, it may be expected to provide important new insights into the functions and standards of capital markets and to furnish the basis for developing rules and legislation that permit the capital markets to fulfill the economic needs for which they were primarily created.[24]

---

24. For a list of the type of studies such a group might undertake, see Sidney Robbins and Walter Werner, "Professor Stigler Revisited," *The Journal of Business of the Graduate School of Business of the University of Chicago*, October, 1964, **pp. 406–413.**

Existence of such a planning group is not a novelty to the SEC. In the first years of its operations, its staff included an Economic Adviser to the Commission "charged with the responsibility of conducting certain economic studies." Included in his office was a Section on Special Studies engaged in "the conduct of research and the drafting of reports for certain studies which Congress has directed the Securities and Exchange Commission to make, and others which the Commission will initiate from time to time in order to facilitate the administration of the Securities Act of 1933 and the Securities Exchange Act of 1934."[25] There was also created a Technical Adviser to the Commission responsible among other things for "the assembly and maintenance of economic, market, capital, and other statistics." By its fourth annual report, for the fiscal year ended June 30, 1938, the Office of the Economic Adviser had disappeared, but under the Trading and Exchange Division, there was a Research and Statistics Subdivision, and the Technical Adviser to the Commission remained. As the years passed, and the Commission became more absorbed in its judicial and legislative activities, its economists left, and the number of its special studies was substantially reduced. If the Commission is to upgrade the planning function, it is indispensable that the head of the planning group be included in the Commission's high councils. Indeed, as has been suggested, it would be preferable if a commissioner would be designated specifically to administer this responsibility.

From Commission to Legislation—A Summary View

The concern of the present chapter has been with the Securities and Exchange Commission. It was pointed out that primarily the character of the Commission depends upon its personnel and that the policies of the Commission will reflect philosophical principles rather than party affiliation. Accordingly, the nature of Presidential appointments to the Commission goes a long way to determine the regulatory path that the agency will travel. Of particular significance is the selection of a Chairman who is not

25. 1st Annual Report of the Securities and Exchange Commission, op. cit., pp. 5–6.

only an able administrator but has the negotiating skills to obtain the backing and appropriations required for the agency to function effectively. Given an interested and active Commission, it is probable that competent divisional heads will be chosen and a vigorous staff developed.

Over the years, however, there is a tendency even for able commissioners to become preoccupied with legislative and judicial functions and for an efficient staff to become burdened with the chores of routine functions. To avoid this, the Commission might periodically undertake, say every ten years, a major over-all examination of the securities business. Special studies of this sort have previously proved effective in introducing significant reforms into the field.

Such investigations, however, represent shot-in-the-arm remedies and recurring studies of a planning nature are also required to assess developments and to evaluate the need for encouraging or taking action. A factor in the way of such studies has been the high percentage of lawyers among the commissioners and chairmen. By inclination and training, it is to be expected that individuals with a legal background will tend to emphasize their current judicial and legal responsibilities rather than the formulation of long-term programs. Some measure of assurance that planning studies will be pursued might be obtained by the appointment of a commissioner whose principal interest is in this area. Also, to provide for the conduct of basic continuing studies, a staff with such responsibility should be maintained within the SEC organization. Such a group, in which an economic unit is included, already has been established. Over the longer term, the ability of the SEC to develop suitable planning programs to underly its policy formulations will depend upon the interest of the commissioners in supporting the activities of this group; otherwise it may fade away.

While the SEC is responsible for administering seven different statutes, two of them—the Securities Act of 1933 and the Securities Exchange Act of 1934—are of particular importance. The principles underlying the Commission's administration of these statutes are considered in the following chapter.

4

The Basic Securities Act and Self-Regulation— An Exercise in Government-Industry Cooperation

Of particular importance to the financial markets, as has been indicated, is the role of the Securities and Exchange Commission in administering the Securities Act of 1933 and the Securities Exchange Act of 1934. A fundamental philosophic issue that had to be hammered out in the creation of the Securities Exchange Act was the form its administration should take.

In the original version of the bill, the Commission (the Federal Trade Commission) was endowed with vast powers. Section 18(c), referred to as a "bundle of happy thoughts" by *The New York Times,* not only gave the Federal Trade Commission direct authority over such matters as conduct of business on the exchanges, election of officers, commission rates, minimum units of trading, and odd-lot transactions, but also incorporated the grandiose injunction "to prescribe such rules and regulations . . . in addition to those specifically provided in the Act, as it may deem necessary or appropriate in the public interest or for the protection of investors."

In the hearings on the bill, this concentration of power was staunchly defended by Landis, then a commissioner of the Federal Trade Commission. He said:

> Now, that makes me want to interject this consideration, namely, that the objection may well be raised that large powers, as I say, are granted, large, wide, and discretionary powers are granted to the Commission. Is not that an enormous step to take? I think we ought to recognize this fact that these powers, these large powers are today being exercised not by the Government, but these powers are being exercised by the governing boards of the exchanges, and the fact that the Government steps in to assume or exercise those powers which work for the public good or public detriment, is not unusual.[1]

A different point of view was taken by the Committee on Stock Regulation, whose chairman was John Dickinson, then Assistant Secretary of Commerce.[2] In its report, the Committee recommended the establishment of a Stock Exchange Authority with discretionary powers of regulation. In order to be entitled to a license, an exchange would have to submit its rules to the Stock Exchange Authority. These rules, in turn, would have to be at least as stringent as those set forth in the statute and developed by the Exchange Authority. The committee, however, further cautioned

> . . . the nonlegal, quick acting, nonreviewable disciplinary measures which an exchange can take, can never be adequately replaced by the slower moving processes of an administrative agency or the courts, and the objective should be to preserve and utilize these private mechanisms to the extent possible.[3]

In testifying before the Committee on Interstate and Foreign Commerce, Mr. Roper elaborated upon this view that the primary responsibility for control rested with the exchanges and that the regulatory function of the Stock Exchange Authority was to be held in reserve. He said

---

1. Hearings before the Committee on Interstate and Foreign Commerce, House of Representatives, 73rd Cong., 2d sess., on H. R. 7852, H. R. 8720, 1934, p. 22.

2. This committee was known as the Roper Committee because it was appointed by Daniel C. Roper, then Secretary of Commerce.

3. U.S. Department of Commerce, Committee on Stock Exchange Regulation, Letter from the President of the United States to the Chairman of the Committee on Banking and Currency, 1934, p. 12.

In the report of the Roper committee, therefore, the action of the Government through the proposed stock exchange authority—which incidentally was to have no other duties than to be a stock exchange authority and was to be free to devote its entire time to the task of exchange regulation—nevertheless the functions, the regulatory functions of this governmental agency were held in reserve and were employed only to supplement and supervise what in the first instance was self-regulation of the exchanges.[4]

Out of these differences, a compromise was reached—biased however in the direction of the Dickinson Committee Report. Section 18 of the bill was rewritten. The nature of the changes is reflected in the difference between the original title, "Special Powers of Commission," and the new one, "Disciplinary Powers Over Exchanges," which eventually became Section 19 of the current Act, "Powers With Respect to Exchanges and Securities." But these powers are largely those of an overseer rather than a performer. The concept that finally emerged was that of self-regulation, much as suggested by Dickinson. In this notion, primary responsibility for insuring that the exchanges meet their public function rests with the exchanges themselves, while the Commission retains the ancillary function of stepping in only when necessary. To Douglas, then Chairman of the SEC, the relationship seemed much like that of a father who relies primarily upon his daughter's own scruples to preserve her honor, but who is ready to adopt protective measures of his own should the need arise. Thus he described the relationship as

letting the exchanges take the leadership with Government playing a residual role. Government would keep the shotgun, so to speak, behind the door, loaded, well oiled, cleaned, ready for use but with the hope it would never have to be used.[5]

Self-regulation thus came to be the major legislative principle underlying the Commission's role in carrying out the functions of the securities acts. The present chapter is devoted to an analysis of this vital idea, as enunciated in the acts and achieved in practice.

---

4. Hearings Before the Committee on Interstate and Foreign Commerce House of Representatives on H.R. 7852, H.R. 8720, op. cit., p. 513.

5. Quoted in Report of Special Study of Securities Markets of the Securities and Exchange Commission, 88th Cong., 1st sess., H. Doc. 95, 1963, Part 4, Chapter XII, p. 698.

As background to this evaluation, there is first provided a review of the purpose and contents of the two major securities acts, including the pertinent amendments adopted in 1964.

The Basic Securities Acts

Prior to the passage of the first of the securities acts in 1933, there was a long period of spadework during which the ground was being prepared for Federal legislation in the securities field. Since 1885, various public leaders, Congressmen, and presidents had made efforts to obtain Federal incorporation or licensing of corporations.[6] In 1909, Governor Charles Evans Hughes of New York appointed a committee to investigate speculation in securities and commodities. Three years later, the Pujo Investigation of the "money trust" was instituted, leading to drastic recommendations for strengthening the stock exchange but not to any legislation.

Probably the most powerful stimuli to action were the stock-market crash of October, 1929, and the depression that followed. These events dramatized the need for reform. In March, 1932, the Senate passed a resolution calling for an investigation, principally of short selling, by its Committee on Banking and Currency. With a new and driving administration in office, the Senate in the following year increased considerably the investigatory scope of the committee's activities. The zealous probe of the field that followed, spearheaded by Ferdinand Pecora, who had been appointed counsel to the committee, paved the way for passage of the Securities Act of 1933.

THE SECURITIES ACT OF 1933

The Securities Act is concerned generally with the initial distribution of securities. Its primary purpose is to make available to the public financial and related information concerning such securities. A second purpose is to prohibit misrepresentation and other fraudulent acts in the sale of securities, whether or not registration is required.

---

6. Loss, op. cit., Vol. II, p. 1181.

The Registration Statement and Prospectus—The primary objective of disclosure is achieved by a requirement in two stages. Firstly, issuers, underwriters for issuers, and persons in a control relationship to the issuer, who are engaged in a public distribution, must file registration statements containing the required information with the SEC. Secondly, purchasers and investors that receive written offers to sell through the mails must be provided with a prospectus containing the necessary information from the registration statement in order to permit them to evaluate the issuer and its securities. So long as a firm continues to act as an underwriter of an original offering or as a dealer effecting transactions in securities that constitute part of his unsold portion of an original offering, the obligation to furnish a prospectus remains, no matter how much time has elapsed since the commencement of the offering.[7]

In a schedule of the Act, there is a long list of requirements to be incorporated in the registration statement, including information on the issuer, its capitalization, its officers and directors, the purpose of the financing, the terms of the underwriting, financial statements, and a number of legal agreements. The prospectus, representing the first part of the statement, is distributed to the public and contains the financial and related information of general interest to investors. The second part of the statement contains the material of a more technical nature such as marketing arrangements, the expenses of the distribution and various legal exhibits.

After the registration statement is filed, a waiting period of at least twenty days is required, during which the Commission examines both documents carefully in order to insure that all the required information has been fully and accurately disclosed. In considering a request for acceleration of the effective date, the Commission has required that a preliminary prospectus be furnished at a reasonable time in advance of the expected effective date of the registration statement to each underwriter and dealer that is expected to be invited to participate in the distribution of the security. This preliminary prospectus must contain substantially the data required by the act except for the omission of information generally related to the offering price. Since SEC rules require

---

7. Securities and Exchange Commission, Release No. 4726, September, 1964.

that the front page of such a prospectus indicate in red ink that it is preliminary in form, the document has become known as a *red herring* prospectus.

After-Market Redistributions—The foregoing policies provide some assurance that the original purchasers of registered securities will receive the required information, but they do not affect purchasers in the immediate after-market, who may be in greater need of the disclosures than the original distributees. Accordingly, the Act provided that, except for unsolicited brokerage transactions, a prospectus also must be delivered in every transaction involving a registered security by any dealer, whether or not he had participated in the original offering, during a forty-day period after the start of the offering.

With respect to seasoned issues, where a prior offering had been made, the Special Study of Securities Markets expressed the belief that the forty-day requirement was sufficient and that, at any rate, there was likely to be a reservoir of publicly available information concerning such issues. With respect to new issues, however, it was found that not only did a substantial redistribution occur in the after-market through trading firms but that many firms made no effort to comply with the statutory requirement of delivery.[8] Accordingly, following a recommendation of the Special Study, the Securities Acts Amendments of 1964 extended the forty-day period of the 1933 Act to ninety days for transactions in a security where no previous public offering had occurred, the Commission having power to shorten this period.

Desiring to put teeth into this delivery requirement, the SEC also adopted rules stating that a prospectus, with specified exceptions, had to display a statement indicating how long (subsequent to the offering date) dealers must deliver it to public buyers of the security. The intention was that this provision would remind dealers, whether or not they participated in the original distribution, of their continuing obligation to deliver a prospectus for the designated period and would put investors on notice regarding this obligation.[9]

---

8. Report of Special Study of Securities Markets of the Securities and Exchange Commission, op. cit., Part I, Chapter IV, pp. 549–550.

9. Securities Act of 1933, Section 4(3); General Rules and Regulations under the Securities Act of 1933, Rules 174, 425A.

The Regulation A Exemption—The Securities Act states that offerings of securities not exceeding $300,000 may be exempted from registration subject to whatever conditions the Commission may prescribe. In accordance with this provision, the Commission has adopted Regulation A which permits companies to make such exempt offerings by filing a limited amount of information and furnishing an offering circular containing such information. Of importance is the fact that the financial statements included need not be certified.

The Special Study found that securities exempt under Regulation A, including equity as well as debt issues, accounted for only a small part of total dollar offerings but represented a large number of issues by small corporations, including many newly formed firms. Thus in the years 1959–1961, less than $160 million of equity issues were offered under Regulation A but in each of the first two of these years, there were about three-fourths as many Regulation A issues as there were registered issues. In 1961 the proportion fell to about 60 per cent because of a large increase in the number of fully registered small issues. Of particular interest was the fact that a much higher ratio of Regulation A issues than registered issues were unseasoned.[10]

The Regulation A exemption confronts the Commission with a delicate problem. On the one hand, the multiplicity of such issues and the susceptibility of small investors to their purchase suggest the need for insisting upon a full reporting of information. On the other hand, the expense of such reporting, including provision for certified statements, could be burdensome to small companies. Thus the Regulation A exemption represents an important grey area where continuing study is required to determine appropriate guidelines of reporting.

Unregistered Distributions—As indicated previously, a public offering must be registered under the Securities Act only when the offering is by the issuer or a person directly or indirectly controlling or controlled by the issuer. If the offering is by someone else, no registration and therefore no disclosure under the Act is required. Moreover, unregistered offerings such as those effected through secondary distributions, which are essentially exchange-authorized

10. Report of Special Study of Securities Markets of the Securities and Exchange Commission, op. cit., Part I, Chapter IV, pp. 484–487.

underwritings of listed securities in the over-the-counter markets, may be completed within a very short period of time, thereby affording buyers little opportunity to make an objective evaluation. Thus, the information furnished and the breathing-spell required between registration and actual sale in a registered offering stand in sharp contrast to the absence of these protective elements in an unregistered offering.

Because of the various forms that unregistered distributions may take and the absence of formal control over these transactions, the SEC has only limited information on the volume that takes place. The Special Study, however, estimated that in 1961 the dollar volume of unregistered distributions of common stock was more than one-fifth as large as the total of registered common stock offerings by issuers and about one-half as large as the total of registered common stock offerings by persons other than issuers for the same year.

The substantial volume of unregistered distributions that takes place and the absence of data provided to investors in such offerings represent a gap in the disclosure system. Contributing to the difficulty of closing this gap is the impracticability of expecting persons not in a control position with respect to the issuer to provide information concerning the issuer. As some solution to the problem, the Special Study recommended that broker-dealers managing an unregistered distribution should file with the Commission information concerning the distribution itself, and that a short waiting period might be imposed between the filing of notification and the commencement of the distribution.[11]

Antifraud Provisions—There are three basic fraud provisions in the securities laws: Section 17(a) of the Securities Act, and Sections 10(b) and 15(c) of the Securities Exchange Act. Prior to the Securities Act, the Federal government could only deal with securities frauds by criminal prosecution for violating the mail fraud statute or for conspiring to violate it. Section 17(a) was a material advance over the mail fraud statute, in that it referred specifically to the sale of securities, afforded the civil remedy of injunction, and was applicable to material misstatements and half-truths. Under the banner of fraud, the Commission in 1939 issued

---

11. Ibid, pp. 559–570.

its famous *shingle* theory, subsequently upheld by the courts, which holds that, even at arm's length, a dealer by hanging out his shingle implies that he will deal fairly with the public. Section 17(b) of the Securities Act is also a limited sort of anti-touting provision.[12]

Summary—In addition to the general question of fraud, a major problem emanating from the Securities Act is the determination of the kind and form of information that should be initially provided investors in a public distribution of securities. It is clearly not sufficient simply to require the filing of more data and its incorporation into the prospectus. The documents may become so complicated that even sophisticated investors could have difficulty interpreting the data provided. Because the operations of the modern corporation are complex and accounting standards are flexible, however, it is not easy to obtain simplification of essentially complicated material into understandable form. This effort to obtain an appropriate balance between comprehensiveness and understandability of reported information represents a major continuing problem of administering the Securities Act. The problem is magnified by the legal niceties that constantly obtrude when an attempt is made to present a portion of the prospectus in a simple manner.

THE SECURITIES EXCHANGE ACT OF 1934

Just as the Securities Act is primarily applicable to distributions, the Securities Exchange Act pertains to the trading markets. Congress recognized that the absence of continuing suitable data concerning a company facilitated the issuance of misleading information, prevented an adequate evaluation of its securities, and encouraged manipulation. Accordingly, a primary objective of this Act is the extension of the disclosure principle to the trading markets; other major aims include the regulation of credit and the prevention of fraud and specific abuses.

Antifraud Provisions—These provisions of the Securities Exchange Act are discussed first because they were mentioned in connection with Section 17(a) of the Securities Act and should be considered with it. Section 10(b) of the Securities Exchange Act makes it unlawful for any person through any means of inter-

---

12. Loss, op. cit., Vol. III, pp. 1423–1425, 1482–1490.

state commerce in connection with the purchase or sale of a security to use any manipulative or deceptive device in contravention of the rules prescribed by the SEC. In 1936, Congress amended the Securities Exchange Act by adding what is the present Section 15(c)(1), under which no broker or dealer may use any means of interstate commerce to effect any transaction (otherwise than on a national securities exchange) by means of manipulative, deceptive, or other fraudulent devices.

Unlike Section 10(b), Section 15(c)(1) is self-operative, limited to over-the-counter transactions, and applicable only to transactions by brokers and dealers. As part of the Maloney Act Amendment several years later, Congress further extended the scope of Section 15(c). Even after these additions, there was nothing in the acts or rules to cover fraud in the purchase of securities by persons other than brokers and dealers. An officer, director, or principal stockholder of a corporation could purchase its securities by fraudulent practices and only be subject to criminal prosecution under the mail fraud statute. To close the gap, the SEC adopted Rule 10b–5, which substantially applies the language of Section 17(a) of the Securities Act to the purchase or sale of securities. While Rule 10b–5 applies to any person, insider or outsider, its most intriguing problems have risen in connection with the purchase of their corporations' securities by corporate insiders. In 1965, as will be discussed, the Commission made use of this rule in a way that had important implications to insiders.

In addition to the basic fraud provisions, Section 9 of the Securities Exchange Act outlaws a series of specific manipulative practices. Falling within its scope are wash sales, matched orders, and pool operations. When not in contravention of SEC rules, however, the Section permits stabilizing transactions for the purpose of preventing or retarding a decline in price of a security during a public offering. Also the Commission is empowered to issue rules regulating puts and calls in relation to any security registered on a national securities exchange.

Periodic Reporting—As a prerequisite to listing, the act requires the filing (with both the applicable exchange and the Commission) of a registration statement similar to that required for registration of new issues under the Securities Act. This information must be kept current by annual and other periodic reports. In its investigation of investment advice, the Special Study found that this valuable source of data, subject to SEC check for accuracy, was not as widely used, even by professional analysts, as might be expected.

As a conspicuous illustration, it cited the case of Atlantic Research Corporation, which operated with a number of subsidiary corporations. During the years 1960 to 1962, several firms recommended purchase of the stock in reflection of favorable profit statements as reported by the Company and published by both major financial services, Standard & Poor's and Moody's. Yet, during the same period, certified financial statements filed with the Commission showed that Atlantic Research had actually sustained losses instead of obtaining substantial profits. The striking difference in reporting was caused by the fact that the publicly released statements were unconsolidated, whereas those filed with the Commission were on a consolidated basis, as required.

Accordingly, among the recommendations of the Special Study to improve the practices of member firms of self-regulatory agencies was that, in printed investment advice which purports to analyze issuers, required references should be made to most recently filed official disclosures by issuers. Also, representations should be provided that such filed information had been examined, with specific identification of issuers for which no officially filed information is available.[13]

Proxy Solicitation—The act authorizes the Commission to prescribe rules governing the solicitation of proxies pertaining to listed securities. Among other things, these rules provide that the proxy shall identify clearly and impartially each matter intended to be acted upon, and whether the proposal is by the management or by security holders. Opportunity must be afforded to specify a choice between approval or disapproval of each item, other than elections to office. Information must be included about the persons on whose behalf proxies are solicited and about nominees for office. Where control is at stake, the names and interests of all participants in the contest must be disclosed. Within the framework of established procedures, minority stockholders may include in management

13. Report of Special Study of Securities Markets of the Securities and Exchange Commission, op. cit., Part 1, Chapter III, p. 387.

solicitations proper proposals to be submitted to stockholder vote.

Financial statements are required in specified instances. Also, if the proxy relates to a meeting at which directors are to be elected, the shareholders must be supplied with an annual report containing adequate financial statements for the preceding fiscal year. Reflecting the discrepancies revealed in the Atlantic Research case, the Commission enacted a rule in 1964 providing that any material differences in the financial statements to securities holders from the principles of consolidation or other accounting principles or practices, applicable to the financial statements of the issuer that are filed with the Commission, must be noted and the effect reconciled in the report.[14]

Insider Trading—In order to prevent corporate officials from using inside information for the purpose of speculating in the stock of their corporations, Section 16 of the Act provides three checks.

1. Each officer, director, and beneficial owner of more than 10 per cent of any listed class of stock must file with the Commission and the exchange an initial statement of his holdings and thereafter monthly reports that reflect any changes in his holdings.[15]

2. Profits obtained by insiders from transactions in the corporation's stock within any six months' period may be recovered by the company or by any security holder on its behalf.

3. Insiders are prohibited from engaging in short sales of their companies' stock.

These provisions afford investors valuable protection against abuses revealed, in the hearings on the act, to have been made by insiders. Each provision has a different aim. The first, like the philosophy inherent in the entire body of securities laws, affords protection, primarily through disclosure. In this respect, the publication of insider transactions suffers from the inevitable delay

---

14. Securities and Exchange Commission, General Rules and Regulations, Securities Exchange Act of 1934, Rule 14a–3(b).

15. In the fall of 1965, Senator Harrison A. Williams, Jr. (Dem., N.J.), chairman of the Senate securities subcommittee, introduced a bill aimed at "corporate raiding." The measure would require disclosure of the identity of any person, or group of persons acting jointly, who acquire as much as 5 per cent of the voting stock of any registered company. It would also give the SEC broader authority to obtain disclosure of the buying of their own stock by corporations.

between the actual transaction and its reporting. Even though this publicity may be too late in influencing a stockholder's investment practices, however, it provides at least useful information to question the insider's actions.

The second provision goes one step further. Armed with the necessary information, the company or a security holder may recover short-term profits for the benefit of the company. This provision has been criticized because it applies only when a profit is incurred although damage may result from the unprofitable misuse of information. Also, recovery under the act aids the corporation rather than the injured party who bought or sold from the insider, and constructive transactions by the insider may be inhibited. Nevertheless, the temptation to abuse probably has been reduced and through long use the effectiveness of the provision has been enhanced.[16]

In contrast to the SEC's general authority to regulate short sales by rule, the third provision establishes a direct prohibition of short sales by insiders. In this context, short selling apparently is associated with speculation and the intent is to relieve the insider from the temptation of using this device for his personal advantage. A short sale occurs when the seller of a stock does not own it or has ownership but does not want to deliver it. In order to make delivery, therefore, he borrows the stock, and at some later time returns it to the lender, ordinarily by purchase in the open market. Often, the short seller is a speculator, who anticipates a market decline and hopes that he will be able to buy, or *cover*, at a lower price, thereby realizing his profit in the difference between the sale price and the subsequent purchase price.

It may appear inherently wrong for an insider to sell the shares of his own company short and, when originally adopted, the provision had considerable justification to ward off danger that an insider could exploit his access to advance information by spearheading a speculative drive on the stock. If the insider is deprived of the opportunity of taking advantage of such advance information, as discussed in the following section, there may be less need for the absolute prohibition against his selling short. Indeed, in these circumstances, such a transaction might even be

16. Loss, op. cit., Vol. II, pp. 1087–1091.

construed to have a constructive result if the stock actually is overvalued relative to the company's basic financial prospects.

Fraud by the Insider—Of considerable importance to insiders is the extent to which their activities may be affected by the legal interpretations given to Rule 10b–5 which, as mentioned previously, is generally concerned with fraudulent practices and misstatements or half-truths in connection with the purchase or sale of securities. Here the emphasis is on fraud in contrast to Section 16(b) which, although aimed at misuses of inside information, permits recovery of insider profits without the need to show actual misuse but with the requirement that the profits are short-term. While Rule 10b–5 was not specifically groomed to fit the insider problem, it has had particularly significant developments in this area because of the obviously disadvantageous position "outside" stockholders could occupy in such transactions.

The Rule has had a jagged history but the tenor of judicial and regulatory action thus far has been to broaden the meaning of the term *insiders,* widen the scope of those who may bring action, and ease the basis of action. Within a year after the Rule's adoption, the Commission published a report of an investigation of a series of transactions involving the Ward La France Truck Corporation in order to call attention to its opinion that they were in violation of Rule 10b–5. In that case, two officers of the Corporation had authorized a broker to buy shares of the Corporation in the over-the-counter market for the issuer's account at prices as low as $3.25, and averaging $9.71 a share. The stockholders were not informed of such pertinent facts as that the Corporation was the buyer, that its earnings had improved from $2.75 to $15.75 per share, and that negotiations were in process to sell the controlling shares at $45 and to liquidate the Company at a figure affording the stockholders $25 per share.[17]

Several years thereafter, the first important judicial decision was issued in a case involving four persons as sole stockholders of a corporation. Here the court sustained the private right of action of a father and son suing two brothers for an accounting of profits resulting from the defendants' purchase of the stock of the plaintiffs, who had not been informed of the prior sale of the bulk of

17. *In the Matter of Ward La France Truck Corp.,* 13 SEC 373 (1943).

the corporate assets.[18] And some four years later, the power of the rule was indicated by an important court decision upholding a claim under Rule 10b–5 that had not been sustained under a common-law action. In this case, Transamerica Corporation, as the majority stockholder of the Axton-Fisher Tobacco Company, gained inside information regarding the latter's considerable inventories, purchased most of the minority-held shares at a price far below their liquidating value and then caused Axton-Fisher to be dissolved. In a common-law suit brought by a selling stockholder, the court granted summary judgment for the defendant on the grounds that it had not been guilty of misrepresentation, while in a later similar action also based on Rule 10b–5 the court held for the plaintiff.[19]

Thereafter, the reported cases continued to extend the implications of Rule 10b–5 to cover actions against the original wrong-doers, even though the plaintiff did not purchase securities directly from them, to stretch the meaning of insiders to include subsequent buyers that might reasonably be aware that they were the recipients of inside information, and to liberalize the type of information to be disclosed.[20] In a landmark decision issued in 1961, the Commission held that the antifraud provision of Rule 10b–5 applied to a partner of the brokerage firm of Cady, Roberts & Co., who had sold the common stock of Curtiss-Wright for his wife's account and for the discretionary accounts of customers on the basis of advance information regarding the reduction of the company's regular dividend, received from a salesman of the brokerage firm who was also a director of Curtiss-Wright.[21] The Commission indicated that even though the partner executing the transaction held no position with Curtiss-Wright, he had received corporate information prior to the first public release. Like an insider, therefore, he had the obligation of disclosing material facts or, if disclosure were improper, to forego the transaction.

In the spring of 1965, the SEC took a dramatic step that had

---

18. *Kardon* v. *National Gypsum Co.*, 73 Fed. Supp. 798 (1947).

19. See Loss, *Securities Regulation,* Boston, Little, Brown, 1961, Vol. III, pp. 1458–1462.

20. See David S. Ruder, "Civil Liability Under Rule 10b–5," *Northwestern University Law Review,* January-February, 1963, pp. 667–684.

21. *In the Matter of Cady, Roberts & Co.,* 40 SEC 907 (1961).

major implications to the role of the insider in the corporation. This action was in the form of a suit in a Federal district court, based on Rule 10b–5, charging that thirteen officers, directors and employees of the Texas Gulf Sulphur Company had used inside information about the company's Timmins, Ontario, ore strike for their own benefit or the benefit of others by trading in the stock before the public was informed of the true nature of the rich copper and zinc discovery. The Commission further claimed that the first press release by the company eventually issued, at the insistence of the New York Stock Exchange, attempted to moderate the significance of the find. The SEC sought recision of the sales made to insiders between November 12, 1963, when it was believed the insiders were in a position to appraise the worth of the find, and April 12, 1964, when the first press announcement was made. The Commission also sought to have the company made directly liable for all sales of the stock between April 12 and April 16 when a more realistic revelation concerning the ore discovery was provided.

The SEC charge against Texas Gulf Sulphur stimulated keen interest in such proceedings and unleashed a number of damage suits by former stockholders against the company and certain officers. Also, similar suits against other corporate managements made their appearance as stockholders sought to obtain profits, presumably foregone by the failure of buyers to disclose material facts. Eventually one of these cases may reach the Supreme Court, which has not as yet had the opportunity to review a Rule 10b–5 suit.[22] At any rate, as more court decisions are reached, they could establish the basis for defining more clearly the extent to which insiders may act on the information at their disposal. At one extreme, insiders have insights into the routines of daily activity that require

---

22. In 1964, the Supreme Court favored a stockholder's private right of action against J. I. Case Company in a suit involving an allegedly false proxy statement issued by the company. The court pointed out that although the language of the applicable section of the Securities Exchange Act "makes no special reference to a private right of action, among its chief purposes is the 'protection of investors,' which certainly implies the availability of judicial relief where necessary to achieve that result." This reference to the famous "protection of investors" clause and the strong statement in behalf of the shareholders' private right of action may have important implications for Rule 10b–5. See, *J. I. Case Co.* v. *Borak*, 337 U.S. 426 (1964).

no special disclosure and that do not prevent them from making executions in a company's stock. At the other extreme, the knowledge to which they have access may exert such a positive bearing upon the company's prospects that it would be a failure to meet their fiduciary responsibilities to stockholders not to make proper disclosure. Included in this category, it has been suggested, is such information as "decreased earnings, dividend cuts, loss of valuable contracts and the like" because "the need for disclosure to public investors of facts material to their investment decisions outweighs any harm to the issuer that might result from such disclosure.[23]

As these two extreme positions narrow, a gray area is created where clarification may be deferred until more decisions on the subject are rendered. In the interim, insiders undoubtedly are learning to proceed more carefully before executing transactions in their companies' stocks. For example, Keith Funston, president of the NYSE, has cautioned the corporate official "who conscientiously seeks to do the right thing" to keep a check-list of questions such as the following: "Has the press reported the news of any development which could be viewed as influencing my decision to buy or sell? Are there any pending developments which need to be made public before I may feel free to participate in the market? Is there anything I don't know about that might prove embarrassing to me after the fact?" And he suggests that a straightforward discussion with the chief executive officer of the company can probably provide the answer to the last question. As another possibility, Funston indicated that the insider might buy stock in his company through a periodic investment plan involving regular purchases under an established program administered by a broker; or he might try to time his transactions so that they occurred during an appropriate period, such as the thirty days beginning one week after the distribution of a comprehensive annual report.[24]

Thus, through SEC and court interpretations, the scope of Rule 10b–5 has been magnified during the twenty-odd years that it has been in effect, principally along the following lines.

1. Defining the insider to include any person who has direct or

---

23. Michael Joseph, "Civil Liability Under Rule 10b–5—A Reply," *Northwestern University Law Review,* May-June, 1964, p. 182.

24. Keith Funston, Address to the *Financial World* Annual Reports Banquet at the New York Hilton Hotel, October 26, 1965.

indirect access to corporate information not available to those with whom he is dealing.

2. Enlarging the group to whom the insider owes a duty to encompass not only the current stockholders but also outsiders who buy shares.

3. Extending the insiders' affirmative obligation to report material facts.

4. Eliminating the need for face-to-face transactions in private actions.[25]

This tendency for the application of the rule to grow has caused concern in some quarters. It has been contended that a continuation of this trend could have detrimental effects upon the economy in various ways.[26] The quality of corporate management may be lowered. For one thing, outside directors may become reluctant to accept assignments because of their enlarged liabilities. Such a development could deteriorate the caliber of corporate management, since inclusion of outside directors generally is considered very desirable in order to enlarge management's perspective and to provide some restraint upon its activities. Then again, management may become reluctant to own stock in the corporation with which it is associated because of the implicit risk in determining whether or not information in its possession is material. As a result, the incentive aspects of such ownership would be lost.

The diminished advantages of stock ownership to management, in turn, could cause the business community to become less aggressive and to dull its enthusiasm for seeking new investment opportunities. A retardation in the rate of new investment would hold back capital formation and dampen the growth of national income, consumption spending, and employment.

Another consequence of enlarging the liability of the insider may be the reluctance of institutional investors to trade in common stocks as vigorously as they once did. A bank trustee, for example, may be uncertain of the use he might make of knowledge derived from his banking connections prior to the public availability of such information. Or a mutual fund that has obtained special in-

25. David S. Ruder, "Pitfalls in the Development of a Federal Law of Corporations by Implications Through Rule 10b–5," *Northwestern Law Review,* May-June, 1964, pp. 191–207.

26. Ibid., pp. 208–214.

sights into a corporation's condition by adroit questioning of management nevertheless may be reluctant to act prior to any general announcement. It is true that an insider presumably is under no obligation to provide the investor with the benefit of his superior financial analysis,[27] but there may be uncertainty as to whether such results are the outcome of independent evaluations or of the transmission of private information. As a result, institutional participation in the securities markets may be restrained with consequent impairment of liquidity and a general lowering of investor confidence.

It is hard to make a prediction concerning the economic effects of Rule 10b–5 without knowing the framework within which it will eventually fall. The foreboding consequences suggested in the above analysis, however, do not seem probable. Even if the rule should be so extended as to result in all investors having access to the same information for the purpose of reaching decisions, there is no reason to believe that management or institutional investors would become disenchanted with stocks as a means of investment. Rather the basis of effecting transactions may shift from seeking priority of information to placing greater emphasis on security analysis, where it probably belongs. If anything, such development could be construed to have favorable economic implications because sharpened tools of security analysis might cause the securities markets to become a more efficient allocator of funds. Thus far, however, the implications to the markets and to the economy of a broadened scope of Rule 10b–5 have been the product of speculation rather than of genuine study. Yet, there can be little doubt that the process of effecting transactions of an important body of investors already has been and may be even further affected by future legal interpretations of the rule. What does seem reasonable, therefore, is that in making these decisions both the courts and the SEC should consider more carefully the economic repercussions of their actions.

Application to the Over-the-Counter Market—As a result of a 1936 addition to the Securities Exchange Act, companies offering securities of a minimum stipulated size had to meet the periodic and other reporting requirements of the Act. These companies,

---

27. Loss, op. cit., Vol. III, p. 1463.

however, were not subject to the proxy or insider requirements of the Act. Because of these limitations, a number of national companies whose issues were actively traded in the over-the-counter market fell outside the scope of the Act. For a number of years, efforts were made to rectify this condition, but no legislative action resulted until passage of the Securities Acts Amendments of 1964.

A major purpose of the 1964 legislation was to afford investors in publicly held companies whose securities are traded over the counter the same fundamental protection as is provided to investors in companies whose securities are listed on an exchange. For this purpose, the new legislation extends the registration, periodic reporting, proxy solicitation, and insider reporting and trading provisions of the Securities Exchange Act to over-the-counter issuers that meet specified tests of size.

More specifically, these provisions apply to all issuers that have both total assets, as generally indicated by the consolidated balance sheet, in excess of $1 million, and a class of nonexempt equity security held of record initially by 750 or more persons, and after July 1, 1966, by 500 persons. Insurance companies are exempt from the new requirements provided they are appropriately regulated by the state in which they are incorporated. Although the Securities Exchange Act applies to banks, administration and enforcement of the provisions (whether listed or unlisted) is by the applicable Federal bank regulatory agency. The Commission may exempt any issuer or class of issuers from these provisions on such grounds as limited trading interest or the nature of the issuer's activities. As some indication of the extent to which such exemptions may occur, in the first year after the new requirements became effective, the Commission received some fifty applications for exemption, granted nineteen, denied three and had the others still pending.[28]

The Extension of Credit—Securities are unique economic assets. Because of the mechanism developed to facilitate transactions, many of them have virtual immediate liquidity, that is, they can be bought or sold at approximately the current price at any time. Liquidity enhances considerably their desirability to lenders and their usefulness to borrowers as collateral for loans. The ex-

---

28. *The Wall Street Journal,* September 8, 1965.

tensive employment of securities for this purpose, in turn, has contributed to the volatility of stock prices and led the framers of the Securities Exchange Act to regulate the extension of credit that is collateralized by securities. Primary authority for administering this area of regulation was given to the Federal Reserve System because of its general responsibility for directing the nation's credit controls. The Board of Governors has tended to view the regulation of stock as another tool in the formulation of broad credit and monetary policies.

The regulatory coverage established in the Act is mixed; under it the Board of Governors has issued only Regulation T applicable to broker-dealers and Regulation U applicable to domestic banks. The net result is a complicated pattern of controls. While the statute enables the Board to prescribe margin requirements both for the initial extension and for the maintenance of credit, the Board has established only initial requirements, leaving the formulation of maintenance requirements to the self-regulating agencies.

With respect to broker-dealers, the statute authorizes the Board to regulate loans for the purpose of purchasing or carrying securities (*purpose loans*) or for a purpose other than purchasing or carrying securities (*nonpurpose loans*), but Regulation T applies only to purpose loans. Under the Act, a broker-dealer, in making a purpose loan, (with certain limited exceptions) could only accept as collateral listed securities or exempt securities, such as Government bonds; but he may accept unlisted securities for a nonpurpose loan. With respect to other lenders, the statute does not apply to nonpurpose loans or to loans for the purpose of carrying unlisted securities. Since Regulation U applies only to domestic banks, lenders (such as factors or foreign banks) are completely free from regulation under present circumstances. In effect, except for the case of broker-dealers, only banks fall within current regulations, and then only on loans for the purpose of purchasing or carrying listed securities, whether such a loan is collateralized by listed or unlisted stock.

It is not easy to keep in mind the varied applications of the statute and the scope of the regulations that the Board of Governors has seen fit to issue under it. In part, the differences arise from the hesitation of the Board to extend substantially a difficult supervising job; in part, they reflect the Board's reluctance to make inroads into the collateral usefulness of an asset. Even though one may understand the reasons for this existence, the gaps and anomalies in the current hodgepodge of statutory and regulatory enactments make difficult the effective functioning of the securities markets. It is with this influence of Federal legislation and rules on the functioning of the markets that the Securities and Exchange Commission is concerned.

Of importance is the lack of any coordinated regulation of initial and maintenance margin requirements. Such coordination is important because the gap between the initial and subsequent maintenance requirements goes a long way towards determining the triggering impact that a drop in prices will have on margin calls, which in turn exert further pressure on prices. Under a 70 per cent margin requirement, for example, the buyer of $10,000 worth of stock would have to deposit margin of $7,000 and borrow $3,000 (*debit balance*) from the broker. The value of the stock could then decline to $4,000 (or by 60 per cent) before the New York Stock Exchange's general maintenance requirements of 25 per cent would be reached. Had the maintenance requirements been 60 per cent, the value of the stock could only shrink to $7,500 (or by 25 per cent) before the maintenance requirements would be in danger of violation.

There is evidence for believing that the triggering influence of margin calls contributed to the great crash of 1929 and that the initial-maintenance margin requirements of later years exerted a strong moderating influence in the market break of May, 1962. Accordingly, it appears logical for the Board of Governors to consider both initial and maintenance requirements in the development of its security-credit policies. In this way there would be assurance of an appropriate spread between these two levels.

During the major 1962 break, bank margin calls on unregulated loans increased much more rapidly than those on regulated loans and in so doing undoubtedly helped the downward push on prices. The volume of stock-collateralized, nonpurpose bank loans is much bigger than that of purpose loans, and this differential may become even wider as employee stock purchase plans spread. It is not at all uncommon for employees to use such stock, acquired through employer sponsored plans, to finance their operating needs. A margin call on nonpurpose loans exerts the same depressing influences on stock values as one on purpose loans. In view of the importance of the nonpurpose category, it would appear logical for the Board of Governors to be granted authority to impose requirements on loans in this area.

Similarly, the absence of regulatory authority over bank collateralized loans to purchase or carry unlisted securities is an omission that could lead to overly slim requirements and heavy margin calls in declining markets. The importance of this absence of legislative control is particularly serious in view of the mounting interest in over-the-counter securities that may follow the greater disclosure now required in this area. On the other hand, the prohibition against broker-dealers accepting unlisted securities as collateral on any loans for the purpose of purchasing or carrying securities appears to be an unreasonable barrier in the other direction. Finally, non-regulated lenders are known to have contributed significantly to the extension of credit prior to the May, 1962, break. Therefore, their full inclusion in any regulatory scheme appears important.

In its annual 1964 report, the Board of Governors commented on the contrasting treatment of brokers and banks. It referred specifically to the authorization in the Securities Exchange Act for the Board to limit the credit that brokers and dealers may extend on listed securities compared with the restriction in the Act forbidding brokers and dealers, generally speaking, from extending credit on over-the-counter securities. It also pointed to the Board's authorization to limit the credit that banks may extend for the purpose of purchasing or carrying listed securities compared with the absence of any credit restrictions with respect to over-the-counter securities. It then urged enactment of legislation "to eliminate this unwarranted difference in the status, for credit purposes, of securities traded on exchanges and securities traded over the counter."[29]

The extension of credit is vital to the national economy. Therefore, assigning the control of securities credit to the Board of Governors, which is responsible for over-all credit policy, is a logical step. In developing its security credit program, however, the Board of Governors, at least until recently, does not seem to

---

29. Board of Governors of the Federal Reserve System, *Fifty-First Annual Report Covering Operations for the Year 1964*, p. 207.

have fully evaluated the implications of this program to market fluctuations. Yet these fluctuations could have an important effect on the national economy. The significance of securities prices and the desirability of maintaining orderly markets are factors within the jurisdiction of the Securities and Exchange Commission. Hence it would appear important for the Board of Governors and the SEC to develop a close working relationship to consider the necessary statutory and rule amendments that are desirable to insulate market prices further from the changing influence of security credit. The cooperation of the staff of the Board of Governors and of the Special Study in the credit phases of the stock-market investigation and the reference to the credit recommendations of the Special Study in the Board of Governors' 1964 report suggest the potential benefit of further cooperation in this area.

Market Manipulation and Surveillance—In the pre-SEC era, the securities markets were a jungle of deception and manipulation. It was estimated, for example, that during the first decade after World War I, fully half of the some $50 billions worth of new securities floated in the United States became worthless. Such a mass collapse of values occurred because of the complete abandonment by many underwriters and dealers of standards of honesty and fairness. "The orgy of speculation which had existed in the stock market, coupled with the fraud, manipulation and other malpractices then prevalent, could lead only to disaster."[30]

Hence the Securities Exchange Act specifically prohibits a number of the types of transactions that were carried out previously, such as pools, wash sales, and matched orders. It also empowers the SEC to adopt rules leading to the maintenance of just and equitable principles of trade. Within this general sphere, the Commission has promulgated regulations on short selling, stabilizing transactions, and similar matters, and has adopted safeguards with respect to the financial responsibility of brokers and dealers.[31]

Summary—Under the Securities Exchange Act, brokers and

---

30. Securities and Exchange Commission, "A 25 Year Summary of the Activities of the Securities and Exchange Commission, 1934–1959," 1961, p. XV.

31. Securities and Exchange Commission, "The Work of the Securities and Exchange Commission," 1962, p. 7.

dealers engaged in interstate commerce must register with the Commission and conform their business practices to the standards of the law and the Commission's regulations. The Act extends the concept of disclosure to encompass periodic reporting, proxies, and insider transactions. Authority to regulate security credit is given to the Board of Governors, which has developed a complex pattern of control that permits sufficiently important loopholes to create the danger that credit transactions could contribute to sharp swings of stock prices. Also, manipulative practices are barred.

To carry out its responsibilities, the Commission has introduced an extensive investigatory and enforcement program. If violations are uncovered, the Commission may apply to the appropriate court for a civil injunction, may refer the facts to the Department of Justice for criminal prosecution, or may institute an administrative remedy of its own. These remedies, instituted after appropriate hearings, involve such steps as the issuance of orders suspending a member from an exchange or denying or revoking the registration of broker-dealers. Important in the enforcement procedure is the Commission's relations with the self-regulating agencies.

The Principle of Self-Regulation

Because of the pivotal role that the New York Stock Exchange occupies in the securities markets, its rules and its relationship to the Federal government are particularly important in shaping the regulatory process. The Exchange is a voluntary association "owned" by its members, who hold *seats*. Through its authority over these members, who are individuals and in turn partners or voting stockholders and directors of member organizations, the Exchange gains regulatory power over the conduct of the member organizations, the other stockholders and partners (*allied members*), and their employees.

From its creation in 1792 to the passage of the Securities Exchange Act in 1934, the NYSE was largely run like a private club and exercised sole jurisdiction over its members. The Securities Exchange Act introduced the new principle of self-regulation, which in the form that it has taken is unique to the securities industry. This principle has its roots in the statute. It has been strongly influenced by several major events in the history of the markets and has been moulded over time by the actions of commissions, exchange officials, and the courts.

THE STATUTORY BASIS

The essential relationship of the exchanges to the Commission is established in Section 6 of the Security Exchange which provides for the registration of national securities exchanges. As part of the registration process, an exchange, among other things, agrees to

1. comply and enforce compliance of its members with the provisions of the Act;

2. file copies of all its rules;

3. include among its rules provision for the expulsion, suspension, or disciplining of a member for conduct inconsistent with just and equitable principles of trade; and

4. furnish the Commission with copies of any amendments to its rules upon their adoption.

Once an exchange has registered, it can adopt and enforce any rule that is not inconsistent with the Act or with rules that the Commission may have issued. This freedom of an exchange is limited by Section 19, which confers upon the Commission the authority to request an exchange to alter its rules. If an exchange does not do so to the satisfaction of the Commission, it may, under the Section, and after an opportunity for hearing, require changes in twelve specified areas of the exchange's operations, including such matters as financial responsibility of members, listing or delisting securities, reporting of transactions on the exchange and on tickers, fixing commission rates, minimum units of trading, and odd-lot transactions. The statute does not expressly require the filing of exchange rules or amendments before they come into effect, does not authorize the Commission to prevent such rules or amendments from becoming effective, nor does it enable the Commission to take action against a member for violation of the rules of an exchange.

In the conduct of its self-regulating activities, according to these provisions, an exchange is given wide latitude to act. However, Sections 10 and 11 of the Act enumerate various vital areas where the Commission, without going through the self-regulatory process, is given direct powers of rule-making. Thus the Commission may enact rules directly affecting floor trading; off-floor trading by members; the operations of specialists and odd-lot dealers; and the use of short sales, stop-loss orders, and manipulative or deceptive practices.

The Act draws a clear distinction between the Commission's authority to take action in regard to an exchange's rules and the action possible for violation of the Federal securities laws. In the former case, as described above, the Commission can request changes in specified areas and can act directly in certain other areas. When a violation of the Act or of its rules is at stake, however, the Commission is given large powers. It may suspend or withdraw the registration of an exchange; suspend or expel members and officers; summarily suspend trading in any registered security for periods of ten days; and, with the approval of the President, suspend all trading on an exchange for a period of ninety days.

THE INFLUENCING EVENTS

Since the passage of the Securities Exchange Act, there have of course been various events that have put their marks upon the self-regulatory process. Several of these have been of lasting influence.

The 1938 Reorganization of the New York Stock Exchange— In conformance with the Securities Exchange Act, the Commission made a study of the rules of the exchanges and developed eleven recommendations for changes. In its reports to Congress in January, 1935, the Commission indicated its preference to have these changes accomplished by voluntary action of the exchanges rather than by legislation. These proposals, along with others made by the Commission, became the subject of extended negotiations between the Commission and the New York Stock Exchange for the reorganization of the Exchange's governmental structure. No agreement as to an adequate solution was reached. Therefore the Commission in November, 1937, publicly requested the Exchange to proceed at once to work out a satisfactory plan of efficient management. In compliance with this request, the Exchange appointed an independent committee, headed by Carle C. Conway, then Chairman of the Board of Directors of the Continental Can Company, to study and report on the need for such a reorganization.

In January, 1938, the Conway Committee submitted its report, which included far-reaching recommendations for converting the government of the Exchange from a largely private affair to a modern administrative organization that recognized its public interests. Subsequent to the release of the Conway report, the Exchange in March, 1938, announced the suspension of the firm of Richard Whitney & Co. and the expulsion of Whitney, who had been president of the Exchange and its recognized spokesman. After the public hearings that followed, the SEC concluded that a "dangerous outmoded philosophy . . . dominated the affairs of the Exchange . . . characterized by the unwritten code of silence respecting the financial condition or misconduct of a member such as Richard Whitney." It added that the Exchange had been administered "as if it were a private social club where the misconduct of its members and officers were regarded as a purely private affair and of no public concern."[32]

With the bogey of the "private club" publicly revealed, the Exchange promptly amended its constitution to adopt the principal recommendations of the Conway Committee. The new organization provided for a salaried president, an executive staff to carry out the administrative functions, public representation in the Board of Governors, and a major simplification in the administrative structure highlighted by a reduction of the standing committees. This reorganization probably is the major landmark separating the outmoded Exchange organization of the pre-SEC period and the current more efficient organization, in which the public interest is clearly recognized.

The Maloney Act—Section 15A of the Securities Exchange Act of 1934—Unlike the organized exchanges which, in effect, had government oversight thrust upon them, participants in the over-the-counter market took the initiative in requesting such supervision. The Securities Exchange Act did not provide any detailed system of regulation of the over-the-counter market, as it did for the organized exchanges, but rather entrusted broad

32. "In the Matter of Richard Whitney," SEC, 177 (1938) as quoted in Report of Special Study of Securities Markets of the Securities and Exchange Commission, op. cit., Part 4, Chapter XII, p. 508.

rule-making powers to the Commission in this respect. Thereafter a strong industry sentiment for organizing the over-the-counter market took place.

The first venture in self-regulation of the over-the-counter market occurred in 1933 under the Investment Bankers Code, authorized by the National Recovery Administration.[33] Despite the fact that the National Industrial Recovery Act was declared unconstitutional in 1935, members of the industry voluntarily continued to meet the standards of the code. It was recognized, however, that there was no legal basis to enforce this form of self-regulation and that, particularly, legislation was necessary to exempt the activities of an industry-wide organization from the antitrust laws. At the urging of the SEC, the voluntary form of organization was kept intact while the industry and the Commission developed a legislative program. In October, 1936, a new group called the Investment Bankers Conference was formed, and through its efforts and those of the Commission, supported by a large segment of the securities industry, there was adopted Section 15A of the Securities Exchange Act, called the Maloney Act after its sponsor, Francis Maloney of Connecticut.

Self-regulation under the Maloney Act followed the self-regulatory principles enunciated in the original Securities Exchange Act but with improvements that reflect the additional experience in this area of control. Any qualified association of broker-dealers may register under the Act and as an inducement to joining, such an association may prohibit its members from dealing with non-members except on the same terms as is accorded to the general public. This is a powerful inducement since it means that only members of the association may grant each other discounts in the purchase of securities.

In conformance with the general principles established in the Securities Exchange Act, associations must register with the Commission. Exacting criteria are established that the Commission must consider in approving registration. While an association is required to open its membership to any broker or dealer who

---

33. Special Subcommittee on Legislative Oversight of the Committee on Interstate and Foreign Commerce, House of Representatives, 85th Cong., 2d sess., "History of National Association of Securities Dealers, Inc.," 1959, p. 2.

uses the mails or interstate facilities to effect transactions in securities other than on a national securities exchange, membership may be denied under certain conditions, such as that the broker-dealer or any member of his firm had previously been suspended or expelled from a national securities exchange.

In important respects, the Commission has more power over the self-regulatory activities of the associations than was established in the basic 1934 Act. Thus associations are required to file rule changes with the Commission before they can become effective, and the Commission may disapprove them. The Commission is authorized to suspend or revoke the registration of an association for failure to enforce compliance of its own rules or for engaging in activities that defeat the purposes of the Act. Of considerable significance is the Commission's power to review disciplinary actions taken by an association against a member or in denial of membership; it may reduce but not increase a penalty imposed by the association. On the other hand, the Commission does not possess the considerable statutory authority to alter the substantive rules of an association that section 19(b) gives it over the exchanges.

The National Association of Securities Dealers, Inc., thus far is the only association to register with the Commission under the Maloney Act. To govern the conduct of its members, it has adopted rules of fair practice; and to formalize over-the-counter transactions, it has developed a uniform practice code. The NASD conducts an extensive program of examination of members' records to enforce its rules of fair practice and has established procedures to govern disciplinary cases.

The Reorganization of the American Stock Exchange—With attention focused on the New York Stock Exchange, the self-regulatory activities of the American Stock Exchange were largely overlooked. The extent to which these activities had sharply deteriorated was brought to public glare with the Commission's order, in May, 1961, to revoke the broker-dealer registration of Re, Re & Sagarese and to expel the Res from the ASE because of numerous violations of the Federal securities laws in connection with transactions in various stocks in which the Res had been registered as specialists. As a result, the Commission directed its staff to study conditions on the ASE. On January 5, 1962, the results of this examination were released.

The staff found that a closely knit group of members, mostly specialists, controlled the government of the ASE. Reliance for administration still rested on a system of standing committees. The activities of the staff were largely confined to mechanical operations rather than regulatory functions. The interest of the public governors in the ASE was small. The staff report devoted special attention to the role of the specialists, particularly as reflected in the conduct of the firm of Gilligan, Will & Co., one of the more influential of the specialist firms on the ASE. It was revealed that the firm had developed an extensive chain of operations, which included bringing listings to the ASE, keeping close contact with the companies listed, and using its relations with these companies to the firm's own advantage. Despite such activities that were clearly antithetical to specialist responsibilities, the firm apparently had an immunity to disciplinary action. The report also pointed to problems related to the activities of the floor traders.

In the interim, with the appointment of a special committee to review its own rules and procedures, the ASE had also instituted a reform movement. The Commission worked with this committee as well as with the new administration of the ASE which assumed control in early 1962. Edwin D. Etherington, who was elected president in March, 1962, and assumed office in September, proved a vigorous and effective leader. A new constitution was adopted, patterned after that of the New York Stock Exchange, in which administrative authority is centered in the president and the system of standing committees was eliminated. Stricter listing and delisting standards were adopted, existing specialist controls strengthened, disciplinary action was taken against members found to have violated ASE rules and Federal law, and in general considerable progress was made in the direction of establishing a regulatory system that met its responsibilities under the Act.

The Securities Acts Amendments of 1964—Out of the recommendations of the Special Study of Securities Markets of the Securities and Exchange Commission came the Securities Acts Amendments of 1964. In addition to extending disclosure principles to a number of companies whose securities are traded over the counter, a major objective of the amendments was to raise the standards of self-regulation. This was accomplished by strengthening the requirements for entrance into the securities business and by making more effective the disciplinary controls of the SEC and the rules of industry self-regulatory organizations over securities brokers and dealers and persons associated with them.[34]

This objective is achieved in several ways. All broker-dealers who are not members of a registered securities association become subject to certain additional regulation by the Commission. A registered securities association is required to classify prospective members; specify the standards of training, experience, and other qualifications that are applicable to any class; and to develop appropriate examinations for these classes. A registered securities association is also authorized to establish standards of financial responsibility for members and to have rules to produce fair and informative quotations.

The Commission is given similar powers to regulate the broker-dealers that are not members of a registered securities association. In this connection, the Commission has given considerable weight, as did the Special Study, to the importance of examinations in upgrading the level of competence in the securities business.[35] By September, 1965, the major stock exchanges, the NASD, and thirty states had imposed examination requirements as a prerequisite for entry by salesmen and others into the business. Following this line, the Commission adopted a rule applicable to nonmember broker-dealers, requiring a qualifying examination for all personnel or supervising personnel engaged in sales, trading, research, investment advice, advertising, public relations, hiring or recruitment of salesmen, training of salesmen, or underwriting and private placements.[36]

The procedure for review by the Commission of disciplinary action taken by a registered securities association against a member is also made more efficient. The amended statute provides additional grounds for the Commission to deny or revoke the registration of a broker-dealer upon finding that it would be in

---

34. Securities and Exchange Commission, Securities Act of 1933, Release No. 4725, Securities Exchange Act of 1934, Release No. 7425, September 15, 1964.

35. Report of Special Study of Securities Markets of the Securities and Exchange Commission, op. cit., Part 1, Ch. II, pp. 47–159; Securities and Exchange Commission, "In the Matter of Hugh M. Casper," Release No. 7479, December 7, 1964.

36. Securities and Exchange Commission, Release No. 7697, September 7, 1965.

the public interest to do so. Disciplinary action may be taken against supervisory personnel whose employees commit violations. This provision, concerned with supervisory responsibility, gives statutory authority to a principle that the Commission has consistently held.

Several important limitations on the authority of the Commission to take action under prior law were rectified in 1964. First, the Commission previously did not possess intermediate powers to discipline broker-dealers. The Securities Exchange Act only called for the extreme measure of revoking or denying the broker-dealer's registration, expelling from or suspending a broker-dealer's membership in a registered securities association, or suspending or removing a member from a national securities exchange. While the Commission had imposed lesser sanctions in offers of settlement, the 1964 Amendments grant it the discretion to impose the lesser sanctions of suspension of registration for a period not to exceed twelve months or formal censure without resorting to negotiation.

A second limitation was the Commission's authority to take disciplinary action only by proceeding against the firm if an individual member or employee defrauded customers or otherwise violated the law. Now the Commission may proceed directly against the individual. As a result of this new authority, the Commission may impose varying sanctions upon individuals and upon the firm as the need may justify.

A third limitation was the restricted power of the Commission to proceed against an issuer by hurling thunderbolts or not at all. Thus, if the issuer of a security failed to comply with the provisions of the Securities Exchange Act or of the Commission's rules, the Commission could only deny or withdraw the registration of a security, or suspend its effectiveness. At present, as a result of the 1964 amendments, the Commission is empowered to conduct administrative proceedings to determine if an issuer has been guilty of violating the Securities Exchange Act and if so to publish its findings and issue an order requiring compliance.

ACTIONS OVER TIME

The framework of self-regulation for the securities business is established in the securities acts. In its actual implementation, the process of self-regulation has been fashioned by certain major developments, as described above, and by the interpretations and actions of the participants. In the latter category, the New York Stock Exchange, as the dominant organized trading market, has been of particular importance.

As a self-regulatory agency, the Exchange has moved far from the cozy, private-club atmosphere of the Whitney era. Much of the efforts of its staff are now devoted to insuring that its members conduct their activities in conformance with required standards. At the very outset, it has been demanding of a company increasingly exacting standards of assets, earnings power, and share distribution in order that its stock be listed; and thereafter the listed companies must meet certain criteria, such as granting their stockholders voting rights, providing for proxy solicitation, and disclosing important corporate developments.

The off-floor conduct of member firms is evaluated through a program of financial questionnaires and visits by Exchange examiners, review of public complaints, and a so-called "stock-watch" operation whereby a computer is used to flag unusual fluctuations in the price of a stock and an investigation is then instituted into the reasons for the movements.

The Exchange has gone a long way in improving its practices over supervising its members with respect to their selling practices, market letters, and advertising methods. For example, new members and allied members, registered representatives, and branch office managers must all pass qualifying examinations. The know-your-customer rule has been affirmed and strengthened by requiring the establishment of adequate supervisory controls. Finally, a method for spot-checking the quality of management, supervision, and sales activities at member firm offices throughout the country has been installed.

In part, this program has been developed under the prodding of the Securities and Exchange Commission. Sometimes it has been sufficient for the Commission to make suggestions to obtain action, such as those suggestions forwarded to the exchanges shortly after the passage of the Securities Exchange Act, most of which were adopted. Sometimes the lines had to be drawn and a confrontation take place before the Exchange would act, as illustrated in the history of the 1964 Exchange rules governing floor trading. In part, too, the Exchange has introduced its own regulatory practices. For example, following the forced liquidation of Ira Haupt & Co., a former old-line member firm, as a result of the failure of its biggest commodities customer, the Allied Crude Vegetable Oil Refining Corporation, to meet its commitments, the NYSE not only took action to bail out Haupt's customers, but also established an insurance fund to protect customers with cash balances from losses in the case of a bankruptcy of a securities firm.

At times, the self-regulatory measures of the Exchange have proved more effective than those of the Commission. An illustration of this situation is the stock-watch program in which the Exchange's computer-aided efforts have been much more searching than the less comprehensive methods of the Commission. In what is perhaps a reversal of the traditional self-regulatory pattern, the Exchange has called violations of the Securities Exchange Act to the attention of the Commission for action. For example, in December, 1964, the SEC charged that a stockholder of Austin Nichols & Co. had been illegally manipulating the stock for two years by placing, through a brokerage house, offsetting purchase and sale orders designed to create a misleading appearance of trading activity; this alleged manipulation was discovered by the Exchange and turned over to the Commission.[37]

Finally, part of the progress in the regulatory practices of the Exchange has been due to independent action that was influenced by the Commission, such as occurred in the 1963–1964 measures to strengthen supervision of selling practices. These measures took place in the atmosphere created by the Special Study of Securities Markets, which gave considerable attention to the subject. Similarly, the NYSE has taken steps, in line with Special Study recommendations, to give greater participation in the exchange government to allied members representing partners or voting stockholders of membership firms, who are presumably more sensitive to the needs of the investors. By the same token these measures have tended to reduce the voice of the floor professionals—specialists, odd-lot dealers, and floor brokers—who have traditionally dominated the Exchange councils.

As a creature of the statutes, the NASD was created primarily

---

37. *The Wall Street Journal,* Dec. 23, 1964.

to provide self-regulation in the over-the-counter market. Because of the heterogeneous character of this market, the diversity in the character of its membership, and the lack of an operating center, the regulatory task of the NASD has been particularly heavy. Despite the difficulties under which it has labored, the NASD has made considerable progress in the area of self-regulation, as evidenced by its transition from an early reliance in conducting examinations upon questionnaires, instituted in 1941, to a more extensive program, adopted in 1947, of actual office examinations on a surprise basis.

Nevertheless, lack of suitably trained examiners has caused serious shortcomings even in this improved program. Following recommendations made by the Special Study, the NASD instituted a number of constructive measures, including an internal re-organization, an improvement in the handling of conduct cases, and more effective control over advertising and selling practices. In mid-1963, the NASD, NYSE, and ASE introduced a program to combine their procedures for administering registered repre-sentatives' examinations.

Self-regulation visualizes a sort of partnership of control between the self-regulatory agencies and the Commission. Much of the effectiveness of the principle, therefore, rests upon the degree of vigor, tempered by understanding, that the Commission displays in fulfilling its responsibilities. It is not easy to summarize the attitude of the Commission over the three decades of its steward-ship in a few words because this history covers many different commissions and many different chairmen, who, as has been in-dicated, have not necessarily revealed the same attitudes. Never-theless, at least during the period intervening between the early years after its inception and those of the Special Study, the Com-mission does not appear to have been a formidable overseer of its self-regulatory responsibilities. Only once during this period did it choose to exercise the vast powers granted in Section 19 to take the initiative in altering an exchange rule; in 1941, the Commission ordered an amendment abrogating the affect of a NYSE rule enforcing a constitutional provision to prevent an Ex-change member from serving as an odd-lot dealer or specialist upon a regional exchange in dually-listed securities. Moreover, until the floor-trading incident in 1964, the Commission never issued a rule under Section 11 but chose instead to suggest the adoption of pertinent rules by the exchanges.

Although, as has been described, the Securities Exchange Act does not call for Commission approval of exchange rules, the requirement that copies of such rules be furnished on adoption created some uncertainty as to the importance of advance notice. The Commission never took steps to clarify this uncertainty but operated primarily under an informal agreement, adopted in 1956, whereby the NYSE gave the Commission two weeks' notice of rule changes prior to their effectiveness.

The Supreme Court made reference to this uncertainty of Commission authority over the rules of exchanges and to the entire question of exchange vulnerability to antitrust charges in a 1963 decision.[38] This opinion is of considerable importance because it is the only expression thus far of the Court's attitude regarding the relationship between the securities and the antitrust laws. A Mr. Silver was the principal of two Dallas over-the-counter brokerage firms that were nonmembers of the New York Stock Exchange. The Silver firms had obtained private wire connections with certain Exchange member firms and ticker service from the Exchange. In accordance with its rules, the Exchange had to grant approval of such wire connections; and, after seven months "temporary" approval, the Exchange, without divulging the reasons, ordered the wire connections severed and discontinued the ticker service. Silver sued for an injunction and damages under the Sherman Antitrust Act and on other grounds. In deciding in favor of Silver, the Court noted the power of the Commission to request modifications in Exchange rules "and impliedly, therefore, to disapprove any rules adopted by an exchange." Although this brief reference might be interpreted as a veiled hint of the Court's belief that the Commission had authority over the rules of the Exchange, there was no further confirmation of this notion in the decision. On the contrary the Court then went on to state that the Securities Exchange Act did not give the Commission jurisdiction to review particular instances of enforcement of Exchange rules, such as was involved in the Silver case, and accordingly no question of conflict with Commission jurisdiction

---

38. Silver v. *New York Stock Exchange,* 373 U.S. 341 (1963).

was involved. Although the Court at least raised the question of possible antitrust exemption in instances where the Commission possessed adequate authority to review the Exchange's action, no conclusion was reached on this subject. This line of reasoning was not pursued on the grounds that the self-regulatory action of the Exchange in this case could not be justified because by failing to inform Silver of the charges against him, unfair procedures had been employed. As a result of these facts—the absence in the Securities Exchange Act of an express procedure for the Commission to prevent an exchange from adopting a new rule, the specification of particular areas where the Commission does have direct authority, and the failure of the Supreme Court to pursue the matter—it is generally felt that the Commission has little jurisdiction over exchange rules in a number of important areas, such as the qualification of members, the government of exchanges, and procedures for disciplining members.

Subsequently, in April, 1964, the Commission adopted a new rule (17a–8), which required a registered exchange to file with the Commission any proposed change in its rules at least three weeks before effectiveness. This new Commission requirement relates to procedure more than anything else, since it makes no reference to the need for Commission approval, although the requirement for advance filing at least implies the authority for the Commission to act. In the specialist rule, issued towards the end of 1964, the Commission went a step further. It established a procedure by which it can specifically review and disapprove new exchange rules relating to specialists if it finds they are inadequate to achieve the purposes required by the rule or are inconsistent with the public interest or the protection of investors.[39] Thus, after a long hiatus of inaction, the combination of the Special Study and a Supreme Court decision motivated the Commission to swift action in issuing two rules under its specifically delegated powers in Section 11 of the Securities Exchange Act— the rules covering the floor trading and the specialist—and in issuing a covering rule defining the procedural relations between the Commission and the exchanges with respect to rules issued by the exchanges.

---

39. Securities and Exchange Commission, Securities Exchange Act of 1934, Release No. 7432 September 24, 1964.

Conclusion

The securities business operates in a way that is unique in American industry. Its members agree among themselves as to the minimum prices they will charge the public; a duopoly of two firms dominates odd-lot transactions and until recently was substantially free to determine the manner of conducting business with the public; the dissemination of quotations represents a communication system that is both vast in scope and vital to the public interest. Yet, self-government largely exists.

Clearly, the reason for this ability of the securities business to conduct itself in the manner of a public utility, without the ordinarily imposed direct governmental restraints, is the associated supervisory responsibility of the SEC. That this responsibility is important in order to free the securities business from antitrust action was made clear in the Silver case. There the Court pointed out that, in the Exchange's action, it had to reconcile the antitrust aim of eliminating restraints on competition with the effective operation of a public policy, contemplating a degree of self-regulation that may have anti-competitive effects. In order to insure that an exchange will not in some cases apply rules that injure competition without furthering legitimate self-regulative ends, Commission guidance is essential. The absence of Commission supervision in the particular action, therefore, led to the Court's conclusion that the application of the antitrust laws was "peculiarly appropriate."[40]

Self-regulation is the foundation upon which the operating mechanism of the securities markets rests. It permits swift, on-the-spot decisions to be rendered in a field whose existence depends upon speed of action, and where the regulatory response often must be immediate and made on delicate grounds. It permits those best aware of the sensitivities built into the industry's price mechanism to create underlying policies governing the activities of its members. But it also exposes the industry to the risk of overlooking its public responsibilities and slipping into the role of a private

40. For a further discussion of the Silver case, see Report of Special Study of Securities Markets, Part 4, Chapter XII, op. cit., pp. 699–701.

club, free from the restraints of either competition or government supervision. Accordingly, the effective implementation of self-regulation depends upon the existence of statutes and rules that clearly define the relationships between the securities business and government; upon a reasonable attitude on the part of the business in administering its public responsibilities; and upon the vigor and understanding with which the SEC, as the principal supervisory agency, fulfills its role.

As we have seen, while much has been done to clarify the implications of self-regulation, its future effectiveness depends upon how the private business–government partnership evolves. When the Securities Exchange Act was originally passed, the principle of self-regulation was clearly in the mind of the legislators but they could not anticipate all the turns in the path of future regulators. Through rule and legislation, if need be, there must be spelled out, as an integrated program and on a uniform basis, the powers of the self-regulating agencies, the supervisory authority of the SEC over the rules and actions of these agencies, as well as the functioning role of each of the members of this partnership. Built into the business are forces that tend to lead the participants to overlook their public responsibilities. An important element—the floor member or market maker—has little contact with the public and easily may fall into the posture of seeing the individual trees of personal problems rather than the over-all forest of public responsibility.

The segment of the business that works with the public is heavily influenced by motivations to sell which may readily obscure the ethical and professional aspects that exist. Association with the field may lead SEC commissioners to develop a confidence in its activities and friendliness towards its participants that make difficult the firmness sometimes demanded of an overseer. The many functioning details in which the Commission is concerned encourage it to take the easy way marked by attention to routine responsibilities, such as registrations, and to minor rule infractions.

Yet of greater long-term significance is the responsibility of anticipating the changing conditions of this dynamic business that call for a carefully planned program of enunciating principles to guide the activities of the self-regulators towards acceptable goals. Thus the basic threat to the principle of self-regulation lies in the danger that either of the partners in the arrangement may relax its vigil in guarding the public-interest aspects of the securities markets, which function as a vital cog in the national economy.

CHAPTER 5

Criteria in the
Securities
Markets

While self-regulation provides the basis for allocating SEC and private-business shares in supervising the securities markets, it is no guide to the kind of control required. For this purpose, regulation must be geared to objective criteria, and in the securities acts the recurring themes are the *public interest* and the *protection of investors*. These twin aims are reiterated again and again. They are most often linked by "or," less frequently by "and," and sometimes one appears independently of the other. The frequency with which they are mentioned clearly points to their importance as statutory standards.

Although study of the acts and of the hearings does not reveal any clear indication of the meaning of these terms, certain general observations may be noted. In the Securities Act of 1933, the terms are used more sparingly; in one form or another they appear perhaps ten times compared with about fifty times in the Securities Exchange Act, which is not very much longer. The additional year of experience with securities legislation may have further convinced the legislators of the significance of the public aspects of the securities markets, or they may have believed that the trading markets exert a more pervasive influence on the economy than the new-issue market. Some reinforcement to the latter notion is given by the repeated references to major economic issues affecting public policy in the section of the Securities Exchange Act describing the necessity for regulation. This need arises, it is indicated, because transactions in securities exchanges and over-the-counter markets are affected with a national public interest. In explaining this interest, five principal factors are cited—all predominantly economic in nature.

Control of the markets is necessary in order to protect interstate commerce, the national credit, the Federal taxing power, and the national banking system and the Federal Reserve System.

Transactions, conducted in large volume by the public, in the securities markets involve the use of credit, affect the financing of trade, industry, and transportation in interstate commerce and influence the volume of interstate commerce and national credit.

The prices established are disseminated throughout the United States and foreign countries and constitute a basis for determining the amount of certain taxes and the value of collateral for bank loans.

Prices of securities are susceptible to manipulation which gives rise to excessive speculation resulting in sudden and unreasonable fluctuations. This condition, in turn, can cause alternatively unreasonable expansion and unreasonable contraction of the volume of credit available for trade, transportation, and industry; can hinder the proper appraisal of the value of securities and thus prevent a fair calculation of taxes owing to the Federal and state governments; and can prevent the fair valuation of collateral for bank loans and/or obstruct the effective operation of the national banking system and Federal Reserve System.

Manipulation and sudden and unreasonable fluctuations of security prices and excessive speculation may precipitate and intensify national emergencies, which, in turn, produce wide-spread unemployment, and the dislocation of trade, transportation, and industry.[1]

Thus at the very outset of the Securities Exchange Act, its necessity is related to economic issues that in turn are identified with the national "public interest," used in this context without its traditional partner-phase, "protection of investors." The term "public interest" is employed by itself several times later in the Act, as is the "protection of investors" and, of course, the joint expression appears frequently. For the most part, however, these

---

1. Securities Exchange Act of 1934, Section 2.

later references are used in a more restricted sense, in connection with specific responsibilities of the Commission. From this usage of the terms, it does not appear unreasonable to conclude that these specific responsibilities are geared to the sweeping objectives enumerated in the Act's introductory section, which describes the necessity for regulation. In the light of the fact that control of the securities markets is tied to economic considerations, it is odd, as was mentioned previously, that the Commission has functioned over so long a period of time without an economic staff. Clearly, such a staff is necessary to ascertain that the Commission's routine functions do not overpower the policy admonitions that are cited, and that the total legal activities of the Commission are undertaken with the economic guides, used to outline the necessity for regulations, in mind.

The Concern with a Market Break

The precipitating element to the economic dangers listed in the Act—the threat to taxes, credit, and banking, and the creation of a national emergency with its enumerated dire consequences to the economy—lies in the market's price structure, that is, in the possibility of unwarranted price fluctuations and excessive speculation. This concern with the potential impact of a market break upon the economy has been expressed repeatedly since the origination of the Securities Exchange Act.

In February, 1934, E. A. Goldenweiser, then Director of the Division of Research and Statistics of the Federal Reserve Board, while testifying on the bill before the Senate Committee on Banking and Currency stated:

The stock exchange is fundamentally an institution which makes it possible to collect capital for the purpose of launching new enterprises, and also makes it possible for persons who own shares in an enterprise to sell them to each other through organized machinery without having to seek for buyers; it furnishes a market place, and those are the legitimate functions of a stock exchange.

When, however, a stock exchange ceases to be, or in addition to being that, when it develops into a place where people from all over the country, without any particular knowledge of what they are doing, are risking their savings and incurring heavy indebtedness on the chance of being able to dispose of their holdings at higher prices, then such a stock exchange is not serving a useful social function. On the contrary, it performs a very dangerous part in our economic machinery, and is destructive and disastrous to many individuals and also to the prosperity of the country as a whole."[2]

Some twenty years later, another economist, John K. Galbraith, testified before the same committee which had initiated a study of the stock market that was prompted primarily by a dramatic sixteen-month price climb. Between September, 1953, and January, 1955, when the study was announced, the Standard and Poor's index of 480 common stocks had risen by 50 per cent. Mr. Galbraith stated:

The breaking of the speculative bubble (the 1929 stock-market crash), which had to come, had in turn a profound effect on the economy. The economy was particularly vulnerable at the time to the effects of the breaking of the bubble. But the effects were real and serious and had a great deal to do with exaggerating the seriousness of the depression that followed.

First there was the effect on consumer expenditures particularly in the higher income bracket . . .

Second, the crash had a serious effect on corporate structures and hence on corporate investment.

And it had a bad effect on bank assets and enhanced the vulnerability of banks to failure, this had further repercussions on economic activity.

And the crash also had a disrupting effect on the balance of payments and, as a result, on exports, particularly of cotton, tobacco, and wheat.

So the speculative upsurge—and the breaking of the bubble—was an occurrence of importance, of original importance, in the economy.[3]

As groundwork for the initial phase of the Senate committee's inquiry, its staff prepared an analysis of the major factors affecting the stock market. In the staff's report to Senator J. W. Fulbright, chairman of the committee, it noted that

2. Hearings before the Committee on Banking and Currency, United States Senate, 73rd Cong., 1st sess., on S. Res. 84, "Stock Exchange Practices," 1934, p. 6439.

3. Hearings before the Committee on Banking and Currency, United States Senate, 8th Cong., 1st sess., "Stock Market Study," 1955, pp. 248–249.

Memory of the bull market of the late 1920's and the stock-market collapse in 1929–1930, followed by one of the severest depressions in our history, has made Americans sensitive to the dangers of fluctuations in total output and in stock prices. There is a widespread feeling that economic stability and the healthy growth of the economy are incompatible with an overemphasis on speculative activity in the stock market.[4]

Shortly thereafter, in its own report, summarizing its findings based notably upon the staff report but also upon an extensively distributed questionnaire and upon public hearings, the committee asserted that:

There is little doubt that the stock market had behaved in its more or less traditional role as a barometer of changing business when stock prices started on their upward climb in the fall of 1953. There is also little doubt that it reflected confidence by the investing public that the 1953–54 business recession would be mild and of short duration. But historical experience has amply demonstrated that, as the rise of stock prices continues to gather momentum, other elements frequently enter which makes it a less reliable indicator of business trends. The continuation and rapidity of the stock-price rise itself increasingly comes to be regarded as the basis for confidence rather than fundamental economic considerations. When preoccupation with the stock market results in widespread distortion of perspective, the stock market may become a potential threat to the stability of the economy. We cannot rule out the possibility of the recurrence of business fluctuations despite the progress that has been made to cope with the problems of instability. Therefore, the development of speculative trends in the stock market bears close watching.[5]

Some eight years later, the Special Study of Securities Markets in analyzing the market break of May 28, 1962, also commented on the implications of stock-market fluctuations:

The markets' erratic behavior prompted concern and caused bewilderment at home and abroad. The frenetic activity of the break resulted in large and sudden losses for many and gains for some. There was concern in Government and business circles that this break, like

4. Staff Report to the Committee on Banking and Currency, United States Senate, 85th Cong., 1st sess., "Factors Affecting the Stock Market," April 30, 1955, p. 27.
5. Report together with Individual Views and Minority Views of the Committee on Banking and Currency, 84th Cong., 1st sess., S. Rep. No. 376, pp. 12–13.

previous breaks of similar magnitude, might signal or provoke a serious business recession. There were unconfirmed but active rumors that "professional speculators" had deliberately triggered the decline. Some corporations reconsidered their plans for capital expenditures and a number of previously scheduled stock offerings were postponed or canceled. Although more than half of the people living in the United States were born after the crash of 1929, the memory of that event still casts a shadow over every major market drop, and, therefore, this break had a strong and immediate psychological impact upon the Nation.[6]

As expressly stipulated in the Securities Exchange Act, therefore, and as recurrently stated thereafter in Congressional investigations and special studies, there is deep-rooted concern about the potential effects upon the economy of excessive speculation leading to serious market declines. Hence it is important to examine the powers of the SEC, as the government agency involved, and of the exchanges, as the pertinent self-regulatory agencies, to control such extreme price fluctuations and the extent to which these powers have been exercised.

THE POWERS OF THE SEC

The Securities Exchange Act gives the Commission several powers to discharge its responsibilities of preventing unreasonable fluctuations, excessive speculation, and maintaining orderly markets. Primarily, Section 19(a)(4) of the Act provides that the SEC is authorized if in its opinion the public interest so requires:

summarily to suspend trading in any registered security on any national securities exchange for a period not exceeding ten days, or with the approval of the President, summarily to suspend all trading on any national securities exchange for a period not exceeding ninety days.

Another grant of emergency power is contained in Section 22(e) of the Investment Company Act of 1940. This prohibits a registered investment company from suspending any right of redemption of investment-company shareholders for more than seven days after tender, except for certain periods, including those when trading on the NYSE is "restricted," or an emergency exists, or

---

6. Report of Special Study of Securities Markets of the Securities and Exchange Commission, 88th Cong., 1st sess., H. Doc. 95, 1963, Part 4, Chapter XIII, p. 821.

when the Commission permits such action for the protection of the shareholders. The Commission may adopt rules to determine the conditions under which trading is deemed to be restricted and an emergency exists. Finally, as a counterpart to Section 19(a)(4), which is applicable to listed securities, the 1964 Amendments, in a new section 15(c)(5), provide the Commission with authority summarily to suspend over-the-counter trading in any non-exempted security for a period not exceeding ten days. Broker-dealers are prohibited from trading in any such security during the period or periods of suspension.

The suspension powers that the Commission has in regard to particular securities and to all securities, although both of an emergency nature, are obviously of different degrees of importance in potential effect on the securities markets. The Commission has suspended trading in a security on an exchange during a number of times, generally because of some event in the issuing company's affairs that casts doubt on the current evaluation of the stock, such as evidence that the company's finances were not as indicated in its financial statements. The power to suspend all trading on an exchange is an extraordinary one, as suggested by the requirement of Presidential approval, and the Commission has never seen fit to invoke it. The power to suspend the right to redemption of investment company shares, which is related to the power to suspend all trading on an exchange, also has never been invoked.

Despite the fact that the Commission has never acted under Section 19(a)(4), it has given clear evidence of an awareness of a responsibility to prevent a market crisis from getting so far out of hand as to lead to catastrophic damage to the economy. It has previously stated:

> The Commission is well aware of the importance of free securities markets to the American economy. Congress, however, in giving the Commission authority to take this drastic step (suspend all trading), with the approval of the President, recognized that occasions could arise in which a chaotic securities market might so disrupt and demoralize general business and might so irreparably damage not only investors but the entire national economy that closing markets would be the only alternative. Obviously no hard and fast rules to govern the closing of exchanges could be laid down in a statute for the reason that there could be no way of telling what particular kind of critical situation might develop. But it is clearly the Commission's continuing duty to so prepare

itself that no crisis can get so far out of hand that catastrophic damage can be done before the action can be taken.[7]

In further recognition of this responsibility, the Commission has previously deemed it prudent to develop measures for closing the exchanges, even though it never has seen fit actually to implement these plans. Thus, after the outbreak of World War II in Europe, the Commission prepared a program of action in case the securities markets became chaotic; it kept in constant touch with the President, furnishing him with reports on market conditions. After hostilities with Japan occurred, a draft of a resolution ordering suspension of the exchanges was approved as to form, and it was determined to watch the market trend closely for further developments but no such order was ever actually issued. Following the outbreak of the Korean war, the Commission once more considered the advisability of acting, and steps were taken to move promptly under its emergency powers in the event that an attack upon the United States created a situation where such measures were considered necessary.

While Section 19(a)(4) clearly is an emergency measure, Congress left determining when an emergency occurs to the discretion of the Commission. The reluctance of the Commission to take action despite the fact that the country has experienced several national crises since enactment of the Securities Exchange Act suggests, in turn, that the emergency conditions must also exist in the market itself. An emergency is not necessary, however, for the Commission to proceed under Section 19(a)(1), (2), and (3), after appropriate notice and hearings, to suspend or withdraw the registration of an exchange, or the registration of a security on an exchange, or to expel any member or officer from an exchange. Neither is an emergency necessary, of course, for the Commission to exercise its powers under Section 10 to regulate short sales and stop-loss orders.

THE POWERS OF THE EXCHANGES

Nothing in the Securities Exchange Act specifically imposes any responsibilities on the exchanges in periods of market stress.

---

7. Securities and Exchange Commission, Sixth Annual Report for the Fiscal Year Ended June 30, 1940, p. 90.

However, the concept of self-regulation embodied in the Act certainly places a duty on the exchanges to help in the statutory goals of maintaining orderly markets and preventing unreasonable price fluctuations. This is particularly true since the powers of the exchanges over trading are quite broad. Like the Commission, the exchanges can suspend trading in specific stocks or completely halt trading if they feel such action is necessary. In addition, the exchanges have complete control over trading activities such as the type of orders which can be accepted and how they can be executed. However, ordinarily they have not prescribed rules under these powers to deal with hectic market periods, and have usually relied upon their emergency powers.

As is properly the case under the concept of self-regulation, the exchanges have been more ready to exercise their emergency powers than the Commission. The NYSE, for example, has gone so far as completely to halt trading on several instances. The outbreak of World War I led the Exchange to stop trading for a relatively long period—from July 31 to November 28, 1914, and to permit only restricted trading from that date to April 1, 1915; the signing of the Armistice on November 11, 1918, once more resulted in the suspension of activity; and the 1929 market collapse caused the Exchange to close on November 1, and 2, 1929. More recently, on November 22, 1963, when President Kennedy was assassinated, the Exchange was closed after 2.4 million shares had crossed the tape and the Dow-Jones industrials had collapsed 24.5 points in the twenty-seven minutes after the first flash of the announcement.

The Exchange also has been alert to take action with respect to individual stocks. When a large imbalance in buy or sell market orders suddenly develops in a particular issue, it is quite common for a floor governor to suspend trading in that stock until sufficient orders can be rounded on the other side, so as to prevent the unfilled orders from causing the price to fluctuate too much. The stock of W. R. Grace & Company was not permitted to open at all on May 29, 1962, because of such an imbalance of orders. Similarly, to maintain orderly conditions, the Exchange has been willing to suspend stop-loss orders and short sales in specific stocks. In 1964, for example, the NYSE banned stop-loss orders in six companies, and during the hectic markets that occurred in the latter part of 1965, it banned such orders in twenty-two companies during a period of some five months. Included were such well-known firms as **KLM** Royal Dutch Airlines, Magnavox, Addressograph-Multigraph Corporation, Radio Corporation of America, Continental Air Lines, Boeing Company, Douglas Aircraft Company, and Lockheed Aircraft Corporation.[8] When the price of the Communications Satellite Corporation fluctuated widely after its original offering in June, 1964, reaching a level of more than three times the $20 at which it was first issued within a matter of months, the Exchange even took the unusual step of requiring only cash transactions in the issue; and did not relax this restriction until some eight months later.[9]

As a further indication of the Exchange's awareness of the possible need to act promptly and to be in a position to move should the need arise, a plan was announced in the spring of 1964 to facilitate the suspension of trading in all securities in a national emergency. For this purpose, the Exchange's rules were amended to permit a three-man committee consisting of the Chairman of the Board, the Vice-Chairman, and the senior floor governor, on a majority vote, to halt trading whenever in their opinion this action would be in the national interest. Following such a suspension, a special meeting of the Board would be called to consider the continuation or termination of the suspension. This meeting

---

8. *The Wall Street Journal,* October 13, 1965; The New York Times, December 26, 1965.

9. Effective August 23, 1965, the Board of Governors of the NYSE reduced from 100 per cent to 50 per cent the Exchange's initial margin requirements on long and on short positions in the common stock of Communications Satellite Corporation. The Exchange pointed out that the Board's ruling applies only to Exchange Rule 431, which establishes the initial and maintenance requirements for margin accounts of customers. In the case of Comsat, the Exchange's initial margin requirement of 50 per cent had to be in the account before the execution of the order. The customer who held Comsat overnight then had to add to his account any additional margin necessary to satisfy Regulation T of the Board of Governors of the Federal Reserve System. This required the deposit of 70 per cent margin as promptly as possible, but in any event within four business days after the purchase or short sale of securities.

The 50 per cent requirement for Comsat was still stricter than that for most other issues because ordinarily a buyer or short seller would not have to deposit any funds until the 70 per cent Federal Reserve margin requirement came due at the completion of the trade.

would be held as soon as a quorum of seven governors could be obtained. Despite these previous instances of quick action and the willingness to prepare in advance to halt trading completely, there has been no indication of the existence of an organized plan to institute intermediary measures, short of a complete cessation of transactions; to control the fluctuations of markets that have become disorderly; nor even to study the relative efficiency of the different measures that could be adopted.

THREATS TO THE PUBLIC INTEREST

Economists have not been able to develop fully the nexus between severely declining security prices and a major business reaction. It is generally accepted that stock prices represent a "leading indicator" and typically precede cyclical turns in business. Nevertheless, it is not unusual for market declines to occur that are not followed by changes in general business. Thus, between the close of World War II and the latter part of June 1962, stock prices, as indicated in the following table, experienced six declines of sufficiently serious proportions to be labelled "bear markets."

Year	Percentage Decline Dow-Jones Industrials	Duration
1946	23%	5 months
1949	16	11
1953	13	8
1957	18	6
1960	16	10
1962	27	6

Except for 1946 and 1962, each of these declines anticipated an economic dip of varying proportions. Although, in 1962 the economy continued its slow but steady advance through the year, by the end of the summer the impact of the drop was felt throughout the securities industry. Trading volume and public interest gradually subsided, the new-issue market shrank severely, and brokerage firms went through a contracting and cost-cutting phase.

Of particular interest was the market break that occurred on May 28, 1962, when the Dow-Jones Industrials closed off 34.95 points, or 5.7 per cent, leading to an investigation by both the SEC and the NYSE. At the low point on that fateful day, widespread concern was felt. There was apprehension about the ability of specialists to stay in the market, about the financial solvency of brokers, about the influence of the decline on corporate expenditures and the raising of capital, and most fundamentally of all, about the effect of all these things on the economy. There can be little doubt that on May 28, the stage was set for a debacle that fortunately was never experienced. It is a sobering thought, however, that another day, week, or month of similarly chaotic markets could have meant economic disaster.

Several years later, in 1965, between May 14 and June 28, the Dow-Jones Industrial average dropped from 939.62 to 840.59, a decline of 10.5 per cent. The shrinkage was sufficiently severe to provoke the usual efforts at interpreting its implications. In the face of the excise tax reduction, the slated increase in Social Security benefits, and the over-all buoyant outlook, the general conclusion was that the decline would not seriously affect economic conditions. After an examination of the business scene, for example, the Morgan Guaranty Trust Company concluded that the absence of paralleling evidence in other areas suggested that the market probably was emitting misleading signals. Nevertheless, the Bank cautioned that "in economic analysis, there is no task more frustrating than trying to read the meaning of gyrations in common stock prices."[10] Reflecting these uncertainties and despite the lack of confirming indications in other areas, the decline, short-lived as it was, began to set in motion the characteristic repercussions stemming from a sharp drop in security values. Both brokers and commercial banks reported some calls for additional collateral or cash on their securities loans, while the scheduled appearance of several large stock offerings was postponed.[11] It certainly is conceivable that in other circumstances, when the economy had less powerful underlying supports, the self-propelling effects of continued market drops, margin calls, and the curtailment of projected capital expansion programs, implied in the withdrawal of contemplated new financing, could dangerously affect business conditions.

Moreover, in the future, it is not unlikely that the national economy will become even more sensitive to the condition of the securities markets as the direct and indirect stake of the public in

10. Morgan Guaranty Trust Company of New York, "The Morgan Guaranty Survey," June, 1965, p. 1.
11. *The Wall Street Journal*, June 29, 1965.

the market grows. The New York Stock Exchange has estimated that by 1980, if present trends continue, there will be 35 million shareowners, compared with 20.1 million by the lastest count in its 1965 Census of Shareowners; some 30 per cent of all listed stock will be owned by financial institutions, compared with 20 per cent in 1964 when the forecast was made; while average daily volume in 1975 will be 10,000,000 shares compared with a then record high of 4,900,000 in 1964. With an expanded interest in securities markets, the psychological reaction of the public to swiftly falling security prices is likely to be more severe than at present and to exert a more immediate and powerful effect on consumer spending and corporate expansion plans. Also, the reduced stock turnover compared with the much higher rates of the 1920s suggests that big blocks have been relatively immobilized in the hands of major owners. As a result, a new element of vulnerability is created in the market because of the possibility that at any time in the future, these large holders may find it necessary to dispose of their commitments within a short period of time. In effect, each important institutional investor occupies a crucial role because the route selected and efficiency employed in disposing of commitments could exert a spreading influence on the market at vital times.

Whatever may be one's conclusions about the influence of an extended market decline on business, there is at least enough evidence of a relationship to provoke concern. Added to this fact, the Securities Exchange Act recognizes this causal relationship in stating that "national emergencies, which produce widespread unemployment and the dislocation of trade . . . are precipitated, intensified, and prolonged by . . . sudden and unreasonable fluctuations of security prices and by excessive speculation." Thus, it could be assumed that the Commission and, by indirection, the self-regulating agencies are charged with the responsibility of taking necessary actions to ward off the dangers of emergencies associated with swiftly declining prices.

CHECKING MARKET ADVANCES THAT PRECEDE DECLINES

Since extreme price gains have been the prelude to subsequent declines, one way of avoiding the threat to the public interest from skidding stocks might be to arrest the advance before it gets out of hand. In apparent recognition of such a relationship, the NYSE has taken modest, ameliorative steps to dampen speculative en-thusiasm that seemed to have excessive taints. To this end, its president has at times issued special cautionary statements. Also, in the latter part of 1965, following a period of hectic trading, the Exchange announced a more unusual move by increasing the re-quired amount of collateral—or margin—that investors had to maintain in their accounts to engage in *daylight trading,* that is to buy and sell particular issues on the same day.[12] It was intended that the increased daylight margin rules would apply to those stocks that had volume activity and price variations exceeding designated standards or had "unusual characteristics." In explaining its new measure, the Exchange observed that "credit often contributes to price and volume activity in such stocks."[13] As mentioned pre-viously, the Exchange also has banned stop-loss orders in issues that have experienced unusually wide fluctuations.[14]

The SEC has not directly attempted to curb speculation al-though it has taken steps to correct flaws in the market that may have contributed to the exaggerated pace of an upswing. For ex-ample, prior to the market break of May 28, 1962, the sharp premiums to which the numerous offerings of small, untried busi-nesses were driven undoubtedly augmented the stock-buying eager-ness of the general public. As rights of entry into the securities field are raised, at least partly because of Commission actions, in-vestment bankers may provide greater discrimination in the financ-ing of new companies and ease the threat that a collapse in the prices of "hot" issues may contribute to a subsequent general mar-ket decline. Similarly, measures taken by the Commission have reduced considerably the degree to which manipulative practices may be employed to produce contrived price gains.

Outside of strengthening the market mechanism so that the

---

12. About a month after the NYSE issued its guidelines for tighter credit rules on daylight trading, the Amex announced similar selective restrictions but applicable to all margin trading in issues that show unusual patterns.

13. *The Wall Street Journal,* November 2, 1965.

14. A stop-loss order, sometimes called a stop order, is generally an order to purchase or sell a security at the market after a designated price is reached or passed. Such an order, therefore, adds to the price fluctuations of a volatile stock by triggering buy orders or sell orders as prices either rise or fall.

possibility of artificial price advances are reduced, there is considerable doubt regarding the degree to which the Commission can or should act to halt a market boom. Much of the reason for this difficulty arises from the problem of asserting with any degree of assurance that stocks are selling at dangerously high levels relative to current earnings. The most extensive studies thus far undertaken of rates of return on common stocks have been those by the Center for Research in Security Prices of the Graduate School of Business, University of Chicago. Depending upon the period of time involved, it was found that the annually compounded rate of return for common stocks listed on the NYSE, ignoring dividends, ranged from about minus 50 per cent to plus 17 per cent.[15] In light of this broad variation, it is clear that a price-earnings ratio, reflecting investors' expectations of future rates of return, that is acceptable at one stage of the economy may not appear equally reasonable at another.

In a later study, the Center for Research in Security Prices expressed as probability distributions the rates of returns for all combinations of month-end purchases and sales of each common stock on the NYSE between January, 1926, and December, 1960. It was found that during 78 per cent of the time common stocks yielded a positive net return—over two-thirds of the time the rate exceeded 5 per cent, and the median rate of return was 9.8 per cent. While such probability data may be used for predictive purposes, the Center cautions that "the past is, of course, not a perfect—or necessarily best—forecast of the future."[16] This caveat is obviously true. Despite the value of such studies, the methods of forecasting security prices have not as yet reached the stage to permit a sufficiently positive judgment regarding the validity of a price advance to warrant the adoption of strong counteracting measures.

Although it appears inadvisable to attempt to control a price advance through special measures, it may be justifiable for the Commission to speak out when its own analysis suggests that prices

---

15. L. Fisher and J. H. Lorie, "Rates of Return on Investments in Common Stocks, *The Journal of Business of the University of Chicago,* January, 1964, p. 7.

16. Lawrence Fisher, "Outcomes for 'Random' Investments in Common Stocks Listed on the New York Stock Exchange, *The Journal of Business of the University of Chicago,* April, 1965, pp. 5 and 11.

are dangerously high. An illustration of this type of action by a government official was the speech delivered on June 1, 1965, at Columbia University by Reserve Chairman William McChesney Martin in which he pointed to the "disquieting similarities" with the 1920s as well as to the comforting changes that had occurred. These comments provoked some indignant responses by administration policy-makers, indicating there is no agreement on the advisability of government officials airing such views. With respect to security prices, it is logical to expect that a statement made by a high-placed official suggesting, even in a prudent way, that they are unduly high would cause a reaction. It is also reasonable to expect that, if underlying sentiment is optimistic, the reaction will be mild; and, if weak, the decline that follows may not be as severe as if it started from an even higher price level. Should the Commission develop an adequate economic staff, it probably could become the agency best situated in the country to evaluate the level of stock prices. In light of the charges imposed by the Securities Exchange Act, therefore, it may be appropriate for the Commission to issue cautionary statements during periods of rapidly rising prices that have earmarks of "excessive" speculation, but it does not seem desirable to initiate any stronger efforts at the moment.

This does not mean that the SEC should refrain from exploring more thoroughly the financial structure of the securities business and its relation to the over-all economy. Quite the contrary, as securities become more deeply interlocked with the public well-being, it becomes increasingly imperative to have a better understanding of this relationship. The business has developed an overhead burden that is geared to large volume and a shrinkage could create serious problems for a number of firms. Because of its cyclical characteristics, a compensatory program may be feasible possibly through the introduction of a flexible commission system that provides some assurance of a more uniform rate of return. In view of the savings and lending aspects of the business, perhaps securities firms should be brought more closely within the ambit of national financial policies—a step that could also imply the possibility of Federal intervention in times of economic stress.

The Japanese situation, which is discussed more fully in a different context elsewhere, is a case in point. As stock prices and activity expanded during the late 1950s and early 1960s, securities firms grew rapidly and relatively fixed expenses, particularly in the form of interest and wages, mounted. The stock market decline that occurred in the latter part of 1963 took its toll in reduced commissions and heavy valuation losses. The condition of the securities firms deteriorated and eventually the Bank of Japan intervened to provide financial assistance. Against this background, the Securities and Exchange Law was revised chiefly on the basis of a license system intended to enhance public trust in securities companies, raising the qualifications of the companies, and improving selling practices. In the United States, steps already have been taken along these lines and the securities firms may be presumed to be in a considerably stronger condition than those in Japan. In that country, however, the issue has been raised whether or not the reforms effected are sufficient to keep the securities field within the province of national financial policy as are the banks.

The securities market, as a market for raising long-term funds, is destined to play an important role in the money market as a whole. The fact that the securities market was placed out of the framework of the general financial policy is considered responsible for the advent of the current dilemma of securities companies. This point should be taken fully into consideration in the future studies of the securities program.[17]

All evidence points to the current soundness of the securities business in the United States. It would seem opportune in circumstances such as the present, when the fires of emergency are not burning, for the regulatory authorities to undertake thorough studies of the securities business to determine if further steps are desirable to insure that it serves as a continued element of strength in the economy rather than an even occasional contributor to economic dislocations. In essence, the question raised is whether financial as opposed to legal relationships have kept pace with the changing structure of the securities field.

Once a serious decline of stock prices has set in, and if suitable data-collecting has been developed to assess its significance, the danger to the economy is much more apparent. In this event, no longer at issue are the theoretical uncertainties of acting during

---

17. *The Oriental Economist,* "Whither Securities Business?," July, 1965, p. 403.

a price boom or of bringing the securities business more intimately within the framework of national financial policy. Under these circumstances, the adoption of a program to stem the downward movement through measures of gradually ascending importance seems feasible.

CHECKING MARKET DECLINES

The Government has developed far-reaching controls through monetary and fiscal policy, as well as through direct public expenditures, over economic conditions. It has developed no effective controls over the securities markets once the toboganning side of stock prices is far advanced. Under these circumstances, the only action presumably remaining is to halt trading. Although the Commission itself has never resorted to this measure, the Stock Exchange, as has been mentioned, has been alert to take such action under emergency circumstances. In most instances, the emergency has been an extraordinary event, external to the economy, such as a war or the assassination of the President. In these cases, the public has been aware of the precipitating factor causing the action and the important related corollary, that it was not the Exchange's or Government's apprehension of the basic strength of the economy that led to the extreme measure. There is a grave possibility, however, that a general halt in trading as a result of a price decline, generated by deteriorating economic conditions, might merely fan the flames of public fear and add to the deepening depression. Under these circumstances, it would appear logical for the Commission or the Exchange, before extreme steps are required, to take corrective action by developing a program of intermediate measures which could be unfolded gradually, as the need arises, to arrest sliding prices.

In order to formulate a program of intermediate measures to help check an accelerating stock market decline that, in turn, might lead to a serious business reaction, two major requirements must be met. First, the Commission and the self-regulatory agencies must have available sufficient information to assess the character of the price slippage and the intermediate measures must be studied beforehand in order to gauge their probable effectiveness.

A major conclusion of the Special Study, as a result of its analysis of the 1962 market break, was the need for disaggregated data in order to understand the factors at work. Thus, it was found that nonmembers characteristically dominated transactions in the eight stocks selected for detailed analysis by the Study, yet in the case of IBM, member purchases were more important than those of nonmembers in eight out of the sixteen days covered. Among nonmembers, public individuals in the aggregate usually were the most important component, but on May 11, the reporting open-end funds absorbed 48.5 per cent of Standard Oil (N.J.) Exchange volume, a higher percentage than that of the public individuals. Illustrative of the further inadequacy of aggregate data is that in only one of the eight stocks did the buying and selling of individuals, as reported by the twenty-five big firms surveyed, result in a duplication of the over-all pattern. It is clear, therefore, that the characteristically reported aggregate data do not necessarily reflect the buying or selling pressures that, at any one time, may be driving prices in a particular direction.

Accordingly, if the NYSE is to be in a position adequately to prevent or meet any emergency situations, it must know from minute to minute the trading by type of participants, at least in selected important stocks or in those issues that change by designated percentages during the course of the day. Current data analyzing the break-down between market and limit orders as well as between cash and margin orders, the volume of short-selling, and the amount of stop-loss orders are all important in evaluating the character of the market. Similarly helpful would be daily information on margin calls, restricted accounts, and the capital positions of broker-dealers. The information gathered for this purpose ordinarily would be nonpublic, but the Commission and the Exchange in consultation could decide the extent to which public releases would be issued within some reasonable period. This enumeration of data is only intended to be suggestive of the type of information needed, the importance of having it available currently, and the necessity for compiling it on a dis-aggregated basis. Through such a program of gathering current information, the self-regulatory agencies could continuously gauge the strength and weakness of existing markets and evaluate the advisability of adopting appropriate measures. The availability of computer facilities makes this type of data compilation feasible. Eventually, as the Commission uses its own computer, the agency, through on-line tie-ins with Exchange facilities, too, could be kept abreast of current developments, so that it could better fulfill its responsibilities under the Securities Exchange Act to prevent unruly price fluctuations from leading to national emergencies.

The second requirement in developing a program to arrest severely deteriorating stock prices is the formulation of the measures that might be introduced. It is important that these measures be evaluated beforehand so that a plan of action may be initiated as the necessity arises rather than that isolated steps be taken under the pressures of an existing emergency. Perhaps the most noteworthy recent effort of governmental concern with and governmental action to check a severe market decline occurred in Japan during 1964 and 1965. The background of these events was reminiscent of the 1959–1961 "hot-issue" period in the United States. In Japan, to entice investors into the market, security houses introduced a *money-boom* promotion program that included daily television shows airing investment advice and newspaper public-relations columns. The results of their efforts lured thousands of housewives, taxi drivers, shopkeepers and bar girls into the purchase of stock. This indiscriminate buying stimulated daily trading and advanced the Dow-Jones average of 225 stocks to an average high level of 1,829 in 1961. Many new offerings of securities reached the market with little regard to the growth potential or operating costs of the issuing corporations. Eventually the inflationary bubble burst as corporate profits dwindled, bankruptcies rose at a record pace, stock prices slid, and trading volume shrank severely.[18]

As the gloomy outlook spread and criticism of the Administration arose, a series of measures was inaugurated to check the deteriorating condition of the market. in January, 1964, the Japan Joint Securities Company was formed by leading securities companies and banks to engage in selective buying and selling operations. Subsequently, the Bank of Japan made additional funds available to the Joint Securities Company, cooperative support buying was undertaken by four major securities firms and listed companies were restricted in making capital increases. In January 1965, a new stock pooling organ, The Japan Securities Holding

---

18. *The Wall Street Journal,* June 1, 1965, June 10, 1965.

Association, was established by member securities companies of stock exchanges for the purpose of buying and shelving for at least three years stock held by securities firms and securities investment companies.[19] Arrangements were made for the holding agency to obtain required funds from the Bank of Japan through the nominal medium of the Japan Securities Finance Co. and, reflecting its governmental relationship, to seek instructions from the Minister of Finance on important managerial decisions.[20]

Initially, the efforts to check the decline seemed successful at about a level of 1,200–1,300 for the Dow-Jones average. Eventually, however, the slide continued, a number of securities firms merged, others went out of business, and one of the country's major houses had to seek a credit reprieve. To stave off bankruptcy, the Bank of Japan granted help to various private securities companies and the Government introduced close regulations over the securities business.

By July, 1965, there was apprehension that the Dow-Jones average might drop below the critical 1,000 level thereby generating a serious psychological reaction on the part of the public. Mounting pessimism in some quarters led to the conclusion that the curative efforts should be abandoned because ". . . even if the market plunges out of sight, Japan does not need one anyway."[21] This viewpoint reflected the extreme reaction that may be engendered by deepening economic gloom, but apparently was not shared by any important economic group. On the contrary, the Government pursued its planning efforts and announced a series of impending economic measures including drastic tax cuts, additions to the national loan and investment program, and the use of public works projects to prime the business pump. The stock market responded favorably to these expanded efforts and the average thereafter gradually rose to a level of about 1,300 in November, 1965.

It is difficult to assess the value of the organized stock-buying program to the sagging Japanese economy. The benefits stem from

19. The Daiwa Securities Co., Ltd., "The Daiwa Investment Monthly," January, 1965, pp. 5–6, February and March, 1965, pp. 3–4.
20. *The Nihon Keizai Shimbun (Japan Economic Journal)*, January 12, 1965, pp. 1 and 4; *The Japan Stock Journal,* weekly, 1964, 1965.
21. *The Economist,* July 17, 1965, p. 274.

the support given to investor psychology and the contribution towards correcting the imbalance between the demand for and supply of stocks. While the pouring of new funds into the markets did not by itself prevent prices from declining, there are financial experts in Japan who claim that without this governmental assist prices would have fallen more severely. As a result, they contend, these buying efforts contributed importantly towards strengthening the faltering Japanese economy and establishing the basis for a future revival.

The Japanese developments have been described in some detail to illustrate the interest of a national government in arresting a serious decline in securities prices, the claimed benefits that may be achieved, and the difficulty experienced in formulating a suitable program in the midst of the financial and political pressures generated by the decline. To permit the adoption of optimum arrangements, intermediate corrective measures should be developed and tested beforehand. In this way, there could be some assurance that any plan of action that has to be adopted will have the benefit of careful advance thinking rather than having to be introduced in the heat of an emergency.

THE TYPE OF INTERMEDIATE MEASURES AVAILABLE TO CHECK A DECLINE

With appropriate information at hand and a plan of action available, the NYSE, under Commission surveillance, would be in a position to judge when to act and the steps to take. There follows a brief analysis of the kind of measures that might be considered.

Public Statements on Market Conditions—Market panics and breaks similar to that of May 28, 1962, usually accelerate and feed upon the absence of accurate information and the multiplication of unsubstantiated rumors. In this area, the self-regulatory agencies and the Commission could perform a valuable service by issuing in such circumstances dispassionate and accurate appraisals of market conditions. Considering their sources, such announcements might well have a sobering and clarifying effect. During the 1962 market-break period a smoke screen of conflicting statements was issued by commentators and analysts without adequate data on hand. It was not until many months later that either the Commission or the Exchange was able to issue the results of their studies.

Consultations with Large Institutional Investors—Since the large institutional investors play an increasingly important role in the markets, the self-regulatory agencies and the Commission at least should be aware of their market actions and investment policies. It is entirely possible that had it been more widely known that on May 28, 1962, the large institutions, such as the mutual funds, were heavy buyers in the preceding week, some of the panic selling might have been avoided. In addition, the Commission might consider encouraging large institutions to exploit their buying and selling potentials to help maintain orderly markets. By an expanded data-gathering program and a closer knowledge of institutional transactions, the Commission would be in a position to show the need for bringing appropriate strength into the market at certain times. In view of the large volume of savings they hold, the institutions occupy a quasi-public role in the economy. Their huge resources plus their ability to reach decisions in a hurry would enable them to respond quickly to Commission requests for action that appeared justified by the facts presented. As a result, they might be able to provide more effectively the balancing role that the Japanese Government attempted to play in its stock-buying program.

Suspension of Stop-Loss Orders—Stop-loss orders generally are used as a profit-taking or loss-limiting device by speculators. Longer-term investors may employ them at times when their own attention is drawn away from the market. While stop-loss orders are not likely to represent a large portion of transactions, they can add materially to the downward pressure during a period of market contraction. On May 28, 1962, for example, they constituted 8.4 per cent of total sales executed on that day. When the effective price of a stop-loss order is reached, it becomes a market order. Thus, if there is no demand at the effective price, the stop-loss order may be executed many points below this level. The Exchange has suspended stop-loss orders in particular stocks, when it appeared that such orders might jeopardize the market in these issues. The American Stock Exchange has banned all stop-loss orders in all stocks and permits only so-called stop-limit orders.[22] The Commission has unlimited authority over stop-loss orders in Section 10(a) of the Securities Exchange Act.

The Commission could announce a suspension of stop-loss orders (whether limited or not) in all stocks on every exchange as a bear market accelerates. Such a step would appear reasonable and justifiable for the protection of investors by helping to prevent a normally reasonable expectation from turning into an unreasonable loss, that is, execution at a price far below that selected by the investor when he entered the order. It would have the further effect of removing the selling pressure of these orders.

Revision of the Short-Selling Rule—Under the current rules of the Commission a short sale can only be effected on a *plus tick* or a *zero-plus tick,* that is, a price above the previous different price. The intent of the rule, however, may also kill incipient rallies by leading to the concentration of short selling on each upward tick.

The short-selling rule approaches the auction market on a transactional basis. It does not regard the over-all market. The available evidence indicates that short selling increases during periods of market decline, thereby adding to the downward pressure. On May 28, 1962, the present rule permitted some short selling, despite the fact that it was one of the greatest market routs in history.

The Commission also has unlimited authority over short sales in Section 10(a) of the Securities Exchange Act. As a bear market deepens, the Commission could modify the short-selling rule to cope more effectively with the potentially depressing effects of short selling during price declines. While the Special Study did not suggest the exact form of such a rule or rules of general application, among the possibilities mentioned for consideration were the prohibition of short selling in a particular stock whenever its sale price was below the prior day's low; or, alternatively, whenever the last sale price was a predetermined dollar amount or percentage below a base price (e.g., the prior day's close or low or the same day's opening) specified in the rule; or, instead, given

---

22. A stop-limit order is one that becomes a market order when a designated price is reached or passed, but in this case, an outer price limit is also indicated; if not consummated within this price range the order is terminated.

the circumstances of such a decline, a limitation of short sales in any particular stock to a predetermined proportion of the amount of stock available at the prevailing market. As a further precaution for times of general market distress, the Commission rules might provide for temporary banning of short selling in all stocks or in a particular stock upon an appropriate finding by the Commission of need for such action.[23]

Suspension of Market Sell Orders—During the severe price decline of May 28, 1962, 70.1 per cent of market orders were for sales, compared with only 35.4 per cent for purchases; while 64.1 per cent of limit orders were for purchases, compared with 21.5 per cent for sales. On May 31, as the market moved upward, a reversal of this relationship occurred; 68.2 per cent of market orders were for purchases, compared with only 51.3 per cent for sales; while 47.2 per cent of the limit orders were for sales, and 31.3 per cent for purchases. Thus, on May 28, the large volume of market sell orders was influential in driving prices down. Apparently, there were insufficient offsetting market buy orders to halt the downward movement, which therefore continued until enough limit orders were set off to permit a matching of demand and supply. On May 31, on the other hand, market orders apparently drove prices up until there were sufficient limit orders to permit a balance between demand and supply.

On such a day as May 28, therefore, the Commission might be empowered to suspend all market sell orders. Trading would then be halted for some specified time, perhaps two hours, while all brokers informed their customers of the event. Investors would then be required either to withdraw their orders or limit them to some specified amount below the last sale which occurred immediately before the halt of trading. The two-hour period, ostensibly for the purpose of allowing brokers to obtain instructions, would serve as a cooling-off period. The very fact that the customer had to limit his order would bring forcibly to his attention the fact that he could expect an execution far below then existing values. It would take a stronger heart knowingly to take a substantial loss than it takes merely to rush in with a market order and hope for the best.

---

23. Report of Special Study of Securities Markets of the Securities and Exchange Commission, op. cit., Part 2, Chapter V, pp. 293–294.

Besides giving the investor a second chance and providing him with a cooling-off period in which to think, the limit order which comes in as a result of this rule would permit a more orderly decline, if it continued. Potential investors could still use a market order to buy, and thus have an immediate reflection of their investment decisions. The efficiency of the auction market would be inhibited on one side but not on the other. While there is no specific statutory authority for such action at this time, the Commission could possibly move along these lines under its emergency powers.

Limitation on Price Swings of a Certain Magnitude—On critical days and in critical minutes, as the psychological factor becomes dominant, the price swings of a few stocks, regarded as market leaders, can have a profound impact on the entire market. It is possible, for example, that had IBM opened on the morning of May 29 down 30 or 40 points, the rally of that day might never have occurred. Rather than let such a drop happen, the Exchange did not open the stock until sufficient buying power was rounded up near the previous close.

Under the duress of extreme market pressures, it is likely that specialists, particularly when their financial situation is at stake, may not be in a position to reach completely objective decisions. Under these circumstances, the Commission, presumably also abreast of the current situation through its computer tie-in, might take the initiative in suspending trading in certain stocks when a prescribed percentage of decline is achieved during a trading session. A variant of this proposal, perhaps the next step, would be to limit price swings in all stocks. This would give the panic mood a chance to dissipate.

Providing an Insurance Fund for the Specialist—During periods of severe market declines, the specialist's role becomes critical. If he is responsible for an important stock, his reluctance to step into a breach might open the floodgates for an indundation of sell orders. Yet despite his obligations to act, the specialist might be restrained from doing so because of the enormous financial risks he would be assuming. It is improbable that capital requirements could be placed so high as to eliminate this consideration in panic markets.

Under these circumstances, the Exchange might consider the possibility of establishing an insurance fund to limit the losses a specialist would take during days that are officially labelled as "emergency." With this fund as a potential support, the specialist could be expected to act more freely in the best interests of the market. Such a provision might go further to protect investors in the long run than the reserve established by the Exchange to be used in the event of future insolvency of a member firm. Like the insolvency reserve, the specialist-insurance fund could be activated at the discretion of the Board of Governors.

Summary—The data-gathering and intermediary-power program suggested are only intended as rough guides. Before suitable measures can be developed, a careful study is necessary as to the information required, the method of compilation, the means of detecting an emergency, and the type of action that could be taken. Despite the fact that the statute calls for such action and the Commission has previously recognized its necessity, no such program has been evolved. When functioning efficiently, the securities markets represent a major cog in the capital rationing and public savings program of the country. When laboring under the stress of rapidly fluctuating prices and psychological panic, the securities markets can be converted into a juggernaut that hurtles the nation towards an economic depression.

The use of intermediate measures would be designed to offset such a national calamity. Part of the reason for the failure of the Commission or the Exchange to develop a suitable program stems from the difficulty of determining the appropriate time to take action and the measures that could be adopted.

As use is made of computers to trace the flow of specific transactions on the floor of the exchanges and their impact upon prices, the gap in self-regulatory knowledge can be filled. It is important, therefore, for the Commission and the self-regulatory agencies to employ the computer for this purpose.

Other Criteria

In addition to the frequently repeated goals of "public interest" and/or "protection of investors," other criteria are employed in connection with the securities markets. Sometimes these are cited in the Securities Exchange Act as statutory standards, while in other cases they have simply developed through usage over time. Despite the fact that reference to such statutory and nonstatutory standards are common, they have never been officially defined. Yet, in order to evaluate the qualities of a securities market, these objectives must be understood. Accordingly, the Special Study of Securities Markets as well as others have made some tentative efforts at framing definitions. Until an official body formally clarifies these uncertainties, however, all that can be done is to theorize upon what are the most logical meanings.

THE STATUTORY STANDARDS

From the point of view of the economist, concerned as he is with the price system, perhaps the most controversial objective set forth in the Securities Exchange Act appeared only once and that in a description of how the rules of an association of brokers or dealers must be framed in order to be registered under the Act. In Section 15A(b)(8), among other things, the Act admonishes that such rules must be designed "in general, to protect investors and the public interest, and to remove impediments to and perfect the mechanism of a free and open market." It is odd that such an important concept—the freedom of the market—made its debut several years after the original passage of the Securities Exchange Act (Section 15A was added in 1938) and then appeared as only one of various standards that were mentioned a single time. Yet, the use of the term *free* and/or *open* in Congressional reports, hearings, and in subsequent discussion of the securities markets clearly indicates that it has a wider applicability than is suggested by its restricted use in the Securities Exchange Act.

A free market presumably is one where prices are determined by the interplay of demand and supply without any outside interferences. The Staff Report to the Committee on Banking and Currency succinctly described such a market as one where "the trading of the security should be governed by the forces of supply and demand."[24] The Special Study of Securities Markets added the notion that in its ultimate sense, the concept might even exclude beneficent extraneous forces such as those of a stabilizing nature and that such markets would be "free" to reflect spon-

---

24. "Factors Affecting the Stock Market," op. cit., p. 118.

taneous bids and offers regardless of the sharpness or duration of the resulting movements. Less interest has been displayed in the implication of "open" markets, which may be construed to mean that anyone can submit buy or sell orders for execution.

Occurring with relative frequency in the Act is the term "fair." At the very outset, Section 2 calls for insuring "the maintenance of fair and honest markets." But the term is used more often either in "fair dealing" or in "fair and orderly" markets. In Section 6(d), the rules of an exchange must be "just and adequate to insure fair dealing"; in Section 11(a), the Commission is authorized to prescribe rules to prevent excessive off-floor trading by members that is considered detrimental to "a fair and orderly market"; in Section 11(b), the Commission's rules governing the specialist "restrict his dealings so far as practicable to those reasonably necessary to permit him to maintain a fair and orderly market"; in Section 12(b) (2), the Commission may require an issuer registering securities on a national exchange to file documents and, in Section 13(a), to file periodical reports in accordance with the governing prescription of being necessary for the "proper protection of investors and to insure fair dealing in the security"; and in Section 15A(k)(1), the Commission may abrogate any rule of a registered securities association or, in Section 19(b), alter certain rules of an exchange if it is necessary, among other things, "to assure fair dealing."

Thus, the term "fair dealing" covers a wide area embracing the rules of the Commission, exchanges, and over-the-counter markets. A reasonable interpretation of its meaning is that no participant in the marketplace should be given an undue advantage over another, and to the extent differences in opportunity exist because of required differences in function and responsibility, such advantages should be held to a minimum. Some confirmation of this meaning is given in the warning contained in Section 15A (b)(8), that the rules of a registered association must not be "designed to permit unfair discrimination between customers or issuers, or brokers or dealers. . . ." The question of unfair advantage was also raised at the hearings on the Securities Exchange Act. For example, in discussing floor traders, Thomas G. Corcoran, one of the architects of the bill, stated:

The justification for throwing them off the floor is that there is no reason why any trading for himself (sic) should have a jump on the rest of the buying public by being on the floor and knowing what is going on whereas the rest of the public has to buy strictly from the ticker outside.[25]

The single reference to "honest" in the section concerned with the necessity for regulation of the markets apparently embodied the idea of eliminating the manipulative practices that are later spelled out in greater detail.

As indicated above, the term *orderly* is used several times in association with the notion of fairness. The Commission is instructed to consider a "fair and orderly" market both in regulating trading by exchange members for their own accounts and in determining the permissive activity of a specialist in his capacity of a dealer. "Orderly" is used to convey the notion of limited changes principally in prices from transaction to transaction and of a narrow spread between bid and ask quotations. Thus, the Commission has referred to a disorderly market as one "in which prices rise or fall several points between transactions—or a market in which no transactions at all are possible because of the wide spread between the bid and asked prices."[26] Apparently the framers of the Act had in mind that exchange members, and particularly specialists, have a responsibility to keep the market "fair," or devoid of special advantages to the extent possible, and "orderly," or moving narrowly from transaction to transaction.

"Just and equitable principles of trade" is another phrase that crops up several times among the subordinate criteria. In Section 6(b), the rules of an exchange must include provisions for disciplining members for conduct inconsistent with "just and equitable principles of trade," and the willful violation of any provisions of the Act or rules adopted under it is considered conduct inconsistent with "just and equitable principles of trade." Similarly, in the Maloney Act amendment the term appears at different points. In Section 15A(b)(4), one of the reasons cited for barring a broker or dealer from a registered association is for violation of a rule which

---

25. "Stock Exchange Regulation," Hearing before the Committee on Interstate and Foreign Commerce, House of Representatives 73rd Cong., 2d sess., on H.R. 7852 and H.R. 8720, 1934, p. 117.

26. Securities and Exchange Commission, Sixth Annual Report, op. cit., p. 91.

prohibits "conduct inconsistent with just and equitable principles of trade"; in Section 15A(b)(8), the rules of an association are designed among other things "to promote just and equitable principles of trade; and in Sections 15A(b)(10) and 15A(h)(1), the disciplining of members requires, as does the review of such action by the Commission a determination (among other things) of "whether the acts or practices prohibited . . . or the ommission of any act required . . . constitute conduct inconsistent with just and equitable principles of trade."

Application of the standard calling for "just and equitable trade" is tied to the self-regulatory concept developed in the Securities Exchange Act. One of the issues considered in the discussions of the Securities Exchange Act was the desirability of requiring Federal incorporation of exchanges. The strongest argument advanced against such a requirement was that it would greatly retard the ability of the exchanges to enforce their rules and regulations. It was recognized that the introduction of exchange incorporation would permit members to have their cases adjudicated in the first instance in a court of law rather than by exchange tribunals. As a result every violator of exchange rules would be provided with a lengthy opportunity, prolonged by the use of delaying technicalities, to indulge in improper practices. Also, use of formal, legal procedures would be an inefficient replacement to the self-regulatory system whereby charges against members may be based not on specific rules and regulations but upon conduct "inconsistent with just and equitable principles of trade."[27] In the latter instance, a tribunal of exchange members with an intimate knowledge of the case may be able efficiently to take disciplinary action based upon information of a less formal nature than that required by legal evidence.

Most of the other subordinate standards listed in the Securities Exchange Act were mentioned only once and generally in connec-

---

27. In the Silver case discussed previously, the Supreme Court decided that the NYSE was liable to Silver, a nonmember of the Exchange, under the Sherman Act for causing its members to discontinue their wire connections with him. The Court decision was based on the unfairness of the Exchange's procedure, including the absence of notice to Silver and the refusal to permit him to meet the "charges" against him. This decision probably assures each NYSE member as well as nonmember of due process in the consideration of the cases.

tion with the over-the-counter market. In Section 15(c)(3), reference is made to the Commission rules providing "safeguards with respect to the financial responsibility of brokers and dealers." Section 15A(b)(8) is a veritable catch-all paragraph containing a number of additional standards that the rules of a registered association are designed to achieve. This long list may reflect the intent to erect legislative safeguards in supervising over-the-counter activity because under the Maloney Act Amendment the NASD was exempted from antitrust laws for actions taken in conformity with the Securities Exchange Act. Among these criteria is the providing of "safeguards against unreasonable profits or unreasonable rates of commission or other charges." This is not designed, however, "to fix minimum profits, to impose any schedule of prices, or to impose any schedule or fix minimum of rates of commissions, allowances, discounts, or other charges." This concern with the profits of the broker-dealers and the charges imposed is of particular interest in view of the SEC's previously relatively lackadaisical attitude with respect to reviewing the entire problem of commission rates.

Reflecting the Commission's concern with the public-interest aspects of quotations systems, a 1964 amendment to Section 15A(b) added a new paragraph pertaining to the standards of over-the-counter quotations. According to this paragraph, the rules of any registered association (the NASD) must be designed to produce "fair and informative quotations, both at the wholesale and retail level, to prevent fictitious or misleading quotations, and to promote orderly procedures for collecting and publishing quotations." Bulwarked by this provision, the Commission subsequently issued a rule eliminating some of the misleading aspects of wholesale quotations and put pressure upon the NASD to revise the method of reporting retail quotations in the newspapers.[28]

THE NONSTATUTORY CRITERIA

Since passage of the Securities Exchange Act, various nonstatutory standards have been employed by the Commission, by the self-regulating agencies, by legislators investigating the securities markets, and by practitioners in the business. Prominent among such criteria are "continuous," "close," and "liquid."

---

28. See pp. 207–210.

The Staff Report to the Senate Committee on Banking and Currency defined "close" as a narrow spread between the price bid for a security and the price at which it is offered for sale and as small variations in successive sales. "Continuous" was defined to mean frequent purchases and sales of securities quickly carried out.[29]

The Special Study associated "continuous" with minimum price variations in a series of consecutive separate transactions, thereby linking it with the Staff Report's description of one phase of "closeness." The Special Study added that it was open to question whether the term implied anything about the volume of trading at any given level or the extent to which a price trend might continue in one direction. It described "liquid" as the ability of a willing seller promptly to find a buyer, or vice versa, at a mutually agreeable price. Whether the term implies anything about the transaction occurring at a level that is close to the current intrinsic worth is open to question.[30]

While the meanings ascribed to the terms differ in specific instances, there is one common aspect about these nonstatutory criteria. In general, they are all concerned with the principle of orderliness. Closely related to this general idea of a close, liquid, orderly market is the question of "depth," which the Special Study defined as the quantity of buying and selling interest and the potential activity on each side of the market. Of prime importance in determining the depth of a stock, in the sense of public interest and activity, are the total amount of shares outstanding and the breadth of distribution among the public, excluding amounts held by "insiders" and other "permanent" holders of large blocks.

Of secondary importance in influencing depth are the prominence of the issuer, current developments affecting the issuer's popularity among investors, the degree of broker-dealer solicitations, the balance between trading and investing activity, and the price. Depth is thus dependent to a large degree on the floating supply of a stock in the hands of the public; this has become an important listing criterion of the exchanges. Despite the significance to the securities markets of this chain—floating supply is the basis

---

29. "Factors Affecting the Stock Market," op. cit., p. 118.
30. Special Study of Securities Markets of the Securities and Exchange Commission, op. cit., Part 2, Chapter V, pp. 15–18.

for listing, which in turn influences depth—there has been little effort statistically to measure the importance of depth. To a large extent, the standards of floating supply required for listing have been arbitrarily established.

Another nonstatutory criterion that has been advanced stems from the "classical" theory that speculators tend to buy stocks when their prices are low and to sell them as prices rise to high levels, thereby stabilizing prices and making profits into the bargain. In order to permit the application of this theory, it is necessary to measure when prices are high or low by means of some market gauge. This is not an easy undertaking because the many techniques of securities trading that have been developed suggest that speculators do not necessarily conduct their transactions in the same manner. One standard that has been suggested, however, is that of an *equilibrium price* defined as the intersection of the investors' demand schedule for a security and the amount outstanding.[31] According to this notion, the equilibrium price changes in accordance with shifts in the demand schedule. To the extent that speculators adequately diagnose these shifts by selling when prices move above the new equilibrium level while buying when they fall below it, the speculators not only earn profits but provide a stabilizing influence.

The equilibrium price does not appear to be a usable market criterion. It reduces to a determination of the demand schedule for securities that in certain periods undoubtedly changes rapidly and is difficult to quantify. The associated implication that the trading profits of speculators may be employed as a criterion because of their stabilizing influence requires the acceptance of a relationship about which there is considerable uncertainty. To make profits, speculators must, of course, sell at higher and buy at lower prices. In the course of doing so, they may very well accentuate or even create trends and will still earn profits so long as they time appropriately the reversing operation.[32] With respect

31. George Stigler, "Public Regulation of the Securities Markets," *The Journal of Business of the University of Chicago,* April, 1964, pp. 126–127.

32. See discussion by Irwin Friend and Edward S. Herman, "The SEC Through a Glass Darkly," *The Journal of Business of the University of Chicago,* October, 1964, pp. 399–402.

to one class of speculators, the floor traders, the Special Study concluded that as a group they tended to trade with price trends, or in a destabilizing fashion. Speculation augments market depth and in the normal sequence of events contributes to the allocation efficiency of the market as speculators base their transactions on their anticipations of future conditions. There does not appear to be sufficient evidence, however, to support the theory that the profits of speculators may be employed as a criterion of market efficiency.

THE BALANCING OF OBJECTIVES

These criteria, statutory and nonstatutory, represent targets at which the rules and regulations governing the operations of the markets are aimed. It is very difficult, however, to hit one target without jarring another. Thus to provide "honest" markets means that the rights of entry must be limited to those likely to observe proper rules of behavior which interferes with the market's "openness." To improve orderliness and its associated concepts means that professional participation should be invited, but "professionals" tend to have an inherent advantage over the nonprofessionals in trading knowledge and opportunities; and their participation, therefore, tends to detract from the market's "fairness." Rules designed to achieve "just and equitable principles of trade" may run counter to "freedom" and "openness." Since these conflicts among criteria persist, the effective regulation of the exchanges requires a delicate balancing to provide rules that maximize the bundle of objectives, rather than any single one.

From the point of view of the investor, whose interests are consistently predominant as an over-all objective, the benefits and costs are offsetting factors. He may be willing to incur more costs to obtain increased benefits until an equilibrium point is reached, when the added benefits are no longer an inducement for the higher costs. Thus, in developing a commission schedule, the investor may be willing to pay higher rates for more services—up to a given level. He may be willing to see the professional obtain a certain amount of special privileges in exchange for providing greater orderliness—to a certain point. He may be willing to sacrifice speed of execution in exchange for obtaining a better price; as a result, in times of emergency, the elimination of market orders may be acceptable, if such action leads to greater orderliness.

Conversely, at any time, rapidity of execution is no necessary virtue if it contributes to price impairment. To most investors, the ability to realize funds through the sale of securities endows these assets with an important advantage over other types of property, such as real estate, where liquidation is more difficult. The unanswered question, however, is how swift must realization be to meet the needs of most investors. If a seller could dispose of a security within a day, for example, at a higher price than within a matter of minutes, he might be willing to accept the delay. The question of developing markets that are structured to optimize the relationship between the two possible elements of liquidity—the time within which and the price at which a transaction is completed never has been fully explored. It is very likely that at some point investors are indifferent to the benefits of time saved in obtaining funds compared with the advantage of receiving more funds through the sale of a security over a longer interval.

Another vital question that requires answering is the degree, if any, to which the criterion of a "free" market may be impaired in order to provide more "orderliness." Some economists have placed the criterion of "free" markets on a pedestal that stands above all others. Thus, it has been argued that "if the impacts on equilibrium are sudden and unexpected . . . the appropriate market response is an immediate and complete shift to the new price level. Under this condition the demand for 'continuity' in a market is a demand for delay in responding to the change in demand conditions, and . . . there simply is no merit in such delay."[33] In a similar vein, the argument runs:

We have already voiced our doubts about the concept of liquidity as the NYSE conceives of it. What about other points? In the case of continuity and stability, it is clear that as long as the information about market conditions remains unchanged, the prices at which transactions are executed will be most efficient economic agents if they are close to the collective appraisal of security value. But when the information changes, are continuity and stability of any real merit? If the heart

---

33. George J. Stigler, "Public Regulation of the Securities Markets," op. cit., p. 130.

attack or assassination of a President are real economic news, why should there not be sharp discontinuities in prices?[34]

To answer these contentions, one must not forget the role of the securities markets in the economy and how prices are determined. It has previously been emphasized that the securities markets must be judged by their contribution to the national interest. A major purpose is their function as an efficient allocator of capital resources. To this end, prices in the markets must reflect, to the extent possible, the intrinsic merits of the issuing company and, as has been explained, a major purpose of disclosure is to enable investors to reach such decisions rationally. The significance of this relationship between prices and values was emphasized at the very outset of the public discussions on the Securities Exchange Act. Thus the 1934 Committee on Stock Regulation, reporting to Secretary of Commerce Roper, stated that one of the three major objectives of regulation of stock markets was:

> So far as possible, the aim should be to try to create a condition in which fluctuations in security values more nearly approximate fluctuations in the position of the enterprise itself and of general economic conditions—that is, tend to represent what is going on in the business and in our economic life rather than mere speculative or 'technical' conditions in the market"[35]

Underlying forces in the securities markets, however, tend to distort the relationship between stock prices and values. Thus transactions in a particular stock on any one day are likely to involve only a small number of shareholders, some of whom may have peculiarly urgent needs to liquidate a position. The resulting sales could cause sudden price variations induced not by changes in intrinsic worth or general economic conditions, but rather by the vagaries of supply and demand at a particular moment.[36] More particularly, such distortions could arise, if the seller is an institu-

---

34. Roland I. Robinson and H. Robert Bartell, Jr., "Uneasy Partnership: SEC/NYSE," *Harvard Business Review,* January-February, 1965, p. 88.

35. "Stock Exchange Regulation," Letter from the President of the United States to the Chairman of the Committee on Banking and Currency, op. cit., p. 5.

36. Report of the Special Study of Securities Markets of the Securities Exchange Commission, op. cit., Part 2, Chapter VI, p. 162.

tion disposing of a large block of stock for portfolio reasons entirely apart from the security's basic value.[37] A sharp break in the price of a pivotal stock, in turn, as has been pointed out, could engender sympathetic selling waves and lead to temporarily panic conditions. In these circumstances, the link between value and price is broken and stocks may be traded as pieces of paper rather than symbols of economic values. Similarly, technical circumstances could be the precursor of unduly sharp price swings that engender overoptimism and send prices to unjustified blue-sky levels.

A market which moves in small fractions probably tends to discourage excessive speculation, which in turn could obscure the valuation basis to price determination. Orderliness is important to preserve the rational character of security trading, which is an imperative requirement for a "free" market. When the economist talks about prices in competitive markets being determined by the schedules of supply and demand, he assumes rational participants who are able to measure the utility or satisfaction derived from the purchase in the light of its cost. If the participants were all rendered temporarily incapable of making such judgments, the pricing mechanism would break down. The stock market is exposed to such dangers because temporary imbalances between supply and demand created by technical factors can cause sharp price changes that in turn generate psychological blocks in investors.

Ordinarily, the basic position of a company, which presumably determines the value of its securities, changes slowly. It is unlikely that the daily passage of events can cause the company's intrinsic worth to move up and down in sharp discontinuous patterns. It is rare for a single event to cause the basic valuation of a company to shift abruptly by a big margin. For example, as events later proved, even so calamitous an occurrence as the assassination of the President did not change the essential economic condition of American companies or of the markets and the sharp drop in stock prices that ensued proved to be a product of emotion rather than of reason.

In very unusual circumstances, a single event, such as the out-

---

37. As discussed later, the organized exchanges have developed various trading methods to facilitate sales of large blocks of stocks without seriously affecting market prices.

break of war, may have such far-reaching economic consequences that the outlook for individual companies is substantially altered, and a sharp price change is justified. Even here, however, a pause in trading would appear reasonable to permit investor evaluation of the situation, rather than to expose the markets to the immediate impact of orders submitted under severe emotional tensions. It is important to realize that the principles of orderliness, with their attendant notions of closeness and liquidity, do not preclude broad price reversals. These ideas imply that the changes should proceed in an orderly fashion so as to prevent sharp price discontinuities from inducing irrational markets.

The desirability of striking a balance between "free" and "orderly" markets has been recognized since the establishment of the Securities Exchange Act. In the original hearings on the Act, Senator Thomas P. Gore commented as follows:

I watched those stocks drop like a plummet, 30 or 40 points in an hour. It ought to be a reasonable market, so far as can be, where some sort of reason prevails. But you have seen times when reason just took flight and people were seized with frenzy. Sometimes you put an individual in a straight-jacket (sic) and in a padded cell to prevent him from doing violence to himself. I want a market place where people can buy and sell, and I only want to guard against those things that are preventable. We do not want to undertake to prevent things that we cannot prevent. Then we would do more harm than good. We would be attacking impossibilities.[38]

And at a slightly later point, Corcoran, in commenting on the need for margin controls, expressed the following view:

To summarize, we have on the one hand the argument of social policy against margin money in the market, both from the point of view of its effect upon business and upon the social fabric which was described to you yesterday, and from the point of view of loss to the individual investor.

Against that we balance the advantages of liquidity in the market from the standpoint of having a place where banks can lend liquid funds and where investors can realize on securities. I am not trying to make that balance. For me there would be no choice. If I had to sacrifice

---

38. "Stock Exchange Practices," Hearings Before the Committee on Banking and Currency, United States Senate, 73rd Cong., 1st sess., on S. Res. 84 and S. Res. 56 and S. Res. 97, 1934, p. 6495.

liquidity of the market in the sense that sales had to be within a quarter of a point rather than within two points to prevent 1929 from occurring again, the decision would be easy for me; but that is a question of policy.[39]

Thus the theory of the securities markets, as it originally evolved and still pertains today, rests on the principle of "freeness," where prices are determined by the forces of demand and supply. At the same time, the theory contemplates that some erosion will be made in the principle to gain "orderliness." Achievement of this delicate balance, which is primarily left to the specialist at present and in emergency conditions to exchange and Commission officials, involves a determination of the degree of the interference to be permitted.

The guiding rule originally established by the Saperstein Interpretation of 1937 was that the specialists' dealer functions should be designed to minimize the effects of temporary disparities between supply and demand. The new specialist rules adopted by the Commission and the two big New York exchanges in 1964 affirmed the positive obligation of the specialist to make fair and orderly markets. Also, in recognition of the desirability of limiting interferences with the criterion of a "free" market, the rules prohibit specialists from changing prices at openings against the direction indicated by public supply and demand. Over the long run, adequate disclosure of corporate conditions, more effective analytic techniques, and the further curtailment of manipulative practices will result in supply and demand for a stock reflecting more closely its intrinsic merits, measured by the present worth of the expected future return. Adherence to this relationship, in turn, tends to enhance the allocational efficiency of the capital markets.[40]

---

39. Ibid., p. 6499.

40. The most effective statistical measure of the improved allocational efficiency of the capital markets since the SEC periods lies in the absence of the enormous losses due to manipulation and excess speculation engendered during the pre-SEC era. Professor Friend and his associates also have provided some statistical evidence of the salutory effect that disclosure provisions have had on the allocational efficiency of the capital markets. See Irwin Friend and Edward F. Herman, op. cit.

CHAPTER **6**

Some Problems
of the
Securities
Markets

Through experience and study, clearer insights have been gained into both the role of the securities markets in the economy and the problems interfering with the effective performance of this role. In the present chapter, some of these issues are discussed, starting with primary distribution of new securities to the public and moving to different aspects of the trading markets.

Primary Distributions to the Public

By means of the distribution facilities of the securities markets, corporations are able to raise funds for their operating and expansion needs, while large blocks of securities in the hands of wealthy individuals or institutions may be transferred to smaller investors. The latter process, known as a secondary distribution is discussed in the next chapter; here we are concerned with the distribution of new issues.

THE MECHANISM OF DISTRIBUTION[1]

Corporations may sell securities to the public through underwriting intermediaries, known as investment bankers; or directly to one or a small number of buyers (ordinarily institutions) by means of a private placement with or without the services of an investment banker; or directly to their present stockholders through the issuance of rights, once more with or without the services of an investment banker that agrees to purchase the unsubscribed shares. In the typical publicly underwritten offering, a buying group pays for the issue, thereby freeing the corporation from the financing risk, and then arranges for its distribution through a selling syndicate.

The gross spread, representing the difference between the amount paid to the issuer and the price at which the security is sold to the public, is divided among the syndicate managers, the underwriting participants and the dealers who are provided concessions and reallowances. Most distributions of corporate securities are done at a fixed public offering price in markets. The underwriters, to prevent a price decline during the period immediately prior or during the public offering, buy the security on the open market in accordance with defined SEC regulations.

In early 1962, approximately 4,000 nonbank broker-dealers and a small number of bank dealers, who operated in the trading markets, also served regularly or occasionally in some sort of investment-banking capacity. These organizations had close to $2.5 billion invested in the securities business and employed over 100,000 persons. The investment activities of commercial banks are restricted to general obligations of states and municipalities and obligations of the U.S. Government, although the question

---

1. Much of the data in this section are from Securities Research Unit, Wharton School of Finance and Commerce, University of Pennsylvania, in cooperation with Investment Bankers Association of America, "Investment Banking and the New Issues Market, Summary Volume," 1965. The full series consists of eight monographs entitled as follows: "Overall View of Investment Banking and the New Issues Market," "Background and Structure of the Investment Banking Industry," "Activity in the Industry," "Inventory Positions and Practices," "Characteristics of New Issue Transactions," "Corporate New Issues in Post-S.E.C. Period," "Underwriting Compensation," "Price Experience and Return on New Stock Issues."

has been raised regarding their legal right to handle revenue bonds.

Investment banking is highly concentrated with fewer than 10 per cent of the firms in 1962 accounting for over 75 per cent of the capital and about the same share of public new issue activity.

In recent years, the gross underwriting spread for new corporate issues registered with the SEC, not counting rights offerings and secondary distributions, ranged from less than 1 per cent of gross proceeds for corporate bond issues over $10 million to 5 per cent or more for issues under $1 million. The rate ranged from 4 per cent for common stock issues over $10 million to over 10 per cent for common stock issues less than $1 million. Underwriting compensation for bonds tended to fall from the pre-SEC period to the beginning of the 1950s and then revealed no consistent trend. The underwriting compensation for stock has been experiencing a long-term downward drift during this entire period. The Securities Research Unit of the Wharton School of Finance and Commerce has suggested that the historical decline in underwriting compensation might be construed to reflect an improvement in operational efficiency of investment banking operations.

THE CHANGING CHARACTER OF INVESTMENT BANKING

During the relatively short history of the United States, the character of investment banking has been substantially transformed, and the changes are still going on. This evolving process reflects both investment banking's adaptation to and its influence on the shifting panorama of the American business scene. Thus the investment banker's confrontation with new problems and the finding of solutions by adjustments in activities is no new thing. In a general way, this development may be roughly divided into several major periods.

Until about 1840, commercial banks in cities like New York, Albany, and Philadelphia engaged in a form of investment banking as an outgrowth of their investment activities. During this period, it became common practice for American banks to hold large amounts of funds in public securities as well as corporations. Gradually a shift of emphasis occurred and resulted in the performance of an embryonic investment banking function. In competition with individual capitalists the commercial banks began to subscribe to new issues of securities, largely those of state governments, for purpose of resale, a form of loan contracting that may be considered the precursor of investment banking. Distribution was also undertaken through *negotiation,* whereby the institution was remunerated for its distribution function by means of a commission. This early transition of American commercial banks from investors to distributors of securities is of particular interest at present because it parallels the current activity of the commercial banks in some developing countries seeking to establish capital markets. In both cases, the accepted position of the banks in the community, their financial insights, and their already available outlets for distribution all pointed to the logic of the transition.

From about 1840 to 1860, the investment banking activity, such as it existed, was largely dominated by the private banker who sold the contracted securities both at home and abroad. While the Mexican War expanded Government flotations, by 1850 investment interest in America was generally shifting to railroad securities. Originally the roads were largely financed by stock distributed locally or to subscribers in communities along the future path of the lines and with payment on an installment basis. When this form of financing proved inadequate, preferred stock was employed to raise funds within the country and bonds to appeal to the English capital market. With the introduction of the standardized railroad bond, investment bankers entered the field more vigorously and some degree of specialization began.

The Civil War and following years until about 1890 was a period of economic and political ferment in the country, during which investment banking began to assume some of its more modern characteristics. The loan contractor of prior years bidding against investors and speculators for commitments was replaced by the investment banker who took whole issues of securities from borrowers. To market these securities, the idea of the *popular* loan was introduced, principally by Jay Cooke, who led the way in the development of a general sales organization employing a network of agents throughout the country and using the powerful tools of advertising. As particular issues increased in size, individual firms could no longer handle them and alliances of investment bankers took place to market both government and rail securities. Additionally, some roads began to form permanent affiliations with certain investment banking firms. This paved the way for the investment banker to play a positive role in the management of a company through becoming a member of the board and exerting an influence on the activities of its officers. This transition from a passive to an active role was probably further stimulated by the absence of sufficient investment information, causing buyers of securities to rely upon the reputation of the investment banker, who in turn considered it necessary to take a closer interest in the company to meet this responsibility. Finally, approximately during this period, firms whose influence persisted long after emerged into the limelight, such as J. P. Morgan & Company; Kuhn, Loeb & Company; J. & W. Seligman & Company; Lee, Higginson & Company; and Kidder, Peabody & Company.

By 1890, the value of railroad investments in land, improvements, and equipment was exceeded by that in manufacturing and industrial areas, but many of these companies were closely held. Over the ensuing years, these private enterprises sought public ownership, partnerships incorporated, the numbers of mergers rose, and public utilities became important. As a result of all these factors, increasing amounts of nonrailroad securities came to the market. This enlargement in the scope of financing afforded expanded opportunities in investment banking. For example, Goldman, Sachs & Company, originating as a commercial paper house some thirty years before the turn of the century, and Lehman Brothers as cotton bankers about twenty years earlier, banded together to underwrite a number of enterprises with very modest beginnings, but which later grew to great size, such as United Cigar Manufacturers; Sears, Roebuck & Company; B. F. Goodrich Company; May Department Stores Company; and F. W. Woolworth Company. During this period about 250 securities dealers, largely concentrated in the East and Middle East, were able to handle most of the burgeoning needs of business, although a handful of major investment bankers were pivotal in the organization of the large-scale private sector of the national economy. Since elaborate distributive systems generally did not exist at that time, sales characteristically were made directly to individual investors through offerings that could last many months. The role of the commercial banks also changed during this period. Prior to the early 1900s, it was considered legal for national commercial banks to hold stock and engage in the broadest investment activity. Subsequent to certain court decisions, the Comptroller of Currency adopted a more limited view, and to circumvent this blocking of their investment-banking activities, the banks organized state-chartered affiliates. Finally, until the outbreak of World War I, the United States was a debtor nation depending heavily upon foreign sources for funds, but the flow of capital reversed its course during American financing of World War I.

Following the war, the nation grew at an unprecedented rate. This rapid expansion led business firms to sell increasing amounts of securities. The surplus savings of individuals rose, and a geographically dispersed class of investors developed. As new issues of securities appeared in the market in rapid succession, the former leisurely distribution methods became inadequate to cope with the pressure for funds. To expedite sales, therefore, dealers formed selling networks that spanned the country and, to lighten their mounting financial burdens, joined into underwriting syndicate systems. New personnel trained in engineering, accounting, and finance was added to the ranks of the investment bankers, thereby providing the skills necessary to discriminate among the large numbers of firms seeking capital and to devise financial plans suitable for the gargantuan enterprises that were emerging.[2]

Starting about 1933, additional political, social, and economic forces began to play upon the investment banking business, the final outcome of which is not yet clear. The Banking Act required mixed banking institutions to make a choice between the commercial or investment banking routes and thereby created a specialized investment banking field. The securities acts provided the basis for an entirely new regulatory structure.

The revival of the nation's economy, following the depression and the long period of general business expansion that has occurred, together with the changed savings patterns of individuals, led to the rise of great financial institutions, such as insurance com-

---

2. The historical description is based on Opinion of Harold R. Medina, C.J., in the District Court of the United States for the Southern District of New York, Civil Action No. 43–757, n.d., pp. 17–37; Fritz Redlich, *The Molding of American Banking, Men and Ideas,* New York, Hafner Publishing Company, Inc., 1951, Part II, pp. 304–423; Merwin H. Waterman, "Investment Banking Functions, Their Evolution and Adaptation to Business Finance," Bureau of Business Research, School of Business Administration, University of Michigan, Ann Arbor, 1958, pp. 15–92.

panies, investment companies, and pension funds. These developments produced notable changes in the characteristics of new corporate offerings. Private placements which bypass the usual investment banking channels became more popular. In 1960–63 over 40 per cent of all new corporate offerings of securities in the United States took the form of private placements, compared with much smaller percentages in the 1930s. The practice of corporations selecting underwriters through competitive bidding rather than through negotiation was more widespread, resulting in some modifications of the previously established relationships between issuer and firms. Of the 1960–1963 totals of new corporate issues and new corporate bonds, additional amounts of 20 per cent and 25 per cent respectively were acquired by investment bankers through competitive bidding rather than negotiation, in .contrast with negligible proportions in the mid-thirties. From the 1930s to the early 1960s, the dollar value of rights offerings increased faster than the total value of new common stock issues, while the proportion of rights offerings underwritten by investment bankers showed mixed trends.[3] The importance of individuals as net buyers of securities diminished as that of institutions rose.

As a result of these factors, the nature of investment banking is once more changing in a striking manner. At one time, the sponsorship of the investment banker was the vital factor in the distribution of securities which, as mentioned, led to an intimate continuing relationship between issuer and banker. While bankers still have a sense of obligation with respect to securities in whose distribution they played a major role, their influence over the issuers' policies and their relationships to the ultimate buyer have been weakened. At present the reputation of the issuer is likely to be the principal criterion in effecting a distribution, and the investor has become a much more sophisticated buyer.

Reflecting these changes in the distributive scheme, investment bankers, in addition to their traditional underwriting functions, now serve as advisers in negotiating private placements; as agents in selling securities on a commission basis in best-efforts transactions; as stand-by intermediaries in rights offerings; and as financial planners in mergers, acquisitions, and refinancing operations. These

3. Securities Research Unit, "Investment Banking and the New Issues Market, Summary Volume," op. cit.

changes are still under way as the industry continues to adjust to the shifting economic environment in which it operates.

THE ALLOCATION FUNCTION

A major responsibility of investment banking is to sift new issues so as to provide for the distribution of securities at prices that reflect the financial risks associated with the issuer. The Securities Research Unit of the Wharton School of Finance and Commerce found that the dispersion of price changes of new issues relative to outstanding issues has declined and mentioned this fact, among other things, as evidence that the allocation efficiency of the securities markets has improved. Also, pointing to a somewhat lower rate of return on new industrial primary issues of common stock compared with outstanding issues, the Securities Research Unit surmised that "there is no evidence that any significant legitimate needs for equity capital are not being met by the new issues market."[4]

This latter conclusion may be strained. Regardless of rate-relationships, the changing character of the business appears to be producing investment-banking firms engaged in more diversified activities, dealing increasingly with large financial institutions, and less willing to evaluate the requirements of small, relatively untried companies so as to allocate funds to such new ventures when justified. This is an old, but yet unresolved issue. The evidence suggests that the smaller, less known investment bankers are more amenable than the established firms to provide financing assistance to new enterprises. Thus, to a large extent, the broker-dealers who managed the underwriting of unseasoned issues[5] in 1961 were relative newcomers to the field. More than half of these underwriters had been organized less than six years prior to the offering, while over one-fourth were formed in either the year preceding or the year in which the offering was made. Also, many of the new underwriters were managed by individuals new to the securities industry, and the more recently created underwriters operated with

---

4. Security Research Unit, *Ibid.*

5. An issue is classified as *unseasoned* if the issuer had not registered stock previously under the Securities Act or Regulation A, and if its stock was not listed on a national securities exchange or known to be traded over the counter. On occasion this classification resulted in the inclusion of large, well-established companies offering their securities to the public for the first time.

relatively modest amounts of capital. Thirty-five per cent of the 271 new firms had net capital of less than $10,000 in 1961 and only 1 per cent ranked among the relatively big underwriters with net capital of $500,000 or more.[6]

Thus, while some substantial underwriters participated in the "hot" issue market of 1961 in which a number of unseasoned stocks were floated for the first time, the big push came from the less-established underwriters. Moreover, as a policy, investment bankers tend to show a risk aversion and to shy away from new companies without demonstrated records of earnings power. For example, in 1964, the author reviewed the investment banking policy of sixteen firms about equally divided between big, medium-sized, and small underwriters. In response to an inquiry as to the disposition of companies applying for an underwriting, the predominant sentiment was that the great majority would be turned down. Typical reasons advanced were

company's earnings too small
lack of history of substantial profits
type of business engaged in—promotional
local nature of company or business
company's future prospects declining
unattractive industries
"bail-out" situations
involved "cheap" stock
not big enough
overpriced
not suitable for our type of customer

Many unseasoned companies that approach investment bankers to obtain assistance in raising funds undoubtedly should be turned away until their proposal appears more promising. By the same token, a number of them are justified in their request and should receive financing help. The Special Study investigated the post-offering experience of a sample of 960 companies going public for the first time between July 1, 1952, and June 30, 1962. Included were 504 "promotional" companies and 456 "operational"

6. Report of Special Study of Securities Markets of the Securities and Exchange Commission, 88th Cong., 1st sess., H. Doc. 95, 1963, Part 1, Chapter IV, pp. 493–494.

companies. "Promotional" was defined as a company organized or incorporated within one year prior to the filing of the notification or registration statement and which had not earned net income from operations, or a company organized or incorporated more than one year prior to such date which did not have net income from operations of the character in which it intended to engage for at least one of the two preceding fiscal years. All other companies were designated as "operational." It was found that 45 per cent of the "promotional" companies were still in existence or had been merged and 15 per cent had shown a profit on the latest income statement. Of the "operational" companies, some 83 per cent were still in existence or had merged and 56 per cent reported a profit in the latest income statement.[7]

It is clear that application of blanket standards barring "promotional" companies would have eliminated a number that were making a contribution to the nation's economic growth. Even in the absence of such blanket standards, there appears to be a bias against the acceptance by established underwriters of the promotional-type company as a client, and therefore, if public financing is desired, such a company must seek assistance from the small, less-established underwriters. The latter type of firm, in turn, seems to be on the decline. Competitive pressures in the investment-banking field has tended to favor the growth of the bigger firms, in order, on the supply side, to handle larger issuers and, on the demand side, to cater to big institutional investors. Indicative of this tendency, as seen in Table 6–1, big underwriters, over the past fifteen years, have grown sharply both in number and capital, and medium-sized underwriters have grown moderately, while the number of small underwriters has actually dropped, although the aggregate capital of this group has remained substantially unchanged. As underwriters go out of business, the small unseasoned company may find it increasingly difficult to make financing arrangements through this intermediary.

As is often the case in the securities industry, the balance teeters between two conflicting principles. On the one hand, it is appropriate for underwriters to establish screening devices that will eliminate unpromising companies from selling securities in the

7. Ibid., pp. 550–553.

capital markets with consequent losses to investors; the lessons of the "hot-issue" period of 1961 highlights the need for such evaluative efforts. On the other hand, the screening should not be so complete as to prevent small deserving borrowers from obtaining capital. Should the established underwriters largely abandon investment banking's historical role of financing the small promising business, their long-term rate of return might very well contract and the firms might seek to diversify into other outlets. Correspondingly, in order to serve the needs of the untried enterprise, other private financing avenues, such as specialized venture-capital firms, would have to be opened, or the Government's activities in the small business program would have to be further extended. An alternative possibility is that the more widespread use of the computer and development of better analytic techniques may encourage the established investment banker to assume greater underwriting risks.

Commission Rates on Trading

Under the umbrella of self-regulation, uniform prices have been permitted in the securities business without antitrust action

Table 6–1—Net Capital of Underwriters by Number of Firms and Amount of Equity Capital (selected years 1948–1964)

Size of Firms	1948	1956	1963	1964
Firms with equity capital of $5,000,000 or more:				
Number	22	44	75	83
Aggregate equity capital (in millions)	$215	$512	$1,055	$1,224
Firms with equity capital of $1,000,000 up to $5,000,000:				
Number	80	132	148	139
Aggregate equity capital (in millions)	$179	$301	$ 343	$ 322
Firms with equity capital of less than $1,000,000:				
Number	212	201	159	147
Aggregate equity capital (in millions)	$ 71	$ 76	$ 79	$ 79
Total firms included in survey:				
Number	314	377	382	369
Aggregate equity capital (in millions)	$465	$889	$1,477	$1,625

Source: Compiled from data in *Finance*, February 28, 1949, March 15, 1957, March 15, 1964, and March 15, 1965. Data are from the annual survey of underwriters compiled by the staff of *Finance* and includes the largest firms reporting in recent years $100,000 or more in net capital.

being invoked until the 1960s when several suits were instituted.[8] The existence of uniform prices means that the investor has no means of protecting himself against unreasonable charges by shopping around among different firms. Accordingly, the direct onus of protection falls upon the self-regulatory agencies and the SEC. But protection means not only guarding the investor against the danger of overpricing but also against that of underpricing which might curtail unduly the profits of securities firms, lead to a contraction of the business, and prevent it from furnishing the services that are to the investor's own advantage. Without the signposts of competition, the determination of appropriate methods of pricing in the public interest is a delicate undertaking.

BACKGROUND OF THE PROBLEM

Under Section 19(b)(9) of the Securities Exchange Act, if the Commission, dissatisfied with an exchange's rules concerning commission rates, requests in writing a change, it may, after appropriate hearings, require the revision to be made if the exchange has not taken appropriate action. The principal guide provided the Commission by the Act for determining the propriety of a change is that the rates should be "reasonable," while the usual over-all charge is used by itself—the changes should be necessary "for the protection of investors." Some further reference appears in a different context; with respect to Section 15A(b)(8), concerned with the over-the-counter market, as has been mentioned, the rules of a registered association of brokers are required "to provide safeguards" against both unreasonable profits or unreasonable rates of commission. This juxtaposition of profits and of commissions suggests that the reasonableness of the commission charges must be considered in relation to the reasonableness of profits.

Between 1937 and 1958, the NYSE effected five changes in rate schedules—all increases and generally justified on the ground of rising costs and, dependent upon prevailing circumstances, inadequate volume. At different times, the Commission indicated some lack of enthusiasm for the changes, obtained modest revisions, and stated the need for further study. Except for such occasional mildly negative reactions, the Commission, at least

8. For a discussion of the antitrust question in the securities field, see pp. 274–280.

until the present, has never interposed any serious objection to the rate increases that have been adopted and, by and large, they have followed the form of the original proposals. The Exchange's program, in turn, generally has set the pattern for the entire field.

At the close of 1964, the cost and revenue committee of the NYSE proposed a revamping of the commission schedule, again including an increase in rates averaging 3.5 per cent, but much higher on small transactions; mandatory charges for securities left in broker custody; and the first volume discount on large transactions. Apparently desirous of reviewing the brokerage community's profit picture and possibly influenced by the surge in stock trading that subsequently occurred, the SEC carefully refrained from giving any official sanction to these changes. The Exchange committee, in turn, never formally presented this plan to the exchange membership but instead continued to study the problem. Indicating an interest in the possibility of introducing some form of commission splitting, the NYSE, in the fall of 1965, requested the SEC to determine whether nonmember broker-dealers that receive preferential treatment might be considered to occupy the status of full members in certain respects. More particularly, the NYSE seemed concerned that in this contingency it would have the responsibility of policing the operations of nonmembers, who might also qualify for coverage under the special trust fund intended to protect the customers of member firms that became insolvent.[9]

Despite this history of consistent increases and the obvious importance of an appropriate schedule of rates for the protection of the investor, neither the self-regulatory agencies nor the Commission has formulated a program for determining and evaluating these charges. In addition to rising costs, the impetus for higher rates in recent years has been more specifically attributable to pressure upon profits. Based upon its 1964 report on its member firms' brokerage business, for example, the NYSE stated that brokerage profits for that year were only 3.6 per cent of total commissions and that 35 per cent of the 310 reporting firms had lost money on their brokerage commissions. Considerable uncertainty still exists, however, regarding the appropriate method of allocating costs in the securities business, where firms often engage

---

9. *The Wall Street Journal,* September 23, 1965.

in diversified activities; of the relationship that should prevail between costs and revenues; and of the contribution that commission business makes to the other profit-making areas of a firm.

THE STRUCTURE AND LEVEL OF RATES

As the lifeblood of the business, the main commission schedule and the applicable rules are set forth in the NYSE's constitution. While the rates represent mandatory minimum charges, in practice they have become the actual charges. Historically, commissions have had to be net, free from any rebates or discounts, and nonmembers had to pay higher rates than members. More recently, there has been a move to permit volume discounts and commission splitting with nonmembers.

The commission-rate problem may be divided into two major parts. The first, generally referred to as structure, pertains to the segments selected for building a schedule and the determination of the relationships which should exist among them. Separate segments, for example, might be assigned to the clearing function, the execution function, and the services performed, or the segment for the professional nonmember might be different from that given to the public nonmember. While these segments have been the ones characteristically considered in building a rate structure, any breakdown or grouping that appears logical could be used. Within a given structure, the second problem involves level which refers to the height of the charges imposed to provide a desired return.

In regard to nonmembers, the commission-rate schedule that the NYSE employs has traditionally been built upon a uniform foundation underlying all the functional segments. The actual charge is based upon a sliding scale on the money involved per round lot. By applying a declining percentage to the dollar volume per round lot, the rate charged is cut as the price per share of a stock rises, but on a scale that results in higher dollar payments. No chipping of the rate has been allowed previously for the size of the transaction, that is, the number of round lots.

The December, 1964, proposal introduced two innovations into the schedule. First the basic commission charge was cut for orders in excess of 3,000 shares submitted from one customer in one day. Second, to cover services rendered a small separate block was created, involving a monthly fee for each security position held by a broker for his customer within a set minimum-maximum range.[10] Recognition that the commission charge actually embraces different structural components coincided with the principles developed by the Special Study. In its report, however, the implication was that the commission charge might be reduced if a client did not want to avail himself of all the components included. In the 1964 proposal, the commission charge was increased at the same time that the mandatory service fee was created to provide for certain services.

Another aspect of the commission-rate structure pertains to the odd-lot customer who trades in less than full lots. He is charged a so-called differential, which is discussed below, and also pays a commission. Presumably, in recognition of the fact that the odd-lot customer's broker keeps the full commission even though execution is by the odd-lot dealer, a $2 discount per transaction from the round-lot rate has been allowed for odd lots. Apparently, there has been little effort to relate the commission that is charged the odd-lot customer to the costs of such a transaction. To the extent that this type of analysis has been undertaken, it has been on the basis of the average costs rather than the marginal or additional costs of handling the odd-lot business. Yet, there is some indication that the elimination of odd-lot business by a broker-dealer would reduce his costs by much less than the resulting loss of revenue, a relationship that, in turn, suggests the odd-lot customer would benefit by having his charge determined on a marginal basis.[11]

---

10. The fee would be automatically applied to all securities in a margin account since they must remain in the custody of brokers. Consequently, on such accounts, a broker might derive earnings from four sources: the basic commission charge, the mandatory service fee, interest paid on debit balances, and the cost-savings from margined securities loaned to short sellers or odd-lot dealers.

11. For example, see the following statement by a member firm as reported in the Special Study of Securities Markets of the Securities and Exchange Commission, op. cit., Part 2, Chapter VI, p. 326:

"There is a serious fallacy, however, in such a method of cost accounting. Such reasoning implies that the elimination of odd-lot business would permit reductions in costs proportionate to the number of transactions handled. This simply would not happen. For November 1945 [5-week period] one of the months used in the association's study, [our firm] had a commission from odd-lot transactions of $207,000. A firm of certified accountants in cooperation with our Internal Statistics Department, has estimated that [this member firm] could have eliminated less than $60,000 if we had handled

Under these circumstances, it seems clear that a much more careful cost evaluation is necessary than has yet been undertaken to ascertain the fair portion of total commission costs that should be borne by the odd-lot customer.

The member rate of the NYSE provides for a separation of the segments for executing and clearing, executing only, and clearing only. Member firms without representation on the floor of the Exchange to execute transactions and without a back-office operation to handle the related movement of paper channel their Exchange orders through other member firms possessing these facilities. For this service, the user firm, acting on behalf of a customer, pays an *execution and clearance commission,* which varies with the price of the stock and is substantially less than that paid by the nonmember. The total member charge for most transactions is split equally between the "brokerage" and "clearance" commissions, depending upon which is used. When a member trades for his own account, the procedures are generally the same except that the clearing commission is substantially reduced.

THE UNDERLYING ISSUES

The principles upon which the NYSE commission schedule is constructed have created certain important issues which have never been squarely resolved.

Basing the sliding scale of rates upon the dollar value of a round lot involves a determination of the degree to which the percentages applied should be related to the price of the stock. If only value is considered, the same charge would be applied to all transactions of the same dollar amount regardless of the number of round lots involved, thereby relegating into the background the importance of costs. If variations in charges are allowed for price differences, then in two transactions involving the same dollar amount, a higher charge would be paid for the one involving more round lots; this distinction would reflect cost differentials but might create a selling bias in favor of low-priced shares. Compare, for example, an investment of $15,000 in one round lot of stock

---

no odd-lot business during that period. Consequently, had we eliminated odd-lot business and its related costs, our net profit would have been reduced $147,000."

priced at $150 per share with an investment of the same amount in 15 round lots of a $10 stock. The same rate applied to both transactions would eliminate any selling bias towards low or high priced stock but would clearly fail to reflect the cost differentials incurred. If higher rates are allowed for the second transaction, some registered representatives might tend to discriminate in favor of the low priced stock.

Another problem area has stemmed from the provision that no commission rebates be allowed. Even if eventually abandoned, the implications of this long-held attitude are worth considering. Adherence to such a policy results in the situation whereby a non-member broker that receives an order for a NYSE stock incurs a loss, represented by his own costs, if he submits it to a member for execution, since the commission he pays probably would be the same as that he charges his customer. If the nonmember refuses to accept the order, he is exposed to the danger of losing his customer.

Since the volume of Exchange business accomplished through nonmember brokers is considerable, the Exchange members created a complicated scheme of arrangements to evade the NYSE non-rebate rule by compensating the nonmember broker. While these arrangements may take a number of devious routes, the most fundamental involves channeling reciprocal transactions to the nonmember. Thus, the NYSE member may place business on a regional exchange with a member of that exchange who is not a member of the NYSE, or he may place orders for unlisted securities with the nonmember to be transacted over the counter. The NYSE member may take this course even though, in the first instance, he is also a member of the regional exchange (a dual member) and therefore could have himself placed the business, or the security is also traded on the NYSE (dual listing), so that the member could have effected the transaction directly in New York.

Indicative of the importance of such transactions, the Special Study found that of 447 members of the four largest exchanges who were nonmembers of the NYSE (i.e., sole members), 298 reported participation in such arrangements in ratios ranging up to three to one, but with two to one most popular; that is, the NYSE member would direct $1 in commissions to the nonmember for each $3 or $2 received. The ratio always favors the NYSE member.[12] In lieu of directing commission business to the nonmember firm on an agreed ratio, the NYSE member may reward the nonmember by furnishing him with special services such as installation and maintenance of wire services, clearance of non-Exchange transactions, office space, special research, and promotional materials and displays.

In evaluating the implications of these devices to avoid the antirebate rule, consideration must be given to the difficulty imposed upon the Exchange to administer them, the possible conflict of interest arising from the fact that reciprocity considerations rather than relative efficiencies might influence a member in determining how to execute a transaction, the complications they contribute to evaluating cost factors, and the resulting dependence of the regional exchanges upon the Exchange's unitary commission structure for an important source of their business.

The American Stock Exchange and various regional exchanges avoid much of these difficulties by providing special treatment to nonmember professionals. The American Stock Exchange, for example, achieves this end by permitting individuals actively engaged in the business of buying and selling securities as members of broker or dealer firms to make application for *associate membership,* which entitles them to have their business transacted on the ASE at substantial reductions from the nonmember rates. As a result of a program of opening full membership to associates, some 100 associate member organizations converted to a regular basis in 1963 and 1964, but at the beginning of 1965, there were 284 associate members still remaining. Although the December, 1964, proposal of the NYSE committee on member firm costs and revenues rejected commission splitting or an arrangement of associate memberships, both these proposals continue to be revived.

Another problem is inherent in basing the commission schedule of the NYSE upon each round-lot sale. This means that the commission on a single transaction involving, say five round lots, is just five times as great as that for one round lot. Since the cost of handling five round lots is clearly not as much as five times that of one round lot, the broker earns a substantially larger margin of profit on the bigger transaction. To the extent that block-discounts

12. Report of Special Study of Securities Markets of the Securities and Exchange Commission, op. cit., Part 2, Chapter VI, pp. 302–307.

are not permitted, therefore, he is likely to be willing to give up a portion of this profit to another member in order to obtain the business. Such a give-up is permissible because the rules of the NYSE allow a split of the commission dollar (above the floor brokerage and clearance portion) among members where directed by the customer. The simplest form of such a directed give-up is a transaction by an open-end fund which directs the NYSE firm receiving the order to give up a specified portion, which may run as high as 60 per cent, in exchange for services performed by the beneficiary, such as the sale of fund shares or providing research, statistics, wire facilities, and quotations.

A variation of this arrangement occurs when a fund directs the primary broker to give up to another member, who in turn renders services to a nonmember as the beneficiary of the give-up; in this case services are provided because of the NYSE prohibition against splitting cash with a nonmember. The path of the give-up may also run through the regional exchanges. In a typical case, the fund places portfolio business with a dual member, who transacts it on the regional exchange and gives up a portion of the commission to a regional-only member. The fund may also take advantage of the rules of those regional exchanges, which permit some splitting with nonmembers, to direct a portion of the commission business to the nonmembers it wants rewarded.

The directed give-up resembles the reciprocal give-up described previously in that the business emanating from a large institution, like that from the nonmember professional, may be substantial and require relatively less sales effort. The consequences of both types of give-ups are also similar with respect to the problem of administration, the distortion of cost data, and the diverting of business to the regional exchanges. Also, in the directed give-up, a fund that provides a portion of its commission business in exchange for sales of its shares, may be exposed to the possibility of a conflict between the interest of the shareowners in lower commissions and that of the investment advisor in stimulating more sales. Finally, the absence of a block discount undoubtedly tends to divert some transactions to the over-the-counter market. While some of these difficulties flowing from the directed give-up would be alleviated by proposed block discounts, the over-the-counter market in listed securities could still be competitive; also there still would remain the possibility of directing give-ups for big orders of less than the minimum block size and for those of more than this prescribed size completed over longer periods than one day. Moreover, should the *block discount* lead to a concentration of transactions that might otherwise have been executed over several days, weeks, or even months, extra pressure on stock prices may be created. An evaluation would have to be made whether or not this extra pressure, measured against keeping transactions on the NYSE, contributed to or detracted from liquidity.

DEVELOPING A THEORY OF COMMISSION RATES

As has been pointed out, important issues must be settled before there can be developed for the securities business a commission structure that fairly allocates the benefits received and the costs that are borne by the participants. These issues include the distribution of charges relative to a scale of prices, the share of the commission burden to be assumed by the odd-lot customer, the treatment of nonmember professionals, the reduction justifiable for block transactions, and the extent to which the commission dollar might be compartmentalized, particularly to allow for service performed. Without such compartmentalization, the imposition of minimum charges shifts the competitive arena to the offering of services and results in some customers paying a commission that includes services for which they have no desire. A knowledgeable investor, for example, may make no use of the research facilities of his brokerage firm, yet the cost of these services are implicit in the price that he pays for executing and clearing his transactions.

The resolution of these structural problems would still leave open the vexing question of the level of rates, although the way the structure is settled could influence the levels that are imposed. Like other businesses affected with a public interest that are subject to rate regulation, the general approach to determining commission levels has been in their relation to costs and their effect upon profits. For this purpose, the NYSE has developed an Income and Expense Report which provides such data for its member firms that do business with the public. While the information included in the report has improved over the years, it still does not provide an adequate picture of operating conditions and cost relationships.

Without a base of reliable data, the determination of "reasonable" commissions become difficult. Accordingly, the development of uniform accounting principles for broker-dealer firms appears to be a logical prerequisite in order to obtain data that are not distorted by individual differences in accounting practices. With confidence established in the uniformity and accuracy of the accounts and with sufficiently comprehensive data available to appraise the factors contributing to profitability in the securities business, attention can be given to resolving the rate problems that are unique to the securities field.

Unlike public utilities, for example, rates cannot be applied to individual securities companies for a number of reasons. Volume is haphazard, and therefore a change in rates may not have the expected effect upon profits, and members compete with each other in contrast to the monopolistic position of a utility in the geographic area served. Also the capital investment of a public utility is relatively much higher than that of the typical broker-dealer firm. These differences aggravate the rate determining problem. Since rate levels probably cannot be established for individual companies, presumably they must be fixed on an over-all basis. In this case, is it more desirable to employ an efficient, marginal, or average firm as the standard? Each criterion has its own limitations and advantages. Fluctuating volume aggravates planning and the diversity of firms affected by the rate schedule means that a change might benefit one at the expense of the other. The lack of big capital investments may reduce the significance of the rate-of-return concept, which is typically related to an investment input.

There is no gainsaying these difficulties. But at best, rate determination is a complex operation. Its history in the public utility field has been long and developed through numerous legal decisions and economic arguments. Other areas have special problems of their own. In fire insurance, it is difficult to anticipate the conflagrations that will occur in any one year and that may upset profit expectations based upon prior rate schedules. Interest-rate regulations in banking exert varying effects on different institutions and, as in the securities business, have led to service competition. As railroads have encountered increasing pressure from other forms of transportation, rate regulation had to take into account the influence of this outside competition.

The fact that rate-making problems differ in each field is to be expected. The existence of special issues in the securities business, therefore, is no justification for the lack of progress by the self-regulating agencies or the SEC in the development of principles that could be consistently applied to determine rate levels that provide reasonable profits to the firms without penalizing the investor. Various avenues could be explored. The industry has consistently referred to break-even levels of volume required at different periods of time. Perhaps rates could be lowered if this level is reached early in a year or raised if attained at a later point to provide a consistent return.

The report of the 1963-appointed Exchange Committee on Member Firm Costs and Revenues considered and dismissed the possibility of a program that called for reducing commission levels automatically as total Exchange volume surpassed certain yearly or other periodic levels and of increasing commissions as volume declined. The reason assigned was that it "deemed the suggestion to be altogether impracticable and unworkable." Over the long term, however, it is clear that a rate-making process that does not provide for adjustments—both down as well as up—as the economic status of the regulated industry changes is a phantom system. This is particularly true in the securities business which notably experiences sharp changes. Thus, in 1962, average daily volume in the NYSE fell to 3.8 million shares, down from 4.1 million in 1961. Thereafter, a steady rise occurred, and in 1964, average daily volume was 4.9 million shares, a new record. In 1965, volume fluctuated widely but in September, not only was a daily level of 10 million shares penetrated but a string of heavy volume days enabled the month's total to surpass the monthly record set in the 1929 market crash.

Since turnover actually has declined, it is clear that the increased over-all activity was caused by the greatly expanded number of shares. At the close of October, 1929, only 1.1 billion shares were listed in the NYSE compared with 9.8 billion at the end of August 1965.[13] Regardless of the implications of the reduced turnover to the Exchange's increased vulnerability to liquidation of big blocks, the enlarged number of shares sets the stage for more commission business. To the broker, it does not make

---

13. *The Wall Street Journal*, September 27, 1965; September 30, 1965; New York Stock Exchange, "Fact Book," 1965.

much difference whether his revenues come from 100 shares that turn over 10 times or from 1,000 shares that trade once at the same price, except that the costs in the latter case are likely to be lower. It seems logical to assume that any continuation of the record activity of September, 1965, would cast doubt on the need for further commission hikes, whereas any long-term trend of this sort would raise the question of reductions. On the other hand, should volume dry up for a prolonged period, the need for commission increases would appear reasonable. The sauce in this case would appear the same for both the goose and the gander.

Rather than adjust rates as volume changed, it might be possible to base rates upon long-term volume expectations so that high profits would result as volume exceeded the long-term average and low profits would follow below-average volume. Through requiring an allowance out of earnings that could be used to reduce and augment profits under these changing conditions, the same rate might be retained in the face of rising and falling volume. Whatever general standard was employed would affect individual companies differently and while curtailment of services could occur in some cases, the over-all result might be in the direction of providing greater over-all efficiency. Clearly, no solution to the development of a suitable theory of rate-making in the securities field will be found, however, until both the Commission and the self-regulating agencies undertake serious studies of the problem with the aim of finding a solution that will be implemented, even if on a tentative basis at first.

To develop a workable and fair system of rate-making and provide adequate subsequent surveillance of its operation would demand a sharp break with the past and require the introduction of a major new activity. It is perhaps not realistic to expect the self-regulating agencies to move in this direction of their own accord because of the magnitude of the problem and the major impact it would have on the entire securities field. Accordingly, the principal stimulus to action probably will have to come from the SEC which thus far has largely avoided this area. Its historic preoccupation with recurring judicial matters may prove a stumbling block that must be hurdled before there can be introduced a long-term program that is designed to develop and implement a sound theory of rate determination. Yet the consistent rate increases that have occurred in the securities business since the creation of the Commission and its lackluster review of these higher schedules at least suggest that in this vital area public interest and protection of the investor have not been served. The Commission's announced intention in December 1965 of obtaining more comprehensive data from broker-dealer firms suggests the possibility of a firmer policy in the future.

COMMISSIONS IN THE OVER-THE-COUNTER MARKET

Section 15A(b)(8) of the Securities Exchange Act prohibits the NASD from imposing any schedule of prices or fixing minimum rates of commission. Nevertheless, in agency transactions, there tends to be a uniformity in the level of commission rates. The Special Study found that approximately 95 per cent of the agency transactions on January 18, 1962, in the stock sample covered were executed at the applicable NYSE commission rate. It was pointed out that the importance of NYSE member firms in handling the public business in the over-the-counter market, and the tendency of such firms to treat these transactions on an agency basis, result in the NYSE minimum commission schedule having a substantial effect upon pricing in the over-the-counter market. Accordingly, any theory of rate making developed for the exchange markets would clearly have an important influence on over-the-counter prices as well.[14]

The size of markups in principal transactions is related to a diversity of factors such as the type of firm, whether the order is a purchase or sale, the size of the transaction, and the general relationship of the customer to the firm. Of importance is the NASD policy which, at present, limits markups to 5 per cent over the prevailing market price of a security. The complications of the over-the-counter market are such that the development of any theory of pricing probably will wait upon prior action in the exchange markets.

The Odd-Lot Dealer

As has been mentioned, virtually all the odd-lot business on the NYSE goes through two member firms, Carlisle & Jacquelin

---

14. Report of Special Study of Securities Markets, op. cit., Part 2, Chapter VII, p. 624.

and DeCoppet & Doremus, while on the American and most regional exchanges, odd lots are handled by the specialists in their respective stocks. The methods whereby these firms conduct their business is of particular importance to the small investor.

THE OPERATIONS OF THE ODD-LOT DEALER

Less than 10 per cent of NYSE share volume but a much higher percentage of its transactions is represented by odd lots. In buying or selling odd lots on the NYSE, the investor at present places his order with a commission firm from where it is eventually transmitted to the odd-lot dealers' representatives on the floor for execution at a price that ordinarily is a fraction of a point away from the next round-lot price—above for buy and below for sell orders. The odd-lot dealers' representatives are associate brokers who are members of the NYSE and not only consummate the odd-lot transaction but undertake the offsetting full-lot transactions on the floor of the Exchange. Each of the odd-lot firms has about fifty-five associate brokers, who are reimbursed by receiving the floor brokerage commissions plus a portion of the differential.

The odd-lot dealers perform a number of services for the commission brokers, including providing information about round-lot transactions, making liberal adjustments of errors, and furnishing interest-free loans through borrowing stock. While the odd-lot houses compete with each other on the basis of these services, the substantial costs involved serve as an effective deterrent to outsiders entering the field. Except for a few small firms and diversions created through friendship ties or money owed, the commission brokers tend to split their business about equally between the two odd-lot houses.

Section 11(b) of the Securities Exchange Act permits the exchanges to regulate the odd-lot business through enacting rules that are not inconsistent with those adopted by the Commission in the public interest or for the protection of investors; Section 19(b) includes odd-lot purchases and sales among the items on which the SEC may request an exchange to effect a change of rule and, if not forthcoming, to require the revision to be adopted after appropriate hearings. While both the exchanges and the Commission thus are given authority to regulate the activities of the odd-lot firms, this power has remained largely unexercised. The Exchange has not only allowed the odd-lot firms to establish the differential that is charged public customers, but in 1938, actually discouraged limited price competition from certain small specialist odd-lot dealers; its position apparently has been that the differential represents a negotiated deal between the odd-lot houses and the commission firms. The SEC, in turn, hitherto has largely remained aloof from interfering with the odd-lot firms in the determination of the differential or of their other activities. This area is, of course, an important one affecting, as it does, so many small investors; the NYSE engaged a major accounting firm to prepare cost analyses and is studying the matter.

THE IMPLICATIONS OF AUTOMATION

In 1956, the NYSE employed the firm of Ebasco Services, Inc., to investigate the implications of automation to the Exchange, including its possible relationship to the odd-lot function. In its review of this investigation, the Special Study concluded that the two odd-lot firms had regarded the possibility of automation as a grave threat to their duopoly and had taken steps to ward off any objective consideration of proposals in this direction. Because much of the activities of the odd-lot firms are done mechanically against full-lot transactions, automation appears reasonable, and therefore the Special Study recommended that the Exchange advise the Commission as to the feasibility of automating the execution of odd-lot orders and as to the possible effects of such action on floor operations, costs, and odd-lot differentials.[15] As a result of its own automation program, it may be possible for the Exchange to provide much of the information now furnished by the odd-lot dealers.

The public attention given to the possibility of automating the execution of odd-lot orders indicates that some steps along these lines will be taken. More specifically, the NYSE has announced that it is undertaking an evaluation program to explore the feasibility of electronically switching odd-lot orders directly from commission firms to the odd-lot houses for computer handling. The question still remains how far possible courses of action will be

---

15. Report of Special Study of Securities Markets of the Securities and Exchange Commission, op. cit., Part 2, Chapter VI, p. 202.

pursued. For example, the minimum unit of trading of 100 shares has prevailed since shortly after the Civil War and has been justified on the ground that it conforms to market needs, the mechanics of trading, and that trading in small units might increase costs and unnecessarily clog the tape. It would appear desirable to reconsider these reasons in the light of current computer facilities and the widening entrance of small investors into the market.

Even if the unit of trading is not cut, the continued requirement of a differential is at least subject to question. At one time, the possibility was considered of developing a bookkeeping system that permitted the aggregating of odd-lot orders and their consummation as full-lots with consequent savings to the small investor. This procedure might not have been feasible previously, but the present availability of computer facilities suggests that the necessary bookkeeping now could be accomplished. Finally, as in the case of commissions, the absence of any positive control by the self-regulatory agencies or the Commission in the presence of an acknowledged duopoly raises the spectre of antitrust action unless there is firmer regulation of the odd-lot system.

The Specialist

The specialist occupies a focal role in exchange markets and around him revolves the continuous auction trading in the securities for which he is responsible. To the extent that he performs his role successfully, therefore, he makes an important contribution to the orderliness of the markets.

FUNCTIONS OF THE SPECIALIST

The specialist's original function, and it remains an important one, is to serve as a broker for other floor members who have limit orders that cannot be executed at prevailing prices. Starting about 1939, when volume in the exchanges was particularly low and commission houses experienced difficulty in obtaining satisfactory executions for their customers, the NYSE began an affirmative program to compel specialists to become dealers. In this capacity, the specialist buys and sells securities as a principal, when there are no public orders at a price reasonably related to the last transaction. Over the past twenty-five years, his dealer function has steadily gained ground until today it is estimated that specialists are purchasers or sellers in about one-third of exchange transactions. A number of specialists characteristically derive more income from dealer profits than from brokerage commissions.

As a dealer, the profits of the specialist are much like that of any middleman; he gains by the *jobber's turn* of buying at a lower price and selling at a higher price. Unlike the public investor, whose market buy orders normally are executed at the offer side and market sell orders at the bid, the specialist usually buys at his own bid and sells at his own offer. Thus, let us assume that a specialist quotes a stock for his own account at a bid of 40 and an offer of 40½. An investor's public market order to sell a round-lot would go to the specialist at 40 while an immediately following public market order to buy would be executed at 40½; thus, the specialist would obtain a jobber's turn of one-half point. Part of the regulatory problem of the specialist stems from his desire to adjust his trading patterns to maximize his profits, a desire that could encourage such tactics as trading heavily in active stocks, quoting stocks at a wide spread, and daylight trading.

The specialist wears various hats. He serves himself as principal and others as agent; he may act for customers on both sides of the market; he has a responsibility to the market as a whole that at times may run counter to his own position. Functioning in these capacities, the specialist is exposed to the danger of conflict of interests. Hence, the advisability of requiring him to shed his dealer or brokerage activities has regularly cropped up as a major issue.

After evaluating this problem, the Special Study concluded that the weight of the evidence presented was not sufficiently strong to justify severing this dual role, particularly in view of the positive service he performs and the importance of his brokerage executions in providing a regular source of income. While the insights into the market afforded the specialist through a monopoly knowledge of the orders in his book give him a trading advantage, his responsibility for maintaining orderly prices exposes him to potentially major financial losses during periods of market stress. In effect, the specialist swaps his willingness to assume market responsibilities with their attendant risks for the trading knowledge provided by his book and opportunities for brokerage income.

As has been indicated previously, the effectiveness of a specialist during crucial moments may be a vital factor in determining the action of the entire market. In its examination of the specialists' activities, particularly during the market break of May 28, 1962, the Special Study found wide differences in performance as well as variations in financial and other capacities. The divergence in performance was corroborated by an SEC study of the behavior of specialists during the tidal selling wave that rocked the market following President Kennedy's assassination on November 22, 1963. In some cases, the Commission found that instead of endeavoring to support the market, some specialists actually sold substantial quantities of stock almost immediately after the news of the assassination.

Towards the close of 1964, there were 358 specialists registered on the NYSE out of a total membership of 1,366. They were organized into 104 units or firms of between one and nine specialists each. On the American Stock Exchange, with a total regular membership of 597, there were 160 specialists organized into fifty-six units. Over the years, a striking decline has occurred in the number of competing specialists. In the NYSE in 1957, fifty units competed in a total of 228 stocks, compared with only two specialist units competing with each other in twelve stocks towards the end of 1964. There are no competing units on the American Stock Exchange.[16] The Special Study of Securities Markets found that this shrinkage in the number of competing specialists and the variations in their performance augmented the need for effective surveillance procedures. Also the Study suggested a number of operating improvements designed to strengthen the system.

REGULATION OF SPECIALISTS

In the spring of 1932, hearings were commenced on an amended Senate Resolution 84, which authorized the Committee on Banking and Currency or its subcommittees to investigate "the practices with respect to the buying and selling and the bor-

---

16. Securities and Exchange Commission, Securities Exchange Act of 1934, Release No. 7432, September 24, 1964.

rowing and lending of listed securities upon the various exchanges." William Gray was counsel to the committee. These hearings marked the opening salvos in the long and complex legislative engagements that preceded the passage of the Securities Exchange Act. In the opening testimony of Richard Whitney, then president of the NYSE, several references to the specialist were made, but the subject apparently had not yet attracted major attention, as indicated by the thirty-two pages of testimony devoted to it out of the 1144 pages that were consumed during the three months of these hearings. The committee resumed hearings in early 1933, and Ferdinand Pecora became its general counsel, a post he held until termination of the investigation in April, 1934.

While hearings continued on various Senate resolutions, President Roosevelt, in the spring of 1933, instructed Secretary of Commerce Roper to form a committee to study the regulation of securities. The first part of this study had an important influence on the Securities Act of 1933 and the second part, dealing with regulation of the stock exchanges, as has been mentioned, became known as the Roper report. The report indicated the usefulness of the specialist's function, noted certain abuses, and recommended that the Stock Exchange Authority should be charged with the task of studying the desirability of segregating the various activities of members of the stock exchanges. In February, 1934, S. 2693 was introduced in the Seventy-third Congress and became the progenitor of the Securities Exchange Act. In this first draft of the bill, the specialist was severely restricted from effecting any transaction on the exchange "except on fixed price orders." In subsequent modifications, the early limitations on the specialist were progressively modified until, when the final bill was approved in June, 1934, as the Securities Exchange Act of 1934, it contained merely the current broad statement in Section 11 that directly pertains to specialists. In effect, the Section now provides that rules of an exchange may permit a member to be registered as a specialist, and if allowed by the Commission, to serve as a dealer so long as his dealings are restricted, as much as practicable, to those reasonably necessary to maintain a fair and orderly market.

The Commission was also directed to study the feasibility and advisability of completely segregating the functions of dealer and broker and to report the results to Congress. Prior to the completion of the segregation study, the Commission's staff, as mentioned previously, recommended various rules for adoption by the exchanges, some concerned with record-keeping and curtailing manipulative conduct by specialists. When the segregation report was issued, it did not recommend separation but recognized the possibility of conflict of interest and indicated the need for further exploration of the matter.

Finally in 1937, the Commission set forth an interpretation of its regulatory position with regard to specialists and their functions. Known as the Saperstein Interpretation (after the Director of its Division of Trading and Exchanges), it defined permitted transactions under the statutory standard as those which enhanced price continuity and reduced the effects of temporary imbalances between supply and demand. It also moved in the direction of minimizing specialist transactions by testing each trade against the standard rather than the total course of dealings. Despite this limitation, the criterion has been sufficiently flexible to permit increased specialist trading when required by market conditions.[17] The Saperstein Interpretation, as it is known, has remained the principal statement of SEC policy concerned with the specialist until the issuance of the Special Study led to the promulgation of a specialist rule by the Commission in January, 1965.

The new rule, complemented by the rules of the New York Stock Exchange and the American Stock Exchange, carries the Saperstein Interpretation one step further in providing a comprehensive system for the regulation of specialists as authorized by Section 11. Both exchanges cooperated in the development of this program, in contrast to the prior conflict that had risen over floor trading. Because of the limited amount of transactions in other exchanges, the Commission exempted the smaller exchanges with specialist systems.

The new rule has three parts. First, it provides that national securities exchanges may register specialists and permit them to act as dealers if the rules of the exchange meet certain standards; second, it establishes a procedure for the Commission to review and disapprove, if considered necessary, new exchange rules relating to specialists; and third, it permits the Commission to

---

17. Report of Special Study of Securities Markets of the Securities and Exchange Commission, op. cit., Part 2, Chapter VI, pp. 66–67.

institute proceedings to require an exchange to cancel or suspend a specialist's registration in one or more of the securities in which he is registered, in the event that he engages in transactions which are not part of a course of dealings reasonably necessary to permit him to maintain a fair and orderly market or to act as odd-lot dealer in such securities.

The areas in which the new Commission rule called for the exchanges to adopt their own rules cover specific criticism leveled by the Special Study; the rules adopted by the exchanges therefore were designed to eliminate these objections. A number of major changes were made. The capital requirements of specialists were raised; in the case of the NYSE, from an amount which would permit the carrying of 400 shares of each specialty stock to 1,200 shares. These requirements were made subject to periodic review. In normal situations specialists will not change prices at openings against the direction indicated by public demand and supply. Specialists are required to avoid liquidating or reducing positions in a manner that would disrupt the market for such stocks. The registration of a specialist may be cancelled if he does not affirmatively apply his own capital and judgment to maintain orderly prices. The concept of market depth is added to the specialist's obligation to keep transaction by transaction price continuity. Various modifications of the specialist's brokerage practices are provided.

The SEC rule is couched in broad terms and the implementing rules of the two exchanges provide a firmer base for effective specialist operations. More specifically, however, the regulatory lines between the exchanges and the Commission have been defined so that the Commission is given more direct control over the specialist.

In order to evaluate the performance of the specialist, the NYSE traditionally has used three measures. The first and most important is the *direct tick* test under which the ratio of the specialist's stabilizing purchases and sales to his total purchases and sales is computed. A stabilizing transaction is defined as a purchase on a minus or zero-minus tick[18] or a sale on a plus or zero-plus

---

18. A zero-minus tick represents a transaction in a stock at the same price as the immediately preceding price but below the previous different

tick. For example, during the abrupt market slide of May and June, 1965, the NYSE estimated that the ratio of stabilizing to total transactions of its specialists was 93 per cent compared with 88.5 per cent in all of 1964.[19]

The second test measures the extent to which a specialist has participated, as a dealer for his own account, in the market for a particular stock. It is calculated by dividing the total shares purchased and sold for the specialist's account by twice the total reported volume in the stock. During the May and June, 1965 drop, the specialists bought or sold for their own accounts an estimated 15 per cent of the shares traded on the NYSE, indicating a greater degree of activity than was normal in 1964, when 13.5 per cent was reported.

The third test is the overnight or *carry-over* position. The unit's position is aggregated and the number of days that the position fell into certain ranges is determined. The size of the carry-over is used to reflect the degree of risk taken by the specialist. In addition to these routine tests, more elaborate studies are undertaken during the year, often involving the reconstruction of the market during a certain period. Despite the fact that there is no specific requirement that the specialists quote a reasonable market, the weight of official Exchange opinion is that they are required to do so, and specialists have been criticized for providing wide quotes.

Various shortcomings to these tests have been mentioned by the critics. Use of aggregate data could conceal considerable individual variations. Thus, on May 28, 1962, the day of the market break, the specialist in American Telephone & Telegraph Company common stock had a stabilizing percentage for the day of 95 per cent for purchases and 81 per cent for sales. On the other hand, the specialist in the common stock of the International Business Machine Corporation had stabilizing activity for the day of 92 per cent for purchases and only 48 per cent for sales; the specialist unit's activity in this stock during the market-break period led to an inquiry by the Exchange, which resulted in criticism of the specialist but no disciplinary action. Then again, depending upon

price; a zero-plus tick is at the same level as the immediately preceding price but above the previous different price.

19. *The Wall Street Journal*, July 13, 1965.

the price-trend of a stock, a high-tick ratio could be achieved, even though the specialist is selling during a broadly declining movement or buying in a rising movement, as illustrated in Figure 6–1. In this case, the specialist sells only on up-ticks, yet the trend of stock prices is sharply downward; similarly, he buys only on down-ticks, but the price trend is clearly upward.

A limitation of the participation ratio lies in the uncertainty of a suitable standard; though routine specialist surveillance has tended to stress greater participation in an active stock, a high participation ratio may merely reflect overparticipation. None of the measures reflects the impact that swiftly declining prices has on the specialist's financial condition and thereby his potential to act. Finally the tests are applied to historic data, but it is necessary to evaluate the specialist contemporaneously if the results are to be helpful in producing orderly markets. The specialist of a major stock who sells at a vital juncture when he should be buying may permit a price drop that will influence holders of other stocks to dispose of their commitments, and the selling movement may spread in ever-widening circles. In the securities markets, the action of the specialist at the critical margin, which is not revealed in aggregate data, may be the influential factor in starting an important market movement.

Reflecting criticism of this type, the exchanges have made progress in refining their surveillance techniques. Specialists are now required to keep records of their commission income and dealer profits and losses by stock. The exchanges have agreed to inform the Commission immediately by telephone if it appears that a specialist unit is running into financial difficulties. Both exchanges have assigned more personnel to the surveillance program and have been endeavoring, through independent studies of their own, to develop new and more effective performance tests. Both exchanges also have been studying the application of automation programs to surveillance procedures.

A long gap has intervened between the original adoption of the Saperstein Interpretation in 1937 and the new specialist rule issued in the beginning of 1965. With respect to advancing the methods of specialist evaluations, these interim years have been largely barren. In the future, much improvement may come from the current programs of the exchanges. No methods, however, are

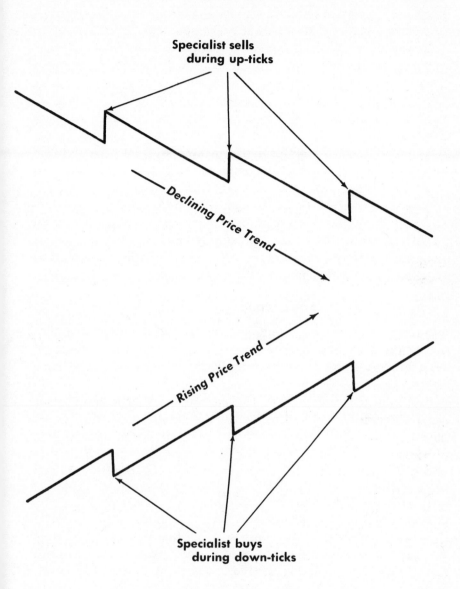

Figure 6–1—Up-ticks During Declining Trends and
Down-ticks in Rising Trends

likely to be fully effective unless they involve, through use of the computer, obtaining information continuously on the performance of the specialist, so that corrective action may be taken immediately should he fail to meet his responsibilities of maintaining an orderly market. The results of historic analyses are useful in identifying prior deficiencies of performance and in determining the need for disciplinary action. Such measures, however, will not help check an incipient disorderly market engendered by the remissness of specialist performance in key issues at critical times.

There may be some reluctance to adapt the extensive computer facilities of the big New York exchanges to evaluate the specialist's performance because such a procedure may be construed to be the first step towards replacing the specialist with the computer. Whispers of such a possibility have been heard for some time and recently have become more audible. For example, two co-authoring analysts have noted:

In a program of computerizing the operations of the NYSE, some systems analysts have argued that certain of the specialists' functions could be programmed quite readily with modern techniques. We are not in a position to evaluate such proposals, but they seem promising enough to merit professional investigation.[20]

The same analysts later indicate a belief that the routine, brokerage functions of the specialist could be automated. They state: "One aspect of the specialists' function should certainly be amenable to this process (computerization): the handling of limited orders." Even if the computer could be presently used to record limit orders, the significance of the specialist's dealer functions would be in no way attenuated. Thus, let us assume the public market in the specialist's book is 25 bid, offered at 30, with the last sale at 30, and market orders to sell and buy arrive in rapid succession. Without the intervention of the specialist, the sell order would be consummated at the bid and the buy at the offer, resulting in three successive transactions at 30, 25, 30. Assuming also that there was no financial reason to justify such sharp changes, the fluctuations would have been caused by the mere mechanics of the trading process; their very sharpness, however, could generate

20. Roland I. Robinson and H. Robert Bartell, Jr., "Uneasy Partnership: SEC/NYSE," *Harvard Business Review,* January-February, 1965, p. 87.

misleading notions about the condition of the corporations represented. On the other hand, an initial intervening specialist bid of 29¾ would have resulted in a much more realistic price sequence of 30, 29¾, 30. Thus, a carefully drawn program incorporating various restrictive provisions would be required even to automate limit orders and a long period of trial would be necessary before its effectiveness could be evaluated.

Under present circumstances, the role of the specialist appears desirable to maintain orderly markets, which are important in holding intact the vital thread of relationship between financial values and prices in the trading markets, a necessary requirement, in turn, for the securities markets to perform their economic functions. No suitable replacement has been found for the judgment he exercises and the risks he takes to meet his responsibilities. His very importance indicates the need of reviewing the specialist's activities currently. This can now be done with electronic equipment.

The age of the computer has just opened. Its immediate applications have been to routine functions, but its greater potential lies in decision-making areas. Clearly, no one is in a position to state what this means to the securities markets in general and to the specialist in particular. All that can be asserted with assurance is that no avenues should remain unexplored because of built-in prejudices. Through simulation techniques on the computer different methods for executing transactions may be pre-tested. By this means some idea may be gleaned of the price action that would have followed under various alternative conditions. Use of simulation for this purpose has not yet been attempted because the vast complications of the securities markets make this approach very expensive. As these techniques are developed further and costs are reduced, their eventual application to the securities markets is likely to occur.

The Floor Trader

In its report, the Special Study observed that floor trading as then carried on was a vestige of the former "private club" character of the stock exchanges and recommended that this practice should not be permitted to continue on either the New York or American Stock Exchanges. This recommendation provoked particularly sharp lines of conflict.

CHARACTERISTICS OF FLOOR TRADING

A member of an exchange who trades primarily for his own account while on the floor of the exchange (except for a specialist or odd-lot dealer) is considered a floor trader. The number of members in this category has been very small, running about thirty during most of the years that the Securities Exchange Act has been in existence. In addition, until 1964, floor trading, including transactions on an intermittent or occasional basis, was conducted by more than 300 members engaged primarily in other floor functions. The total amount of floor trading, however, has never been very large, and in 1961, when examined by the Special Study, amounted to 2.1 per cent of aggregate purchases and sales on the NYSE. Also, most floor trading on the Exchange has tended to be concentrated in the hands of a relatively small number of members and traditionally has been centered on the more active stocks.

The principal objections that have been advanced against the practice are that floor traders enjoy a competitive trading advantage over all other traders and that floor trading accentuates price movements. The competitive advantages of the floor trader arise from the elimination of the costs of floor brokerage and the opportunity afforded him to assess at first-hand, and to respond instantaneously to floor developments. Both the SEC, in prior years, and the Special Study examined the relationship between market trends and floor traders' net balances and concluded that the floor traders predominantly traded with and therefore accentuated the trend. On the other hand, the exchanges argued that even though floor traders accounted for only a small percentage of total volume, their contribution to liquidity was far greater than suggested by the number of shares involved and that they aided in maintaining market stability.

REGULATION OF FLOOR TRADING

Section 11(a) of the Securities Exchange Act authorizes the Commission to prescribe rules to regulate or prevent floor trading by members of national securities exchanges. Despite various investigations and some tentative steps towards abolition, the Commission did not take any direct action. Regulation was accomplished by the exchanges, with both the New York and American Stock Exchanges adopting rules that restricted to some extent the latitude allowed the floor traders. Also, floor traders had to file reports that were subject to daily review to detect rule violations, although little in the way of disciplinary action was ever actually taken.

When the SEC finally revealed an intent to follow the recommendation of the Special Study to eliminate floor trading, both exchanges at first adamantly opposed any such step. Eventually a compromise was struck that leaned heavily in the direction favored by the Commission. In mid-1964, the Commission adopted a rule that prevented a member of a national securities exchange from trading on the floor for his own account, with certain exceptions. These include transactions by a specialist or odd-lot dealer in a security in which he is registered, and transactions effected in conformity with a plan adopted by an exchange and approved by the Commission to eliminate floor-trading activities that are not beneficial to the market.

To implement this agreement both the New York and American Stock Exchanges announced plans that established a number of new rules. Among them was provision for a new class of members, *registered traders,* who must have stipulated minimum amounts of capital, must pass an examination showing familiarity with the required standards of performance, and are prohibited from executing brokerage orders and floor trading in the same security during a single session. Another series of rules is designed to compel registered traders to engage in transactions that contribute to the orderliness of markets and to prevent them from engaging in transactions that have disruptive market effects.

Measured against the number of floor traders involved and their total volume of business, the heat generated by the floor-trader conflict and the time devoted to the problem seem out of proportion to the actual effect on the market. Considered in the light of a governing principle applicable to public markets, the issue has considerable significance. In public markets, no members are entitled to special privileges unless they assume offsetting responsibilities. Thus, floor brokers and specialists must meet fiduciary standards of behavior in executing agency orders, and associate brokers consider themselves obligated to fill every odd-lot order placed with them. Only the floor traders operate outside this circle of market responsibility expected of floor members. For this reason, the Special Study visualized the possibility that floor traders could perform a highly useful function as "auxiliary specialists."[21] While this recommendation was not adopted, the Commission rule, supplemented by the exchanges' plans, circumscribed severely the latitude permissible to the floor trader and prescribed much more positive standards of performance. As a result of these factors, floor-trading activity dwindled perceptibly; for the twelve months ending July 31, 1964, prior to passage of the new provisions, on-floor purchases and sales amounted to 62,242,000 shares, representing 2.48 per cent of total transactions, compared with 17,006,000 shares or only 0.66 per cent of the total for the twelve months ending July 30, 1965.

The Over-the-Counter Market

The diffuse, sprawling nature of the over-the counter market vests it with an aura of uncertainty and even mysteriousness that makes it particularly vulnerable to abuse and difficult to regulate. Some light on the operations of this market was shed by the Special Study of Securities Markets which provided fresh insights into and data concerning activities of the participants in this market. On the basis of this information, a number of major improvements were incorporated into legislation and formulated into rules and practices both by the SEC and the NASD. The Special Study, however, was a one-shot affair and special problems still remain that will have to be resolved over the years as increased knowledge is gained of this market.

THE STRUCTURE OF THE OVER-THE-COUNTER MARKET

The Special Study found that there were over 6,000 broker-dealer firms in the United States engaged in some aspect of the securities business. The bulk of these firms, of course, have no

---

21. Report of Special Study of Securities Markets of the Securities and Exchange Commission, op. cit., Part 2, Chapter VI, pp. 241–242.

exchange affiliation and confine their activities to the over-the-counter market while many deal only in mutual fund shares. Although there are a number of giant firms, both with and without exchange affiliations, operating over the counter, the vast majority of registered broker-dealers are small and do business from only one office. These small firms have a particularly high rate of turnover.

As the industry grew, it attracted a large number of inexperienced personnel. The ranks of its salesmen became swollen with part-time employees whose merchandising efforts often did not conform to the presumed professional character of the industry. Lack of suitable information in the over-the-counter market made this area particularly vulnerable to "hard-selling" tactics.

Much of the effort at regulation has been directed to eradicate these difficulties. With respect to disclosure, the relatively big companies in the over-the-counter market, as a result of the Securities Acts Amendments of 1964, are now subject to similar periodic reporting, proxy regulation, and insider-trading restrictions as are applicable to listed companies. A new Section 14(c) of the Securities Exchange Act, supplemented by an SEC rule, requires dissemination of information to shareholders of both listed and unlisted companies if proxies are not solicited. To raise the standards of operations in the business, firmer controls have been established at the portals of entry and over the subsequent conduct of its participants. Broker-dealers must be members of a self-regulatory agency or become subject to the direct regulation of the SEC. Most authorities with regulatory responsibility over the securities business, as has been mentioned, now require successful completion of a general securities examination as a prerequisite for salesmen and others to participate in the field. In the fall of 1965, the Commission adopted a rule establishing such a qualifications examination for registered over-the-counter brokers and dealers that are not members of a national securities association registered with the Commission; at present, of course, this means the NASD.

As more individuals become owners of securities that are regarded as a means of savings, the financial position of the broker-dealers becomes of greater public concern. Accordingly, recent regulatory measures have also been in this direction. These efforts are particularly important in the over-the-counter area where the bulk of the small and financially less secure firms operate. In the course of buying and selling securities, customers not uncommonly leave with broker-dealer firms free credit balances that are used in the ordinary course of the firm's business. In effect, therefore, the broker-dealer serves in the capacity of a banker keeping his client's money on deposit. To provide some control of this practice, the SEC, in the summer of 1964, under Section 15(c)(3), giving it authority to provide safeguards with respect to the financial responsibility of brokers and dealers, enacted Rule 15c3–2, which requires such firms to send a written statement at least once every three months to customers with credit balances. This statement is to inform them of the amount due, the fact that such funds are not segregated, and that they are payable on demand. In the following year, the Commission amended Rule 15c3–1 which originally provided that brokers or dealers shall not permit their aggregate indebtedness to exceed twenty times their net capital. Among other things, the expanded provision now also calls for broker-dealers engaged in the general securities business to have and maintain a minimum net capital of $5,000; this amount could be scaled down to $2,500 for firms that do not hold customers' funds or securities and whose business is substantially limited to the area of mutual funds and soliciting accounts for certain insured savings and loan associations. The addition of a minimum net capital requirement stems from conclusions of the Special Study that no firm handling customers' funds or securities should have such a small amount of its own resources in the business to result in its customers' assets becoming its principal working capital; that the smooth functioning of the market mechanism requires persons to have confidence in each other's stability and responsibility; and that broker-dealers should not, in effect, be rendered judgment proof because of an inadequate financial stake in the business if the liability to customers for violations of state and Federal laws is to be a deterrent to improper conduct.

The foregoing requirements raise substantially the personnel, ethical, and financial standards of the industry. These improvements, however, are only one side of the coin. The other side encompasses the operating problems of the over-the-counter market, a number of which still persist.

The range in caliber and varied sense of obligations of the

market-makers result in big differences in the quality of the markets for individual securities. In comparison with the market-maker or wholesaler, who uses his interdealer quotations and transactions to adjust his positions, the integrated firm that does both wholesaling and retailing often uses its retail outlets to dispose of inventories acquired through trading activities. This dual function may lead to conflicts of interests. In the retail end of the business, considerable variation marks the diligence with which firms represent their customers' interests in obtaining the best prices for their transactions. Moreover, in riskless transactions, where the dealer sells as principal to his customer and concurrently buys the security sold, customers have tended to pay relatively higher charges despite the absence of risk to the firm. In order to understand better how to eliminate these problems, the Special Study pointed to the need of identifying, classifying, and obtaining information from the different participants in the over-the-counter market. Such a procedure appears to be a necessary preliminary step to the eventual development of more effective regulatory procedures in this field.

QUOTATION SYSTEMS AND REPORTING

Wholesale or *inside* quotations are disseminated among professionals principally by the National Quotation Bureau, Inc., controlled by Commerce Clearing House, Inc., since 1963. Broker-dealers in the business use the *sheets,* as the reproduced lists in which the quotations appear are called, to find and communicate buying or selling professional interest. The Bureau exercises some restraints on who may insert quotations in the sheets by imposing modest listing requirements. An important gap that the Special Study pointed out was the failure to require disclosure when one broker-dealer inserted quotations for the benefit of another. Such a beneficial insertion might be for legitimate reasons, such as the use by a correspondent located in a different city of its own name in order to increase the likelihood that other broker-dealers, located in the same city as the correspondent, would respond to the quotation. Or the insertion might be for misleading reasons, such as to give the appearance of a degree of trading interest that does not exist.

Similarly, a broker-dealer might insert a fictitious quotation

in order to create an impression of trading activity and not respond
to the quotation if an order was transmitted at the level indicated.
To avoid such shortcomings, the SEC placed into effect, in the
fall of 1964, Rule 15c2–7, concerned with the identification of
quotations. In general, under this rule, there must be identification of the beneficiary broker when a quotation is inserted by a
correspondent and of the brokers participating in a special arrangement, such as a joint account. Also the category or categories for
which the quotation is submitted must be disclosed through appropriate symbols.

While the wholesale quotations in the sheets are not generally
available to the public, retail quotations are designed for public
information through the newspapers. The retail system is run by
the NASD which includes a national and various regional and
supplementary local lists. The Special Study criticized the traditional way of reporting retail quotations which involved a bid,
supposed to be simply the wholesale figure, and an asked price,
determined by adding to the submitted wholesale bid an amount
from a suggested but not uniformly applied NASD schedule. Calculated in this manner, the NASD retail quotation system did not
provide either a reliable reflection of the underlying wholesale
markets or an accurate indication of the actual price range of
consummated retail transactions. Moreover, institutions and other
favored investors had regular access to the sheets through NASD
members. This resulted in unfair discrimination among customers.

Of perhaps greater significance was the Special Study's contention that investors required additional disclosure about the
markets in order to make informed decisions regarding their transactions. Contributing to this condition is the close relationship
between the retail quotation system and the NASD markup policy.
In a principal transaction, the public does not know how the price
he pays compares with that prevailing in the interdealer market.
To prevent abuses arising from this condition, the SEC in 1942
suggested a rule, based upon the principle of disclosure, that provided for the reporting of inside prices by broker-dealers. The
Commission eventually withdrew this proposal, principally because
the NASD had adopted, in 1943, an alternative approach that
relies upon direct regulation in the form of a policy statement;
this asserts that markups in over-the-counter transactions should

take into account all relevant factors, such as the type of security, its price, and the amount of money involved, but ordinarily should not exceed 5 per cent. Considerable difficulty has been experienced in enforcing this policy, not only because of the vast problem of administration but also because of sheer uncertainty regarding its meaning. There is confusion, for example, as to when the base of computation is the dealer's own contemporaneous cost and when it is the prevailing wholesale offer.[22] The net result is that the costs of executing principal transactions have differed markedly and could exceed the 5 per cent limitation.

In the light of these circumstances, the Special Study recommended that the retail quotation system generally should show the best prevailing interdealer bid-and-asked quotation that could be reasonably ascertained. Under the prodding of the SEC, the NASD eventually agreed, starting about the middle of February, 1965, to revise its reporting procedure. Under the new system, the NASD publishes the wholesale or interdealer quotations for the 1,300 issues on its national list as of a specified time of the day. Initially, the reform did not apply to the much larger number of other over-the-counter securities that are publicly quoted but generally are traded locally.

The Special Study also ascertained that principal markups ordinarily run higher than agency commissions, which generally are executed at the applicable NYSE commission rate. To provide investors with some insight into the costs of their principal transactions, therefore, the SEC suggested that broker-dealers who sell stock from inventory should indicate on their confirmations the prevailing independent wholesale price. Finally, it was noted that markups tend to be higher on riskless transactions where the dealer sells as principal to his customer and concurrently purchases the security sold. Since these transactions constitute a substantial portion of the retail activity of dealers as principals and resemble agency executions, the idea was advanced that a broker who is neither a primary market-maker nor has a bona fide inventory generally should be required to execute customers' orders on an agency basis.

Modifying the method of reporting retail quotations does not

---

22. Report of Special Study of Securities Markets of the Securities and Exchange Coommission, op. cit., Part 2, Chapter VII, p. 676.

appear to have created any serious ripples in the over-the-counter field. Nevertheless, grumbles are still heard, particularly with respect to the possible incorporation of the other changes. It is contended that such changes would have an especially serious impact on the small firm, which cannot compete with large organizations on a principal basis and therefore would have to function increasingly as an agent. Moreover, by revealing his charges, the small firm might experience difficulty in marketing the shares of new companies where charges usually are high because of the greater risks involved. As a result, the small firm as well as the enterprise seeking new capital might be hurt. Finally, concern is typically expressed for the small, rural dealer who must maintain salesmen to solicit customers and therefore incurs higher costs, which it is asserted could no longer be recouped because his customers would shy away from paying the premium charges they now knew were being incurred.

These arguments are not fully convincing. The over-the-counter field is heavily concentrated, with a relatively small number of firms doing a large proportion of the business. Moreover, agency dealings appear to be relatively more prevalent for small, inactively traded issues where presumably a greater markup might be necessary to cover the added costs of solicitation and research. Then again, there does not seem to be a tendency towards principal executions among firms doing low volumes of business and therefore presumably incurring higher costs.[23] Nevertheless, before attempting to extend the new pricing system or for adopting the Special Study recommendations for disclosure of sales markups, by broker-dealers in confirmations, and for curbing riskless transactions, both the SEC and the NASD have desired more information concerning their potential effects upon the securities business. For this purpose, the management consulting firm of Booz, Allen & Hamilton was engaged to conduct a broad study of the quotations issue, the riskless transaction, and the disclosure of sales markups.

THE QUESTION OF AUTOMATION

In its analysis of the over-the-counter market, the Special Study indicated that it appeared technically feasible to use a cen-

---

23. Report of Special Study of Securities Markets of the Securities and Exchange Commission, op. cit., Part 2, Chapter VII, p. 666.

tral computer to record and report interdealer quotations and possibly to match buy and sell orders so as to accomplish actual executions.[24] Following this conclusion, various companies began to experiment with proposed automated arrangements based upon a central computer linked by wire to dealers' offices throughout the country. The NASD has been studying these proposals and its eventual recommendations will undoubtedly strongly influence the type of program that is adopted.

Automation in the over-the-counter market may take different forms. Most basically, the computer might serve as a giant National Quotation Bureau into which the dealers could feed their quotations for individual stocks to be sorted and distributed, as high bids and low asked prices, to the investment community. A more elaborate system would also provide such information as the day's high and low price in different stocks, the total number of shares traded through the computer, last sale prices in the stocks, net changes, and dividend payments. Each day a summary of these statistics could be provided to the newspapers enabling investors to gain a more realistic picture of trading conditions in the over-the-counter market. In addition to automating quotations, the computer could function as a huge switchboard permitting dealers to communicate through its equipment while leaving the execution of trades to them. On a different level, the computer could serve the purposes of a specialist's book so that unfilled orders would be retained until execution; when buy or sell orders could be matched, the computer would print on the teletypewriter the name of the dealer on the other end of the transaction, along with the price and other pertinent details. In an even more elaborate arrangement, subscribing dealers could be commissioned to trade for their own accounts to maintain orderly markets.[25]

Presumably it would not be difficult for dealers to adjust to a system limited to the automation of quotations since they need this information anyway in the course of their present negotiations. In addition to the technical problems that would have to be resolved, the major drawback to the introduction of such an arrangement would be the price. There are many small dealers who would probably find the costs of subscribing to such a service heavy in

24. Report of Special Study of Securities Markets, op. cit., Part 2, Chapter VII, pp. 668–669.
25. *The Wall Street Journal,* December 2, 1964.

light of their relatively limited operations. Accordingly, continued operations outside the system might be necessary, or the means of functioning through larger dealers on a less expensive basis might be developed. Moreover, an automated quotation system could serve as the basis for providing centralized bookkeeping services to small, over-the-counter dealers, thereby lowering their overhead costs. Automation of trading, on the other hand, is another matter. Such a system would radically change the present over-the-counter method of operation, where prices are established by negotiation, to a procedure where prices are determined in accordance with prescribed rules fed into the computer. Trading on such a basis probably would resemble more closely the auction process and could be a step towards converting the over-the-counter market into a giant organized market. Such a revolutionary movement does not seem probable at present.

The NASD study committee has indicated a rejection of the idea of a totally automated over-the-counter securities market while leaning towards some limited plan.[26] It is logical that the first steps at automation in the over-the-counter market should proceed slowly. It is probable, however, that whatever measures are adopted will represent an initial venture and, as experience with the computer is gained and costs are reduced, the process of automation in the over-the-counter market will become more extensive.

The Problems of the Securities Markets in Perspective

In an industry as dynamic as securities, functioning in an environment that has been shifting rapidly, it is inevitable that needs will change. In the present chapter, an effort has been made to highlight some of the currently important issues upon which action has been taken but which still remain unsettled in varying degrees. Included was a discussion of the new-issue market, commission rates, odd-lot dealer, the specialist, floor trader, and the over-the-counter market.

---

26. *The Wall Street Journal,* July 20, 1965.

As steps are taken to eradicate the difficulties existing in each of these categories, new questions undoubtedly will continue to arise in response to changing circumstances. It is difficult to visualize the securities markets ever reaching a static condition. In the interim, one issue of major significance which has been on the horizon for a number of years, and which is looming increasingly large as it comes closer, is the role of the institutional investor. This question is considered in the following chapter.

CHAPTER 7

The Institutional
Investor

Apart from the other developments affecting the securities markets, the growth of institutional investors warrants special attention. Although in the aggregate they own less stock than individuals, their holdings are large, increasing, and concentrated in a relatively small number of issues compared with the millions of other public investors. As a result, investment decisions with respect to the particular stocks bought and the method of executing the transactions can have a major influence on the securities markets. The growth of the institutions and their importance to the securities field led the NYSE, in October, 1965, to establish an Institutional Investors Department. The announced objectives of the department are to help institutional customers and member firms understand and make more effective use of the NYSE market; to assist the membership in developing and servicing institutional business; and to develop programs to better the Exchange's service for institutional investors. This move represented a positive effort on the part of the NYSE to concentrate more vigorously on the expanding problems of dealing with the institutions.

Institutional Investment Holdings and Policies

The amount and kind of securities that institutions own are
dependent upon their size and investment policies.

THE GROWTH OF INSTITUTIONS AND THEIR PORTFOLIOS

The rapid growth of financial institutions is an important and
well-known economic phenomenon that has been taking place
over a number of years. Thus, between 1945 and 1962, the total
assets of the major savings and nonsavings institutions grew from
$88.6 billion to $432.5 billion, a rise of 388 per cent.[1] This
advance has been much more rapid than that of the general
economy which during the same period, measured by the gross
national product, gained 160 per cent. Various factors have contributed to the swift progress of the institutions. They have bene-
fitted by a growing desire for financial security on the part of
individuals as well as by a developing social consciousness that
stresses the responsibility of both the government and private
firms to provide continued income payments during periods of
unemployment and old age. Aware of these changes, the institutions have been alert to develop programs to facilitate the savings
process and attract the funds of an expanding middle-income
class. Similarly, higher incomes and resulting wider ownership of
property have stimulated the need for increased insurance, while
tax pressures have encouraged contributions to endowments and
foundations.

Because of their financial responsibilities to others—depositors, beneficiaries, or those insured—most institutions have followed a conservative investment policy. As a result they dominate
the bond market. At the close of 1961, it is estimated that institutional investors owned about 80 per cent of the total amount

1. New York Stock Exchange, "Institutional Shareownership, A Report
on Financial Institutions and the Stock Market," June, 1964, pp. 1–13. The
savings institutions include life insurance companies, mutual savings banks,
savings and loan associations, non-insured corporation pension funds, state
and local government pensions funds and mutual funds. The nonsavings institutions include fire and casualty insurance companies, college and university endowments, and foundations.

of corporate bonds outstanding.[2] A long-term trend towards price inflation, steadily mounting stock prices, and lack of suitable investment opportunities elsewhere, however, have attracted the institutions' attention to equities. This interest, coupled with a relaxation of legal restrictions, has led to their acquisition of substantial amounts of stock, much of which has come from sales by individuals as indicated in Figure 7–1.

This dual trend of absorption by institutions and disposal by individuals has increased considerably the institutions' share of the equity market. At the close of 1964, they owned an estimated 20.4 per cent of the market value of all NYSE-listed stock compared with 12.7 per cent in 1949.[3] Among the institutions, the principal holders of NYSE-listed stock are the non-insured corporate pension funds and open-end investment companies as shown in Table 7–1. The former group also increased its stock portfolio at the most rapid rate.

INVESTMENT POLICIES

The policies followed by the institutions are outcomes of legal restrictions, the nature of their business, and their investment attitudes. Legal restraints keep such major institutions as the commercial banks, which own some corporate stock acquired through defaulted loans,[4] and the savings and loan associations substantially out of the stock market. The nature of the business determines the amount and timing of the drains that may be made on an institution's resources, and therefore, the type of security it may reasonably buy. Thus, life insurance companies, which can predict with assurance their cash flows, rely principally upon

2. Ibid., p. 15.

3. In addition, bank-administered personal trusts held an estimated 13 per cent or about $61 billion.

4. Through their customer relationships, however, banks exert considerable influence in the execution of stock transactions. Thus banks act in a fiduciary capacity or as agents for trusts and estates, pension and profit-sharing plans, and a number of different institutions. In the October, 1963, NYSE public transaction survey, 35.2 per cent of the share volume on the Exchange from these sources was channeled through commercial banks and trust companies. Moreover, the proportion of all bank volume where the banks had full investment discretion was 43.5 per cent compared with 27.8 per cent in 1955. The New York Stock Exchange, "Institutional Share-ownership," op. cit., pp. 51–56.

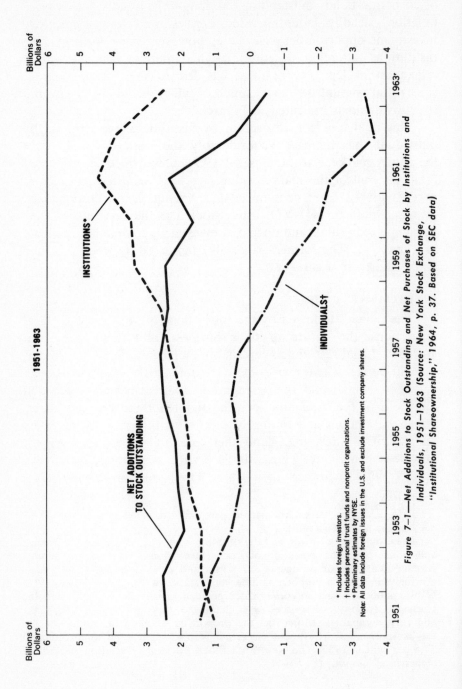

Figure 7–1—Net Additions to Stock Outstanding and Net Purchases of Stock by Institutions and
Individuals, 1951–1963 (Source: New York Stock Exchange,
"Institutional Shareownership," 1964, p. 37. Based on SEC data)

* Includes foreign investors.
† Includes personal trust funds and nonprofit organizations.
° Preliminary estimates by NYSE.
Note: All data include foreign issues in the U.S. and exclude investment company shares.

long-term fixed-income securities, while open-end funds, generally concerned with maximizing return within stipulated investment objectives, invest heavily in common stock. The attitude to the market is a reflection of the prevailing economic outlook, as illustrated by the growing institutional interest in equities as the post-World War II bull market continued its climb. Some gauge as to the significance of investment policy is provided in Table 7–2, in which the total assets of the major institutions are compared with their stock holdings.

By far the biggest institutional investors are the life insurance companies followed by the mutual savings banks, yet because of their restrictive investment policies, neither is a relatively big holder of equities. The laws of New York State are particularly influential on life companies' portfolio policies since companies licensed to do business in that state account for about 85 per cent of the assets of all life companies. These laws include the following investment provisions: Common-stock holdings may not exceed 5 per cent of total assets or 50 per cent of capital and surplus,

Table 7–1—Estimated Holdings of NYSE Listed Stocks by Financial Institutions

Type of Institution	1949	1956	YEAR END 1962 Billions of Dollars	1963	1964†
Insurance Companies:					
Life	$ 1.1	$ 2.3	$ 4.1	$ 4.6	$ 5.3
Non-Life	1.7	4.5	7.1	8.2	9.2
Investment Companies:					
Open-End	1.4	7.1	15.4	18.6	21.8
Closed-End	1.6	4.0	5.3	5.7	6.5
Non-Insured Pension Funds:					
Corporate	0.5	5.3	17.9	22.6	27.4
Other Private	*	0.4	1.0	1.3	1.7
State & Local Government	*	0.2	0.8	1.0	1.3
Nonprofit Institutions:					
College & University Endowments	1.1	2.4	3.3	4.0	4.5
Foundations	1.1	4.1	6.7	8.1	9.2
Other	1.0	3.1	5.0	5.9	6.8
Common Trust Funds	*	1.0	1.7	2.4	2.7
Mutual Savings Banks	0.2	0.2	0.4	0.4	0.4
TOTAL	$ 9.7	$ 34.6	$ 68.7	$ 82.8	$ 96.8
Market-Value of All NYSE-Listed Stock	$76.3	$219.2	$345.8	$411.3	$474.3
Estimated Per Cent Held by all Institutions	12.7%	15.8%	19.9%	20.1%	20.4%

* Less than $50 million.
† Preliminary estimates.

Source: New York Stock Exchange, *The Exchange*, March, 1965, p. 11.

whichever is less; the amount in each issue may not exceed 2 per cent of total assets or 2 per cent of the issue's outstanding shares, whichever is less; and requirements are imposed pertaining to earnings, dividends and listing. In New York, which is the most important state for mutual savings banks, each institution may hold up to 3 per cent of its assets or 30 per cent of its surplus, undivided profits and reserves, whichever is less, in common stocks. Because of their relatively high and fixed rate of return, mortgages constitute a principal investment of both the life insurance companies and the mutual savings banks.

Non-insured corporate pension funds ranked third in size among the institutional investors but second in the amount of common stock held. The bulk of these plans is administered by trustees and is financed by means of employee and employer contributions determined actuarially on the basis of assumptions regarding future rates of employee retirement, required benefit payments, and earnings from interest and dividends. Since possible future market appreciation is not taken into account when the amount of company contributions to the pension fund is determined, these contributions may be reduced as the market moves upward. Accordingly, there has been an incentive to invest in common stock within the framework of the underlying trust agreement, which ordinarily grants considerable discretion to the trustee; if there is no such agreement, state laws apply but this is relatively unusual. At the

Table 7–2—Comparison of Total Assets and Stock Holdings of Major Institutional Investors, Year-end 1962

YEAR END 1962

	Total Assets	Common Stock	Per cent Common Stock to Total Assets
		(Dollars in billions)	
Life Insurance Companies	$133.3	$ 4.1	3.1%
Mutual Savings Banks	46.1	1.0‡	2.3
Non-Insured Corporate Pension Funds	36.0	13.9	38.7
Fire and Casualty Insurance Companies	34.2	10.4	30.4
State and Local Government Pension Funds*	23.3	0.7‡	3.0
Open-End Investment Companies	21.3	17.6	82.7
Foundations	13.8	6.7†	48.6
College and University Endowments*	7.5	3.8	50.3

* Year-end June 30, 1962.
† NYSE-Listed Stocks.
‡ Common and Preferred Stocks.

Source: Assets and stockholdings from: The New York Stock Exchange, "Institutional Shareownership," op. cit., pp. 11-26.

close of 1962, the assets of the non-insured corporate pension funds were almost equally divided between stocks and corporate bonds with very small amounts held in other media such as mortgages and Government securities. The investment freedom of the non-insured corporate pension funds plus their rapid growth explain their substantial holdings of common stock.

New York State law, which is the most influential affecting fire and casualty insurance companies, permits comparatively liberal investment of surplus and residue reserve accounts. In general, therefore, fire and casualty companies provide a stable foundation for their investment portfolio by placing a substantial portion of their funds in Government bonds and rely on equity securities to increase their over-all return. As a result, they rank third among the institutional investors in their ownership of stock.

State and local pension funds have large amounts of assets derived from employee and government contributions. Investment policies in general have been conservative, and in some states the funds are precluded by law from purchasing common stocks. Consequently, the great bulk of their commitments are in corporate and government bonds, and despite the considerable size of these funds, the amount in stock is small, but growing.

At the close of 1962, open-end investment companies were sixth in size based upon total assets but ranked first in the amount of common stock held. Although the investment policy of the funds varies with their underlying objective, the pressure for performance is strong and therefore, in the aggregate, they characteristically place the bulk of their funds in common stock.

The remaining two categories listed—foundations, and college and university endowments—have less total assets at their disposal than the other institutions. Since each has close to half of its investments in common stock, however, they rank ahead of several of the bigger institutional types with respect to their equity holdings.

The amount of common stock that the institutional investors will hold in the future depends upon their rate of growth and investment policies. The tendency has been for legislators to relax investment restrictions, such as the permission now given by various states, including New York, for life insurance companies to segregate their pension fund accounts from the rest of their assets, thereby freeing funds for investment in common stock.

While there is no reason to expect a halt in the growth of the institutions, especially in view of their aggressiveness in attracting funds, some slackening in the rate of advance may take place. Based upon such an assumption, the New York Stock Exchange has estimated that the institutional investors will own about 30 per cent of the total market value of NYSE-listed shares as of 1980, compared with the 20 per cent held at the end of 1963.[5] This forecast further assumes that the reduction in the rate of institutional growth will occur particularly after 1970, because of changes in the age distribution of the working population and a diminution in the net money flow to non-insured private pension funds as their pay-out requirements rise.

Effect Upon the Channels of Distribution

In the ordinary course of events, when an individual buys or sells a security, he places the order with his broker who executes the transaction in the issue's primary market, unless reciprocal arrangements or other special considerations cause a detour from the ordinary paths. With respect to institutions that hold large amounts of each stock in their portfolios the problem is more complicated. For one thing, the institution may be interested in directing business to brokers that have performed some service, such as the rendering of investment advice or the sale of fund shares, or in the case of a commercial bank that controls trust accounts, to brokers that keep deposits at the bank. Outside of these special factors, the institution also considers the effect upon price because, depending upon how the transaction is handled, different results may be experienced.

Orders for an institution's portfolio stocks may be handled by its own *internal* trading department. They also may be arranged by the *external* trading department of its nonbank investment advisor or that of a bank acting as its trustee and/or investment advisor. While the trading department may have substantial discretion in selecting broker-dealers, more generally, it is provided with a list of such firms among which the business may be spread.

5. New York Stock Exchange, "Institutional Share Ownership," op. cit., pp. 59–61.

Decisions with respect to price and market channel, however, are normally made by the institution's investment committee or trading department and transmitted to the broker-dealer.

When an institution is processing a large transaction in NYSE stock, it has a number of courses open. Orders may be funnelled to the floor of the Exchange for execution through the facilities of the regular auction market; a negotiated arrangement on the floor of the Exchange may be worked out; or one of the seven special methods sponsored by the NYSE may be selected. Then again, the order may be routed to a regional exchange or over-the-counter market. Thus, dependent upon the choices of a relatively small number of persons, the amount, timing, and method of buy or sell orders coming to a particular market at a particular time may be importantly affected.

METHODS NOT REQUIRING SPECIAL PERMISSION

Even when an institution is working on a large block of listed stock, by far the most common way of executing its program is through placing a number of relatively small transactions on the floor of the Exchange. Thus, the Special Study, in its examination of the transactions of ninety-one different institutions in March, 1961, and April, 1962, found that the average size of transaction on the NYSE in each of the two months was around 500 shares and the median around 200 shares.[6] As a result, it might take several months to complete a very large program. In order not to have brokers competing with each other on the same transaction, the institution may select a *lead* broker, who will obtain the co-operation of other firms if considered necessary.

Another method of executing large transactions on the trading floor without involving the use of a special method is through *crossing* of buy and sell orders. In this transaction, the broker assembles matching orders in advance, possibly with the assistance of the specialist, and then actually consummates the purchase or sale on the floor at a price between the current bid and offer. Since the matching orders may have been rounded up off the floor this procedure resembles more closely a "negotiated" rather than a

6. Report of Special Study of Securities Markets of the Securities and Exchange Commission, 88th Cong., 1st sess., H. Doc. 95, 1963, Part 2, Chapter VIII, p. 850.

"pure" auction transaction, in which the price is freely determined by the competitive process of bidding and offering. The price limits, however, are established within the framework of the auction market; other broker-dealers presumably may intervene in the cross; and Exchange rules govern the procedure. It is believed that prearranged crosses may be the second most important method of handling block transactions.

In order further to encourage institutions to use the apparatus of the organized marketplace for consummating their big orders, the Exchange has sponsored a program of bringing the office partners of the member firms and the specialist into closer cooperation. In such arrangements, the specialist is promptly informed of any large orders received by the brokerage house and is included in the negotiations to buy or sell the stock as soon as possible. It is intended that the specialist will both participate in the transaction as principal and help to accumulate offsetting orders from other floor members. The sale of 191,811 shares, worth $10,549,605, of Gulf Oil Corporation in April, 1964, supposedly the costliest single order in stock exchange history until that time, was handled in this way. When the order came to the floor, the specialist obtained buyers for 50,000 shares and personally absorbed the remaining 141,811 shares, with the whole transaction taking about a half hour.

As part of this program, the Exchange has been moving to strengthen the financial position of specialists by requiring them to obtain additional resources or by enlarging the number of specialist units operating as teams. In this way, it is hoped that the specialist will be in a better position to assume the financial risks necessary adequately to service the accounts of big institutions. As a further backup to the specialists, some member firms have offered to take positions with them. Such an arrangement can cut down the time of the transaction materially; for example, in 1964, 154,000 shares of Pan American World Airways was sold in ten minutes, with the specialist absorbing 129,000 shares, and the selling broker the rest. It was reported in early 1965 that about a dozen and a half houses engaged in this activity, known as *block positioning*.[7]

---

7. *The New York Times*, March 14, 1965; *The Wall Street Journal*, January 25, 1965.

As some indication of the relative importance of large transactions, during the final quarter of 1964, when the NYSE initiated its quarterly tabulation of blocks involving 10,000 shares and up, there were completed 399 such transactions—most of them institutional orders—totalling 8.8 million shares, or 2.9 per cent of reported volume. Of these blocks, 14 were consummated by exchange distributions and one by a special bid, both types of transactions representing special marketing procedures developed by the NYSE as described below. The remaining 384 blocks were traded through the machinery of the auction market, frequently by means of "crosses" in which one member firm is involved at least partially on both the purchase and sale side. If the institution is a seller in such a transaction, for example, the broker may assemble a buying group and submit a bid, which if not acceptable to the seller, may be negotiated to reach a mutually acceptable price. Thus, while the transaction is handled within the framework and rules of the NYSE, a form of negotiation may be added to the pure principles of auction trading. Excluded from the NYSE survey of big trades are off-floor transactions such as secondary distributions or blocks executed through smaller lots. In succeeding periods, the amounts absorbed through blocks were somewhat higher, representing 3.6 per cent of NYSE volume in the first quarter of 1965, 3.3 per cent in the second quarter, and 3.2 per cent in the third quarter.[8] With respect to individual securities, the proportions represented by blocks may, of course, be substantially larger.

THE SPECIAL METHODS

Through its efforts to improve the operating efficiency of the auction process and to provide for pre-arranged methods, the NYSE has been able to expand its absorptive capacity to handle big blocks. Nevertheless, the continued pressure of such transactions over a number of years has impelled the Exchange to develop specific plans that are largely insulated from the regular auction system and that enable large orders to be executed within reason-

8. The New York Stock Exchange, "Institutions and the Stock Market," February 1965, May 1965, August 1965; The New York Stock Exchange, "The Modern Auction Market, A Guide to Its Use for Institutional Investors," March, 1965.

ably short periods of time. In the case of the NYSE, seven methods are available, each of which must receive special approval before adoption. Four of the plans, adopted prior to 1956, are designed to assist in disposing of large blocks, while the three other plans, adopted in 1956, are intended to aid in purchases but have proved less popular.

Secondary Distributions—In secondary distributions, a member firm combines with other members and nonmembers to accumulate sufficient orders to permit the sale of the block off the floor, usually after trading hours. This distribution ordinarily is handled like an underwriting through a selling group or syndicate at a fixed price that does not exceed the last sale price on the floor. The seller pays a commission or spread generally equal to three to six commissions. This method, which may be used only when a special offering or exchange distribution does not appear feasible, has proved the most popular; in 1964, 14,741,000 shares were offered in this manner, representing about 1.2 per cent of reported stock volume on the NYSE for the year.

Exchange Distributions—Exchange distributions involve the accumulation of the necessary buy orders by a member firm, acting singly or with other members, and the crossing of these orders with the block being sold on the floor of the Exchange between the bid and asked quotations. Their distinguishing feature from an ordinary cross is that the seller's broker is able to give extra compensation to its own registered representatives and to the other participating broker-dealers. The seller pays a minimum of two commissions while the buyer pays a net price. This method has proved the second most popular, with 2,629,000 shares handled in 1964.

Special Offerings—In special offerings, the seller offers a block at a fixed price that is not above the last sale or current offer on the floor, whichever is lower. The terms of the offer are flashed on the tape and it is open to all members and their customers. The seller pays the equivalent of two to four commissions, and the buyer pays a net price. Use of this method has dwindled over the years and in 1964 was not used at all.

Specialist Block Purchases—Specialist block purchases permit the specialist to buy a block without executing the purchase orders on his book at prices at or above the per-share price he pays for the block. Through this means, the specialist obtains the shares and then distributes them in the ordinary course of his regular activities. A regular commission is paid based on the negotiated price. This method has never been widely used and no transactions were undertaken in 1964.

Acquisition Plans—The three acquisition plans are simply the reverse of their distribution prototypes. A *specialist block sale* involves an acquisition from the specialist rather than a sale to him; an *exchange acquisition* is the same as a distribution except that the initiator is a purchaser rather than a seller; a *special bid* is the same as the special offering except that the initiator is a bidder rather than an offerer.

OTHER METHODS

Institutions also execute transactions through other methods. Like any investor, they may obtain securities by means of underwriting, although their large size sometimes places them in a relatively privileged position. Also, issuers frequently offer securities directly to the institutions through private placements, thereby avoiding the public market entirely.

Of interest are the direct transactions that institutions may execute with each other. As has been indicated, since the number of decision-makers in this area is relatively small and portfolio compositions are generally known, it is sometimes convenient for one institution to arrange a purchase or sale directly with another. By avoiding the broker-dealer as an intermediary, commission charges are saved. This method has provoked some interest in recent years and even has been described as the *fourth market*. Since no matching of orders is involved, it can hardly be described as a market, nor does this procedure appear to impose a serious threat to the exchanges. In the long run, the institutions depend upon the existence of continuous channels, whereby transactions can be consummated with reasonable speed at objectively established prices. Direct transactions can only be done in isolated circumstances, whereas to insure the arms-length bargaining expected of them, fiduciaries require the price-determining mechanism of public markets as a guide. Accordingly, the institutions are not likely to make serious inroads into the basic securities markets by means of direct exchanges, although such transactions may become more frequent.

More important as a competitive threat to the exchanges is the purchase or sale of listed securities in the over-the-counter market. Called the *third market,* this method, as well as the *fourth market,* is discussed in the following chapter.

THE IMPLICATIONS OF THESE METHODS

Of the methods described, the most popular, as has been mentioned, involves the ordinary use of the auction market by institutions through the splitting of a large block into a series of small orders. In the typical transaction, therefore, institutions contribute depth and liquidity to the auction market as they gradually and carefully execute their large-scale transactions over time. Moreover, since the major pressure upon prices comes from market orders, as occurred during the break of May 28, 1962, when some 70 per cent of total sales were at market, the institutions, by their reliance upon limit rather than market orders, reduce the likelihood that they will be the instigators of disorderly market conditions.[9] In its survey of institutional practices, the Special Study found that institutions, as a whole, reported limit orders for 60 per cent of their transactions in March, 1961, and 58 per cent in April, 1962; discretionary orders were employed for 20 and 22 per cent respectively of total volume; and market orders for only 8 per cent and 10 per cent of volume.[10]

Another institutional influence on the auction market, that has been mentioned by some analysts of the securities markets,[11] is the smaller number of stock transactions by institutions relative to the size of their holdings (portfolio turnover) compared with other investors, although the aggressive institutions tend to have more active policies. The reason generally ascribed for the lower turnover of the institutions is that they tend to buy stock for long-term investment. Also, the tax laws favoring long-term capital gains, high margins that discourage some speculation, and a growing tendency to view stocks as a means of saving, have all con-

9. The New York Stock Exchange, "The Stock Market Under Stress," March, 1963, p. 37.

10. Report of Special Study of Securities Markets of the Securities and Exchange Commission, op. cit., Part 2, Chapter VIII, pp. 851–852.

11. Roland I. Robinson and H. Robert Bartell, Jr., "Uneasy Partnership: SEC/NYSE," op. cit., pp. 77–78.

tributed to the reduced annual over-all turnover rate in recent years compared with the very high rates of the pre-World War II period. In 1937, for example, the annual turnover rate on the NYSE was thirty times compared with only fourteen times in 1964. During the same period, the number of shares listed on the Exchange increased from 1,412 million shares to 9,229 million shares, but data are not available to show the changes in activity of all the different classes of holders of these shares. At any rate, there probably is little doubt that orders generally may be executed more swiftly now than some three decades previously, when turnover was higher, thereby suggesting the improvement in the market mechanism that has taken place. As a final note on this matter, annual turnover over the past decade on the NYSE seems to have largely stabilized, at least for the present.[12]

Of considerable interest at present are the transactions of the institutions that are consummated outside of the Exchange floor. These include, particularly, use of the over-the-counter market for executing transactions in listed securities and secondary distributions. The Special Study found that for the two months covered in its survey, about 20 per cent of the total institutions' transactions was accomplished off the Exchange. Even more striking was the fact that 26 per cent of the volume in public utility common stock and about three-fourths of the total volume in preferred issues was accomplished off the Exchange.[13] To a large extent, because of institutional domination, the bond market is virtually over-the-counter, the preferred stock market largely so, and therefore, the query logically rises whether the institutions, as they continue to grow, will have a similar effect upon the market for common stock. Essentially, the answer to this question rests upon the ability of the exchanges to service the institutions sufficiently well with respect to the size, price, and speed of completing transactions in order to arrest these inroads into their volume. For this purpose they have encouraged the use of on-floor trading methods that do not follow strict auction procedures. In these cases, the offsetting orders to a block bid or offer are largely solicited and the price is negotiated but in relationship to the auction trading.

---

12. The New York Stock Exchange, "Fact Book," 1965, pp. 36, 39.
13. Report of Special Study of Securities Markets of the Securities and Exchange Commission, op. cit., Part 2, Chapter VIII, p. 848.

The net result of all these factors is the existence at present of four identifiable markets in listed securities. The first is the traditional auction market. Then, within the limits established by this means, there are three types of negotiated, solicited markets including one that is exchange sponsored with the transactions consummated on the floor (crosses, exchange distributions, block positioning); an exchange sponsored over-the-counter trading (secondary distributions); and an over-the-counter trading outside the regulatory structure of the exchange (the so-called third and fourth markets). It is difficult to determine at this juncture how these different sectors will grow or what other methods may be developed, but the demarcation appears to be reasonably clear between the traditional auction market in listed securities and a negotiated market of some sort, whether or not under jurisdiction of the organized exchanges. It also seems clear that these developments impose upon both the self-regulatory agencies and the SEC the responsibility of determining the extent of further reporting, review, and controls that are desirable in order to insure that the interests of the public, generally, and investors, particularly, are protected.

Effect Upon Stock Prices

Because stock prices are influenced by moment-by-moment actions, it is extremely difficult to isolate the effect of over-all transactions upon price changes over a period of time. Some insight into the influence of institutions on stock prices may be gleaned, however, by the concentration of their ownership and trading in specific issues.

CONCENTRATION OF INSTITUTIONAL OWNERSHIP

By and large institutions prefer to hold NYSE-listed securities to those traded elsewhere. As shown in Table 7–3, on an over-all basis, NYSE-listed stocks represented 78 per cent of the institutional stock portfolios at the end of 1961, compared with 74 per cent in 1956. The range of the ratios reflects, to some degree, institutional preference for certain types of stocks. Thus, the heavy investments of life insurance companies in preferred stocks; and of fire and casualty companies, mutual savings banks, and other institutions in bank and insurance stocks, which usually are not listed, tend to hold down their ratios.[14]

With respect to the listed stocks, the institutions reveal a concentration in a relatively small number of large issues. Table 7–4, for example, shows that 41.4 per cent of the holdings of the institutions, at the close of 1962, was in 51 big issues out of 1,168 listed.

The percentage of the outstanding market value of big stock issues that the institutions hold is not very large. In the highest valuation category, the institutions had only 4.5 per cent while their largest single percentage concentration, in the $800–$999 million category, was only 10.7 per cent. These ratios do not show a domination of any size category of stock. What is more important, however, in evaluating the influence of the institutions on stock prices, is to study their actual transactions.

OVER-ALL INSTITUTIONAL TRANSACTIONS

Since 1952, the NYSE has conducted one- or two-day public-transaction studies, which are designed to provide a sequence of

Table 7–3—Holdings of NYSE-Listed Stock as Per Cent of All Stock in Institutional Portfolios 1956 and 1961

Type of Institution	1956	1961
Life Insurance Companies	65%	73%
Fire & Casualty Insurance Companies	62	65
Mutual Funds	82	79
Closed-End Investment Companies	79	86
College & University Endowments	83	78
Foundations	60	73
Other Nonprofit Institutions	NA	NA
Non-Insured Corporate Pension Funds	86	87
Common Trust Funds	86	86
Mutual Savings Banks	26	31
TOTAL*	74%	78%

NA: Not available.
* Assumes 85% in both years for Other Nonprofit Institutions.
Source: New York Stock Exchange, "Institutional Shareownership," June, 1964, p. 33.

14. As a result of the extended disclosure requirements of the Securities Acts Amendments of 1964, the Chase Manhattan Bank obtained listing on the NYSE in early 1965. Several insurance companies were already listed at that time and others were in the process of listing.

portraits of the stock market over the years. Table 7–5 shows the changing relationship of the share volume of institutions and intermediaries measured against total volume during this period. The institutional participation has risen rapidly but so has total volume; as a result, the relationship is varied but generally tends upward. In March, 1965, the ratio was 31.4 per cent, the highest during the period, but the NYSE indicated that, on the day of the survey, the funds of many public individuals may have been diverted to the secondary offering of General Aniline & Film Corporation that was taking place at that time. As a result, the implications of the sharp spurt in the relative activity by institutions could not be fully evaluated. The Exchange, however, stated that if the past growth rate was resumed, institutions and intermediaries could be expected to account for some 40 per cent of all NYSE volume by 1980.

Behind the facade of the single ratio of institutional to total volume is considerable diversity. Institutions do not behave in the same way at the same time. For example, the Special Study found

Table 7–4—Holdings of NYSE Listed Common Stocks by Over 1,800 Institutional Investors Distributed by Value of Total Issue Outstanding Year-End 1962

| Market-Value of Total Issue Outstanding ($ Million) | No. of Issues | PER CENT DISTRIBUTION OF TOTAL MARKET VALUE | | Per cent of Market Value in Size Class Held by Over 1,800 Insts. |
		Holdings by Over 1,800 Insts.	All NYSE-Listed Common Stocks	
$10,000-30,000	5	14.5%	23.6%	4.5%
$ 3,000- 9,999	8	9.4	11.7	5.9
$ 1,500- 2,999	16	8.3	9.7	6.3
$ 1,000- 1,499	22	9.2	7.6	9.0
$ 800- 999	20	7.7	5.2	10.7
$ 600- 799	36	9.7	7.3	9.7
$ 400- 599	64	11.9	9.3	9.4
$ 200- 399	126	14.0	10.9	9.4
$ 100- 199	167	9.4	7.0	9.9
$ 50- 99	200	4.1	4.2	7.2
Under $50	504	1.8	3.5	3.8
ALL STOCKS	1,168	100.0%	100.0%	7.3%

Method: All NYSE-listed common stocks were ranked by size in terms of outstanding market value—from the largest issue to the smallest. This ranking was divided into the eleven categories shown above. Institutional holdings were distributed over these groups and compared with the distribution of the entire list. Also, within each size category, the proportion of outstanding stock held by the institutions was determined.

Data on institutional holdings were taken from the Standard & Poor's *Stock Guide*, February 1963. However, since this analysis was intended to reflect the aggregate portfolio structure of institutions with *diversified* holdings, the holdings of several nondiversified institutional investors were eliminated, the most important being Christiana Securities.

Source: New York Stock Exchange, "Institutional Shareownership," June, 1964, p. 30.

that in March, 1961, when market conditions were generally buoyant, no-load investment companies were selling slightly more securities than they were buying, whereas the sales of the college endowment funds were more than twice as great as purchases. The dollar purchases of all the other institutional groups exceeded sales by a substantial margin. On the other hand, in April, 1962, when attitudes were relatively pessimistic, the institutions as a group contracted their gross dollar purchases by about 21 per cent under their March, 1961, level, yet four of the groups raised their gross purchases to a higher level than those in March, 1961. Similarly, the open-end (load) funds, conspicuous by the high amount of their trading relative to the size of their portfolios, had a total dollar volume of purchases and sales in April, 1962, that was more than three times that of the pension funds, but their net acquisi-

Table 7–5—Relative Importance of Share Volume of Institutions and Intermediaries† to Total Volume

SHARE VOLUME PER DAY
Institutions and Intermediaries

Period*	Total Volume	Shares	% of Total Volume
	——— Thousands ———		
March, 1965	11,144	3,499‡	31.4%
October, 1963	12,227	2,921	23.9
September, 1961	7,389	1,936	26.2
September, 1960	6,607	1,606	24.3
June, 1959	6,670	1,521	22.8
September, 1958	8,887	2,036	22.9
October, 1957	4,880	1,136	23.3
March, 1956	7,121	1,429	20.1
June, 1955	6,790	1,319	19.4
December, 1954	7,696	1,346	17.5
March, 1954	4,098	962	23.5
March, 1953	4,954	956	19.3
September, 1952	3,101	762	24.6

* 1959, 1960, 1961, 1963, and 1965 are based on transactions for one day. The previous eight studies are based on two days. The 1958 data are projections from a 10 per cent sample.
† Institutions include: savings banks, educational institutions, foundations, religious groups, nonprofit organizations, life and other insurance companies, investment clubs, mutual funds and closed-end investment companies, nonfinancial corporations, partnerships, personal holding companies and nonbank-administered estates, guardianships, pension funds, personal trusts, and profit-sharing plans having legal ownership of the shares bought and sold.
Intermediaries include: non-member channels through which orders for public individuals, institutions, and other legal owners are processed. Most important in this category are commercial banks, trust companies, and non-member broker-dealers. Includes transactions for individuals which are processed through an account in the name of any of the various intermediaries.
‡ The Study reported the share volume of institutions and intermediaries was 31.4 per cent of total volume on the NYSE of 11,114,000 shares including customers' odd-lot transactions. Actual volume as shown in the table is the product of these two reported figures.

Source: New York Stock Exchange, "Institutional Shareownership," June, 1964, p. 46; "Public Transaction Study," March 10, 1965, p. 5.

tions were less than 90 per cent of those of the pension funds.[15]

These differences in practice by type of institution do not go far enough to appraise the significance of the variations. What is necessary is a detailed study of transactions by individual securities over a period of time.

ANALYSIS OF INVESTMENT COMPANY TRANSACTIONS

In order to assess the degree to which insiders, in a position to know in advance the projected purchases or sales of investment companies, use this knowledge to their own advantage, the Special Study examined the portfolio transactions of 51 open-end investment companies during the seven months from December 1, 1960, through June 30, 1961, a period of heavy activity in a rising market. The net assets of the fifty-one funds aggregated $14.9 billion as of December 31, 1961, an amount equal to 65.4 per cent of the assets at that date of the 169 open-end investment companies that were members of the Investment Company Institute. The responses of the fifty-one funds revealed a maximum of 154 portfolio issues traded by a fund during the period, a minimum of twenty-one, and an average of seventy. The Special Study used this information as well as other related material to determine conflicts of interest among the insiders and published its findings in Chapter XI, Part D of its report. After this phase of the investigation was completed, several members of the Study analyzed the records of the institutions' daily purchases and sales in individual stocks to provide some measure of the net buying and selling pressures generated by the funds during this period and, therefore, at least an indication of their influence on stock prices. Since it was outside the framework of the Special Study's interest at the time, these data were not used in the report. They are analyzed at the present time from several points of view.

Transactions in NYSE-Stocks Compared with Other Stocks— During the seven months from December 1, 1960, through June 30, 1961, the fifty-one funds made total common stock purchases in all markets of $1,471 million and sales of $1,129 million, divided according to market place as shown in Table 7–6.

15. Special Study of Securities Markets of the Securities and Exchange Commission, op. cit., Part 2, Chapter 8, p. 847.

Table 7–6—Purchase and Sale Transactions of Fifty-one Funds Classified
by Type of Market* Dec. 31, 1960—June 30, 1961

	PURCHASES		SALES	
	Amount ($000)	Per cent	Amount ($000)	Per cent
All Markets	$1,470,606	100%	$876,660	100%
New York Stock Exchange	1,128,830	77	744,763	85
All Other Markets	341,776	23	131,897	15

* Respondents to the questionnaire identified stocks by name and did not indicate where the trade actually occurred. To the extent that transactions in NYSE stocks were effected outside the Exchange, the depth of the NYSE market would have been further reduced.

The 77 per cent of total purchases made in NYSE stocks and the 85 per cent of total sales in such issues clearly dominate the total value of transactions. In appraising the influence of the funds' transactions, however, it is important to trace the relationship between the source from which the money to effect purchases is obtained and the markets in which the purchase actually is made. To the extent that institutions simply buy shares in a given market with money derived from the sale of stock in the same market, they neither add to nor subtract from the amount of money held in the securities of that market. To the extent, however, that purchases of shares exceed or are less than sales in the same market, new money is either channeled into or taken away from the market. For the purpose of ascertaining this differentiation, the focus of the prior table is shifted in Table 7–7 to highlight the distribution of net purchases.

Table 7–7—Transactions in Different Markets of Fifty-one Funds Classified
by Type of Transaction Dec. 31, 1961—June 30, 1962

	ALL MARKETS		NYSE		ALL OTHER MARKETS	
	Amount ($000)	Per cent	Amount ($000)	Per cent	Amount ($000)	Per cent
Purchases	$1,470,606	100%	$1,128,830	100%	$341,776	100%
Sales	876,660	60	744,763	67	131,897	39
Net Purchases	593,946	40	384,067	33	209,879	61

From the preceding breakdown, it is clear that during these seven months, on an over-all basis, the investment companies obtained 60 per cent of the money required to make purchases from sales effected during the same period. The remaining 40 per cent represented new money placed into stocks that may have been obtained from the additional investment companies' shares sold to the public during the period or from a shift of the companies' own portfolios from non-equity to equity issues. When a similar analysis of the sources' funds is made for NYSE stocks, on the one hand, and all other issues, on the other hand, the picture changes sharply. During this period, 67 per cent of purchases of NYSE shares were made from sales of such stock compared with a ratio of only 39 per cent in all other markets. As a result of this difference in market policies, 35 per cent of the total amount of new money derived by the investment companies was directed to purchases of securities not listed on the NYSE; this figure may be compared with the 23 per cent total of purchases placed in non-Exchange stocks.

These findings indicate that the investment companies were predisposed either to hold a relatively large portion of the stocks that were not listed on the NYSE or chose to commit a proportionately large amount of their new money to such stocks, or engaged in both these practices. Continuation of such a policy would tend to add depth to the non-Exchange markets at the expense of the NYSE. As has been indicated, this comparison is distorted to some extent because some of the transactions in Exchange stocks were undoubtedly made outside the Exchange but such a diversion, if anything, would contribute further to the same effect.

Since the period covered was one of market buoyancy and speculative enthusiasm, it is possible that it is not entirely representative of what might happen under other conditions. Nevertheless, it provides another piece of evidence suggesting the basic influences affecting the relative volume of trading in the different market places. Institutions may not have the same policy with respect to the trading of securities already in their portfolios and those obtained with new money. To the extent that such differences exist, gradual inroads may be made into the depth of one market at the expense of another, providing a competitive thrust to each market to protect its own position.

Relative Importance of Transactions in NYSE Stocks—During the seven-month period, the fifty-one funds purchased 22,935,000 shares of stock listed on the NYSE and sold 15,585,000 shares of such stock. Relative to total volume on the Exchange these transactions were small, with the purchases amounting to only 3.5 per cent of volume and the sales to 2.4 per cent of volume. This comparison however greatly understates the direct importance of the institutions. Since the institutions did not buy and sell all the listed stocks during this period, it is clearly inaccurate to compare their transactions with total transactions on the Exchange. As a first step in disaggregation, therefore, a relationship may be drawn between the funds' activity in the stocks that they bought or sold and the total volume in these same shares.

There were 605 different NYSE issues in which the funds had some transactions. Although this represented only slightly more than one-half of all the common issues listed in 1961, it was a broad representation of issues and gives some indication of the over-all participation of investment companies. The 605 issues, in turn, accounted for 442,240,000 shares or some 60 per cent of the total volume on the NYSE during this period. Because of the large volume of total transactions in these issues, the funds' share was still relatively small, with purchases amounting to 5.2 per cent and sales to 3.5 per cent of total trading.

While the investment companies did some business in about half of all listed issues, they concentrated the great bulk of their transactions in only a handful of stocks. Out of 529 different issues in which they had some purchases, the top forty stocks, or only about 8 per cent of the total number of issues purchased, accounted for 38 per cent of the total amount of shares purchased. And while the funds had some sales in 413 different issues, the top forty or about 10 per cent of the number of issues, accounted for 47 per cent of the volume of sales in shares.

With respect to those issues on which they concentrated, the combined buying or selling of the investment companies, in a number of instances, represented a considerable percentage of total purchases or sales. Thus, in eighteen of the principal issues bought, the investment company purchases exceeded 20 per cent of total purchases on the NYSE and in seventeen of the principal issues sold, the investment companies' sales exceeded 20 per cent of total sales on the NYSE. Moreover, in several stocks the participation of the funds ran over 40 per cent of total volume during the test period.

Whatever offsetting factors may have been at play to blunt the full impact of the investment companies' buying and selling efforts, their purchases or sales of stocks, in which they had a major participation clearly created upward or downward pressures, as the case may be. By and large, these stocks tended to be active issues of well-known companies.

The Extent to Which the Institutions Bought and Sold the Same Stock—Thus far attention has been given to the buying and selling patterns of the funds during the seven months, without considering the extent to which their transactions may have been in the same securities. Yet to the extent that the funds were merely "swapping" shares of the same stock with each other, their net influence in any given direction would have been significantly reduced. For example, four separate issues appeared among the stocks that were both most heavily bought and sold by the funds, thereby largely creating offsetting pressures in these issues.

In the 605 different common stocks listed on the NYSE in which the funds had transactions during the period, they had only purchases in 192 stocks and only sales in seventy-six stocks. Their effect on the price of these issues, regardless of degree, therefore, is clear-cut; on the first group they exerted an upward force and on the second a negative or depressing force.

The funds had both purchases and sales in the remaining 337 issues; in these stocks the greatest part of the activity occurred— some two-thirds of purchases and four-fifths of sales—and the effect of these transactions was uncertain.

Accordingly, an attempt was made to determine if, in a large sense, the firms were simultaneously buying particular securities and at the same time selling others, or if their purchases and sales in specific securities had a tendency to balance one another so that in effect they were buying and selling among themselves. Either of these situations if true could have important theoretical implications, for if the funds were buying heavily in a select group of securities while selling heavily in another group, the transitions would tend to magnify any influence they might have on the markets of those securities. If these procedures were normal, it would be reasonable to assume that any influence that the funds projected upon a specific security would be in a definite direction not offset by opposite orders from other funds. On the other hand, if it were found that the funds largely bought and sold in balance, so that in effect the purchases of one fund were offset and moderated by the sales of another fund, there would seem to be less direction or thrust in the funds' total influence on the market.

In order to throw light on these various possibilities, the 337 issues in which the funds both bought and sold were classified on the basis of the relationship between the purchases and sales. It was desired to ascertain the number of issues and shares of stock in which purchases about equaled sales, in which purchases exceeded sales by a moderate or wide margin, and in which sales exceeded purchases by a moderate or wide margin. The results of this analysis are summarized in Table 7–8.

Table 7–8—Transactions of Issues in Which Funds Had Both Purchases and Sales Classified by Ratio of Purchases to Sales and Sales to Purchases

Ratio	No. of Individual Issues	No. of Shares Purchased (thousands)	Per cent of Total Purchases	No. of Shares Sold (thousands)	Per cent of Total Sales
	337	16,414	100%	13,049	100%
PURCHASES ABOUT EQUAL SALES					
1.4 to 1	60	2,585	15.8	2,575	19.7
PURCHASES EXCEED SALES					
1.5–2.4 to 1	34	1,610	9.8	1,226	9.5
2.5–3.4 to 1	11	535	3.3	172	1.3
3.5–4.4 to 1	12	991	6.0	360	2.8
4.5–5.4 to 1	9	472	2.9	329	2.5
5.5–6.4 to 1	7	307	1.8	114	0.8
6.5 and over to 1	70	7,722	46.9	576	4.4
SALES EXCEED PURCHASES					
1.5–2.4 to 1	39	1,149	7.2	2,097	16.2
2.5–3.4 to 1	19	398	2.4	928	7.1
3.5–4.4 to 1	12	247	1.5	842	6.4
4.5–5.4 to 1	12	72	0.4	344	2.6
5.5–6.4 to 1	7	91	0.6	562	4.3
6.5 and over to 1	45	235	1.4	2,924	22.4

Examination of the table reveals three outstanding clusters of issues and shares. The first is where purchases about equal sales, which includes sixty issues, representing 2,585,000 shares purchased or 15.8 per cent of all shares purchased and 2,575,000 shares sold or 19.7 per cent of all sales. The second is where purchases are 6.5 times or more greater than sales, which includes seventy issues, representing 7,722,000 shares purchased or 46.9 per cent of all purchases and 576,000 shares sold or 4.4 per cent of all sales. The third is where sales exceed purchases by 6.5 times or more, which includes forty-five issues representing 2,924 shares sold or 22.4 per cent of all sales and 235,000 shares bought or 1.4 per cent of all purchases.

From this analysis it is evident that in the stocks where they have had both purchases and sales the funds were exerting a mixed influence. In a significant number of stocks, they were merely swapping with each other, buying and selling approximately the same number of shares of each stock. On the other hand, in a larger number of cases, they were clearly on either the buy or sell side, and often the differential was quite substantial. In these instances, on balance, they were exerting an influence in one direction.

The fact that the institutions center their attention on a relatively small number of active stocks does not mean they have little or no direct influence on the price movements of the other issues in which they do less business. It is entirely possible that their purchases or sales may have been minor relative to total transactions in these other stocks, but if they were made at crucial junctures during the trading period of any of the stocks, these purchases or sales could have been effective in contributing to the creation or halting of a trend. Moreover, even when the institutions have net purchase balances, they could be selling bellwether or market-leader stocks and buying less popular or less focal issues, thereby providing a depressing influence. Finally, the analysis of activity in individual issues reveals that at times the transactions of the institutions may be the dominant factor involved.[16]

Implications of Investment Company Transactions—Evidence of the fact that institutions, on balance, may be buying or selling large amounts of a particular stock at least suggests that they may be influencing its price movements in a given direction. Support to this idea is given by the study of investment companies made by the Wharton School for the SEC which included an investigation into the influence of the funds' activities on stock prices. This phase of the study was based on replies to a Wharton-SEC questionnaire covering 185 companies that provided monthly, weekly and daily statistics on their purchases and sales for different periods during January, 1953 and September, 1958.[17]

---

16. See for example, "Report of Special Study of Securities Markets, op. cit., Part 2, Chapter V, p. 6.

17. "A Study of Mutual Funds," prepared for the Securities and Exchange Commission by the Wharton School of Finance and Commerce, Report of the Committee on Interstate and Foreign Commerce, 87th Congress, 2d Session, August 28, 1962, Chap. 6, pp. 359–397.

Because price changes are the outcome of total demand-supply relationships at a particular moment, it is difficult to draw precise conclusions on the basis of aggregate analysis of data covering a segment of the market. Allowing for these difficulties, the Wharton tests indicated that increases by the funds in their monthly net purchases of a particular security were followed on the average by increases in the price of that security relative to general market prices. Similarly, that decreases in their net purchases were followed generally by relative declines in the market price. These findings are consistent with the hypothesis that the funds were at least partially responsible for some of the major price movements in the individual issues.

As has been indicated, the impact of institutional transactions at a specific crucial time on an individual security may be cascaded into a broadening effect on the over-all market. To gauge the influence of the institutional investor on stock prices, therefore, it is important to follow their actions at the margin in addition to their aggregate transactions. For this purpose, the surveillance techniques of the exchanges might be broadened to identify all major transactions of an investor over time (on a confidential basis). Such information would be helpful to the specialist and exchange officials in ascertaining the need for taking balancing actions and the type of measures that might be instituted. Additionally, it would facilitate reaching a decision relative to the advisability of undertaking direct discussions with institutional investors during emergency conditions and determining which institutions to approach, should the SEC ever want to move along these lines. With computer facilities available, it would appear possible to have this type of information provided through ordinary reporting channels.

Summary

Various economic and social factors have led individuals increasingly to employ the services of institutions, resulting in a considerable increase in their assets over the past years. Because of differences in the nature of their business and legal restrictions, the amount of stocks the institutions are in a position to buy differs sharply. Reflecting these differences and their rates of growth, the non-insured corporate pension funds and the open-end investment companies have emerged as the principal holders of stocks among the institutions.

By and large, the institutions do not necessarily act in the same way—one group may be selling while another is buying, and even within the same category variations may occur. For example, an examination of the trading practices of investment companies during a seven-month period in 1961 revealed a considerable amount of intercompany trading, with a number of institutions buying and selling the same stock. These differences reflect variations both in investment policy and in attitudes with respect to prices and values.

In the final analysis, the purchase or sale of a stock rests upon the judgment decision of an individual, or in the case of an institution, on a group of individuals. This back-and-forth trading, the tendency of institutions to concentrate on active stocks, their extensive use of limit orders, and the care employed in executing transactions all contribute to the liquidity of markets. Moreover, their greater degree of sophistication permits them to act against market trends and the actions of individual investors. As an illustration, during the May 28–31, 1962, period of rapidly declining and rising prices, institutional investors as a whole tended to provide a counterbalancing influence by purchasing equities in substantial quantities on May 28 and 29 while selling them on May 31, after prices had recovered to a large degree.[18]

Buried in these aggregate movements of the institutions are the individual differences that could play an important role in affecting over-all market trends. At any one time that funds are buying or selling on balance, individual institutions may be moving heavily in the opposite direction. This characteristic was seen in the activities of the investment companies during the seven months of 1961 that were studied. During a period of generally rising prices, they had only sales in seventy-six stocks (out of 605 stocks in which the investment companies had some transactions) and sales exceeded purchases by 4.5 times or more in an additional sixty-four stocks.

---

18. New York Stock Exchange, "Institutional Shareownership, A Report on Financial Institutions and the Stock Market," op. cit., p. 38.

The theoretical implications of this separate influence of the investment companies lie in the possible explanation provided for the market's inability to respond consistently to the influence of the new money that the investment companies and other institutions have been placing in securities. Despite the inflow of such new money, selling pressures in crucial issues could act strongly in the opposite direction. This is particularly true since the concentration of funds' activity on particular issues may make their influence dominating on these issues which not uncommonly are market leaders.

Their huge size means that the institutions have large blocks of stock that they either want to buy or sell. Whether this decision is made internally, by the institutions' own employees, or externally, by outside advisors, the final determination is in the hands of a relatively small number of individuals. Their handling of transactions, therefore, could have an important influence upon the market. The institutions are well aware of this fact and characteristically place their orders with great care by either feeding them into the market over a period of time, working carefully with a lead broker, who may try to arrange a cross or other type of essentially negotiated arrangement, or by using one of the special methods sponsored by the exchanges. The growing use of transactions consummated on the floor of the organized market place, but relying upon solicited orders and negotiated prices that are related to but outside the auction stream, is a significant development. On the one hand, these methods reflect the vigor of the organized exchanges in responding to the problem of handling big orders and to the challenge of the over-the-counter markets. On the other hand, their importance and unique features suggest the desirability of obtaining more information concerning their operation to assess their economic implications and to determine if further regulation would be desirable.

CHAPTER **8**

Market
Interrelationships

The history of the trading markets in the United States begins with the history of the United States as an independent government. Following the Revolutionary War, the newly-born nation required financial power to operate the machinery of commerce, industry, and trade that underlies economic growth. For this purpose, the first Congress authorized an issue of bonds, and large amounts of stock appeared in the process of creating local banks and the United States Bank in 1791. This flood of securities led to the establishment in Philadelphia of the first board of brokers to deal in securities, currency and specie, while shortly thereafter, in 1792, a group of brokers signed a trading agreement that became the nucleus of the New York Stock Exchange. This agreement pledged the signers to give preferences to each other in their trading and to charge commissions to outsiders, but not much was known about their activities until in 1817 a formal constitution was drawn and the name "New York Stock & Exchange Board" was adopted. Thus, both in and outside of New York City, stock markets had their beginnings about the same time.

Thereafter, the markets grew, spread, and changed in form to reflect the shifting financial needs of the rapidly growing nation. In the grand design, as it has finally emerged today, the trading markets represent a complex interlocking communication network that spans the country and makes possible the rapid exchange of orders and information. In turn, four principal components of these markets serve sufficiently important roles in the over-all system to require special attention. Of these, the two big New York exchanges, constituting one component, and the over-the-counter market, representing another, already have been discussed. Accordingly, attention is now given to the other two segments—the regional exchanges and the over-the-counter market in listed securities or the so-called *third market*. In recent years, as has been mentioned, the term *fourth market* has been used particularly with reference to the practice of institutions directly swapping securities with each other. This designation may be somewhat imposing for the scattered activity that occurs but individual transactions have been extremely large and the number may increase in the future. Accordingly, some consideration also is given to this area. Thereafter, the issues implicit in the relationships among all these markets is considered.

The Regional Exchanges

The fourteen stock exchanges that are located outside New York City are generally identified as *regional exchanges*. Of these, three, in Colorado Springs, Honolulu, and Richmond, are local in character and are exempt from registration under the Securities Exchange Act. Three of the remaining eleven exchanges, in Salt Lake City, San Francisco,[1] and Spokane, deal chiefly in mining

1. At the time of this writing, the SEC has instituted proceedings against the San Francisco Mining Exchange to suspend its registration. In his report on this subject, the hearing examiner indicated that all of the officials of the Mining Exchange during the past ten years or more had been guilty of major transgressions and violations of the Federal securities laws and that remedial action had to be adopted in the public interest. He also found, however, that responsible persons in the area and recognized professional and civic bodies believed that the Exchange had played an important part in the develop-

shares and are outside of the main stream of market interrelationships. One of the others is inactive as a stock market; the regional-exchange category, therefore, usually refers to seven exchanges: Boston, Midwest, Philadelphia-Baltimore-Washington, Pacific Coast, Cincinnati, Detroit, and Pittsburgh.[2]

BACKGROUND

As local financing was employed in the development of different regions of the country, stock exchanges were formed to provide facilities for trading in the newly issued securities. Without modern means of communication, direct confrontation of the participants was necessary in order to arrange the transactions. Thus, the regional exchanges were the outgrowth of regional financial needs that had to be satisfied through local investors who would experience difficulty in executing trades with parties located at a geographic distance. The NYSE grew to its predominant position because of the rise of New York City as the nation's commercial and money-market center, but during these formative years, the regional exchanges played a part in financing the growth of local areas.

The outpouring of securities that occurred during the 1920s contributed to a mounting interest in the markets and to a sharply enlarged number of issuers seeking listing on the regional exchanges. Abetting this tendency was the exemption from registration accorded to listed securities by a number of state blue-sky laws. During this period the regional exchanges attained their high-tide of growth as indicated by the increasing proportion of national trading that they absorbed; in 1915, for example, share volume in Chicago was only 0.41 per cent of NYSE; in 1923,

---

ment of minerals in the West. Accordingly, he concluded that the public welfare would be better served if the San Francisco exchange were permitted to continue operations provided that a complete reorganization occurred involving new personnel in every department of management and evidence of financial responsibility in the new management.

2. The Chicago Board of Trade is registered as a national securities exchange but has not traded securities since 1953, although it is an important commodities exchange. The National Stock Exchange, which started operations in 1962, is located in New York City, but does only a minor amount of business.

it rose to 5.6 per cent, and by 1929 reached a peak of 7.3 per cent.[3]

The 1929 debacle ushered in a period of decline as share volume shrank and the regional exchanges suffered the loss of their functions in the distribution of securities and the elimination of their blanket exemption from blue-sky registration. Mergers, reorganizations, and dissolutions cut the number of previously listed stocks, and a severe blow to the position of the regionals was experienced in the withdrawal of bank issues, once the backbone of their lists. By 1932, Chicago's trading volume once more shrank to a level equal to 3.7 per cent of NYSE. Thereafter, the passage of the Securities Exchange Act with its investor safeguards for listed securities enhanced the attraction of the over-the-counter market to issuers who preferred their activities to remain shrouded in a veil of secrecy. Also, technological advances made over-the-counter trading on a national scale more feasible, relatively liberal merchandising methods facilitated transactions, and dealers found attractive the higher markups often possible in an over-the-counter transaction. Pressure was also felt from the other side, as issuers skipped the period of seasoning at the regionals to seek direct listing in New York. As a result of all these factors, a long-term shrinkage occurred in the number of securities solely listed on the regional exchanges.

The major offsetting influence to the declining status of the regional exchanges was the growth in the number of securities traded on more than one exchange, known as *multiple trading*. The practice of unlisted trading which is largely responsible for multiple trading was not provided for in the original draft of the Securities Exchange Act, but the statute, as adopted, allowed unlisted trading under prescribed conditions until mid-1936. In view of the temporary nature of this provision, the Commission was directed to study the subject and make its recommendations to Congress. The report, submitted in January, 1936, pointed out that two-thirds of the shares then available for trading on the regional exchanges were not listed, and that the future of these exchanges would be jeopardized if unlisted trading were not continued.

---

3. Special Study of Securities Markets of the Securities and Exchange Commission, 88th Cong., 1st sess., H. Doc. 95, 1963, Part 2, Chapter VIII, pp. 916–917.

Following the recommendations of the SEC, Congress adopted an amendment to the Securities Exchange Act designed to allow each type of market to develop according to its "natural genius." The amendment provided for three ways of conducting unlisted trading: The first was through a *grandfather clause* permitting an exchange to continue unlisted trading privileges in a security that had been admitted prior to March 1, 1934. In the second method, the Commission was empowered to extend unlisted trading privileges to any security listed on any other national securities exchange; this provision has proved the most important. According to the third method, the Commission was allowed to extend unlisted trading privileges under certain circumstances to unlisted securities that comply substantially with the requirements for registered securities, but this method was rarely used.

In order to be granted permission to maintain unlisted trading privileges in a security listed elsewhere, an exchange had to establish to the Commission's satisfaction that there existed in the vicinity of such exchange enough distribution and trading of the security to justify unlisted trading privileges in the public interest. The early strict interpretation of this restriction gradually was relaxed until eventually it became the practice to extend, with relative ease, unlisted trading privileges to any security already listed on another exchange. In addition to this encouragement to multiple trading, a growth occurred in the number of members of regional exchanges who also held seats in the principal New York exchanges, referred to as *dual members*. Nevertheless the two-way pressure on the regional exchanges from both the over-the-counter market and the New York giants continued to be severe and led to a series of mergers between exchanges in the same general region but in different cities and to a reduction in the number of independent exchanges.

CURRENT STATUS OF THE REGIONAL EXCHANGES

The effect of the historical forces that have been working on the regional exchanges is seen in their current position. Today the great bulk of the dollar volume of trading on the major regional exchanges is represented by stocks that have their primary market on the two big New York exchanges. Many of the common stocks that are traded on the NYSE are also traded on one or more regional exchanges, which in turn have shown varying capacities to adapt to new conditions and differ considerably in size.

In terms of dollar volume, the largest is the Midwest Stock Exchange, a 1951 consolidation of four prior exchanges. Next in size is the Pacific Coast Stock Exchange, which in 1957 consolidated the San Francisco and Los Angeles exchanges. The next two are the Philadelphia-Baltimore-Washington Stock Exchange, which assumed its present form in 1953, and the Detroit Stock Exchange. These four exchanges have held their own relatively well in recent years, but the Boston Stock Exchange, which a little more than two decades ago rivalled the Midwest (that is, the four constituent exchanges), has now slipped to fifth place (Table 8–1). As a result, in early 1965, the Boston Exchange engaged

Table 8–1—Market Value and Volume of Sale of Stocks Effected on Registered Securities Exchanges 1964

The Exchange	MARKET VALUE		NUMBER OF SHARES	
	Dollars	%	Number	%
1. American Stock Exchange	5,923,050,464	8.21	397,043,056	19.42
2. Boston Stock Exchange	310,107,457	0.43	5,925,854	0.29
3. Chicago Board of Trade	0	0	0	0
4. Cincinnati Stock Exchange	46,306,336	0.06	830,240	0.04
5. Detroit Stock Exchange	481,319,021	0.67	11,538,925	0.57
6. Midwest Stock Exchange	2,286,202,057	3.17	50,584,823	2.47
7. National Stock Exchange	644,920	0.00	633,325	0.03
8. New York Stock Exchange	60,424,051,675	83.75	1,482,256,735	72.49
9. Pacific Coast Stock Exchange	1,790,447,442	2.48	52,780,907	2.58
10. Philadelphia-Baltimore-Washington Stock Exchange	827,924,991	1.15	18,618,998	0.91
11. Pittsburgh Stock Exchange	45,304,864	0.06	1,059,996	0.05
12. Salt Lake Stock Exchange	3,650,517	0.01	8,847,981	0.43
13. San Francisco Stock Exchange	566,760	0.00	6,573,870	0.32
14. Spokane Stock Exchange	9,419,720	0.01	8,178,388	0.40
Total	72,148,996,024	100.00	2,044,873,098	100.00

Source: Securities and Exchange Commission, Statistical Bulletins, March, 1964—February, 1965.

a consulting firm to diagnose its problems with the intent of regaining its position or possibly going out of business.[4] Following the recommendations of this firm, the Boston Exchange then embarked upon a major program of rehabilitation including employment of a full-time president and staff to replace the former voluntary committee system of administration and revamping the

4. *The Wall Street Journal*, February 3, 1965.

procedure for executing orders on the floor.[5] The president selected was youthful, vigorous, and eager to obtain new listings;
he was hired from the SEC and had previously been a senior
attorney on the staff of the Special Study.

Of the 687 regional exchange member firms on June 30, 1962,
449 were sole members, 205 were members of both big New
York exchanges, while thirty-three were members of either one
or the other of these exchanges. The dual members, who are affiliated with the NYSE and a regional exchange, constitute the
most important source of business for the regional exchanges,
but the great majority of these dual members earn the bulk of
their income from NYSE commissions, from profits in over-the-
counter transactions, and from underwritings. Similarly, sole members as a group, who do a smaller share of the business on each
regional exchange than do the dual members, obtain most of
their income from activities in the over-the-counter market and
the sale of mutual funds. Nevertheless a larger number of sole
than dual members draw from the regional exchanges their principal source of income.[6]

With respect to methods of trading on the regional exchanges,
different procedures characterize the handling of transactions in
solely and dually traded stocks. The former are traded in much
the same manner as securities on the New York exchanges, with
the specialist also serving as odd-lot dealer, as in the case of the
American Stock Exchange. For dually traded stocks, the regional
exchanges are secondary markets and therefore the prices of their
transactions are tied to the NYSE tape. Within this framework,
there have been developed various trading practices that are dependent upon the willingness of the specialist to meet the competition of the principal exchanges, his capital resources, and his
imagination in arranging deals.[7] Odd-lots have constituted a more
substantial portion of total trading volume on the regional than on
the primary exchanges although very recently, transactions in big
lots have grown increasingly important as institutional volume
has gained. Odd-lot orders in dually traded stocks are executed

---

5. *The Wall Street Journal*, March 8, 1965.
6. Special Study of Securities Markets of the Securities and Exchange
Commission, op. cit., Part 2, Ch. VIII, pp. 928–931.
7. Ibid., pp. 931–935.

routinely at the round-lot price appearing on the NYSE tape, plus or minus the odd-lot differential, several minutes (approximating the time it takes for the tape to reflect an execution on the floor of the NYSE) after the receipt of the order.[8]

An important aspect of the trading volume on the regional exchanges is their dependence upon policies adopted by the NYSE. A dual member that does not have executing or clearing facilities in New York, may trade a dual stock on a regional exchange because he may keep a larger part of the commission by handling the transaction in this way. Or, a dual member that has such facilities in New York may still favor the regional exchanges either to keep the business local or to generate reciprocal commissions. This latter type of arrangement, as has been indicated, arises out of the withholding of preferential treatment by the NYSE for nonmember professionals. As a result, a sole member is encouraged to place an order on the principal exchanges via a member of that exchange with full facilities in order to provide the basis for the reciprocal commission business forwarded in return by the dual member for execution on the regional exchanges. Another NYSE policy that has contributed to activity in the regional markets is limiting cash give-ups to exchange members on NYSE transactions. Consequently, a mutual fund may direct a give-up to a sole member whom it wants to reward for selling its shares or for supplying it with statistical and other services. Even further, an institution might not only funnel portfolio business for execution by a regional sole member but also to be further shared with nonmembers, as in the cases of those exchanges, that permit this type of transaction.

The Third Market

Members of the NYSE are required to execute transactions in NYSE-listed stocks on the Exchange, except for dual members trading multiply listed stocks in a regional exchange, for stocks on a special exempt list which may be handled over-the-counter, or for cases in which special permission is obtained to go off board.

---

8. Ibid., pp. 935–936.

Similarly, members of other exchanges, under certain conditions, may execute away from the exchanges, orders in securities traded on the exchanges. Different from these transactions is the over-the-counter trading in issues listed on an exchange by nonmembers of that exchange; by far the most important segment of such trading is in NYSE-listed securities. Because of the unique characteristics and importance of this market—in form and structure like the over-the-counter market but bound to the price movements of the exchanges—it has been labelled the *third market*.

CHARACTERISTICS OF THE THIRD MARKET

It was estimated by the Special Study that since 1941 the third market in NYSE stocks alone has grown from $84 million, when it was about 1.6 per cent of the value of sales on the Exchange, to a level just under $2 billion in 1961, or 3.8 per cent of the value of Exchange sales, and the percentage may have risen since then. In specific instances, the ratio runs still higher, as indicated by the fact that of the full group of 270 NYSE common stocks for which off-board markets were made in 1961, forty-three had sales that amounted to more than 10 per cent of sales on the Exchange.[9] In the case of the American Stock Exchange, fifty-six stocks that traded regularly in the third market from March through August, 1964, accounted for 15 per cent of the total floor volume during the same period. The first SEC release covering a new reporting series on the third market, for the month of January, 1965, showed that out of the seventy-five common stocks most actively traded in the third market, eleven had a ratio of over-the-counter volume to NYSE volume of over 50 per cent.[10]

Both the firms participating in the third market and the type of stock traded have changed. Of the nine major and eleven minor firms which might be considered market-makers at the beginning of 1965, only a handful reported any activity in 1941. In the earlier period, the principal stocks traded were high quality, inactive issues with stress on preferreds and to a considerably lesser extent on the common stocks of financial, real estate, and utility

---

9. Ibid., pp. 873, 902.
10. Securities and Exchange Commission, Statistical Series, Release No. 2037, March 12, 1965. The third market volume includes odd lots as well as round lots.

groups. Today, the third market continues to be favored for the handling of preferred stocks, but the significance of these transactions has waned considerably. As in the earlier period, utility and railroad issues are still prominent but the major change has been the growing importance of industrial equities from established blue chips to comparatively less seasoned stocks. Among these industrial stocks are now included some of the most active Exchange issues representing companies of substantial size with wide stock distributions.[11]

The principal dollar volume of business in the third market is conducted by institutions who believe they can obtain a better price, reduce their cost, or execute the transaction in a shorter period of time. Among the institutions, the investment companies occupy a relatively small role in the third market since they apparently prefer to give their off-board business in NYSE securities to the regional exchanges where give-ups are possible. At the opposite extreme, there is a high proportion of odd-lot transactions in the third market, ordinarily through broker-dealers or commercial banks rather than directly with the market maker.

At the heart of the third market is the small group of market-makers that are actively engaged as principals in buying and selling exchange securities over the counter and that hold themselves out as making a market in these issues. The firms range from those of small size to substantial organizations, and the extent to which they depend upon their third market activity as a source of income also differs sharply. In April, 1965, Blyth & Company, one of the largest securities firms and formerly prominent in the third market, became a member of the NYSE. The market is largely "professional" in character since the market makers trade almost exclusively with institutions and with broker-dealers. Reflecting this characteristic, the firms that concentrate in this field provide few of the fringe services offered by the member firms, such as securities research, sales representatives, customers' rooms, and safekeeping of securities.

The price at which a round-lot transaction is executed in the

---

11. Special Study of Securities Markets of the Securities and Exchange Commission, op. cit., Part 2, Chapter IV, pp. 874–875. See also SEC, Statistical Series, Release No. 2037, March 12, 1965.

third market ordinarily falls within the range of the exchange price plus the commission. Within this boundary, substantial variations may occur, dependent upon such factors as the market-maker's inventory position, his judgment of the market, his desire to be competitive, and the size of the block being offered. Moreover, the market is one involving both considerable shopping as the broker-dealers or institutions seek the most favorable price among different market-makers, and substantial negotiation of terms with individual market-makers. Prices of odd-lots, on the other hand, ordinarily are established in a more mechanistic way by applying Exchange differentials to the last round-lot price on the NYSE (rather than to the next round-lot price following receipt of the order on the floor, as in the case of the NYSE).

Unlike his specialist prototype, the market-maker is free to make or discontinue a market in a particular stock at will, characteristically communicates directly with his institutional customers in executing transactions, and is not subject to the regulatory limitations or responsibilities of the specialist. On the other hand, the specialist, through his book and his focal role on the floor, plays a more direct role in the determination of prices than does the market-maker, who is tied to the levels established on the exchange floor. The market-makers also employ the exchanges in a small way to offset inventory positions, to execute transactions requested by customers, and to share in crosses in which they may have been invited to participate. Despite the growing importance of the third market, the great bulk of institutional trading in NYSE stocks takes place, of course, on the Exchange, and the third market often is used as a complementary means of executing block transactions.

REGULATING THE THIRD MARKET

The broker-dealer participants in the third market deal in listed securities and yet are not subject to either the self-regulatory or SEC restrictions that apply to member firms in the exchange markets. This differentiation has provoked the objections of officials of the organized exchanges, who have argued that the third market is inadequately regulated, that the public interests are not served by this dual standard, and that the third market erodes the liquidity of the organized exchanges.[12] Accordingly, representatives of the organized exchanges have urged the application of more comprehensive regulations to the third market, including registration of market-makers based upon such standards as minimum capital and examinations to determine competency; a requirement that market-makers meet trading standards established by the NASD to assist in making fair and orderly markets; demanding that market-makers obtain NASD approval before commencement or cessation of market-making activities in any stock; and extending surveillance procedures by the NASD and SEC to the third market to cover efficacy of performance, detection of manipulation, and conformance with short-selling rules.

While the Special Study provided more insights into the scope, operation, and role of the third market than had yet been available, it recognized that further investigation was necessary before a decision with respect to the extent of regulation could be reached. Toward this end, it recommended, among other things, that market-makers be identified and a continuous reporting system be instituted. In July, 1964, the SEC proposed Rule 17a–9, concerned with reporting requirements in the third market and, after obtaining the comments of interested parties, augmented its original proposal somewhat in the rule that finally was adopted in December, 1964. In general, provision is established for identifying firms making off-board markets in listed common stocks and for reporting summaries of over-the-counter trading in these stocks on the exchanges which had sales of securities in the most recent calendar year of over $20 million; on the basis of 1963 data this standard resulted in the exclusion of only the National, Salt Lake, San Francisco Mining, and Spokane exchanges. Also, the market-makers must file certain information on the individual stocks in which they had transactions, and other broker-dealers must file on certain transactions of $25,000 or more.

The SEC indicated that it plans periodically to conduct detailed transaction studies for the purpose of analyzing particular aspects of activity in the off-board market. It was intended that the data and the studies would provide the basis for an evaluation of the need for more detailed reporting and further regulation of

12. G. Keith Funston, Speech before the National Association of Investment Clubs, October 24, 1964.

the market. While the Special Study reached the general conclusion that the over-the-counter market for listed stocks had been beneficial to investors and in the public interest, it recognized that the extent of regulation that might be desirable would become clearer as more information was gathered about the third market.

The Fourth Market

For a number of years, large institutions and, occasionally, wealthy individuals have directly bought and sold securities with each other, thereby bypassing the use of a broker in either the exchange or over-the-counter market. Little notice was given to this practice until the publicity received by the third market, following publication of the Special Study, attracted some attention to it. Although little was known about these transactions, they did represent a different way of doing business and it became popular to refer to them as the fourth market.[13]

CHARACTERISTICS OF THE FOURTH MARKET

Increased interest and a title have not significantly thrust aside the veil of secrecy that tends to shroud trades occurring in this way. Institutions often are reluctant to reveal this information for fear of antagonizing brokers, receiving criticism on the terms arranged, or simply because they feel there is a stigma of impropriety about such transactions. On the other hand, the principal reason advanced for their use of the market is the expectation of obtaining a better price. Other factors mentioned are the commission savings, speed of execution, and the ability to diversify without registering. Although the Special Study observed that institutions may execute block transactions by direct arrangements, it did not investigate this area, because at that time such arrangements appeared to be relatively infrequent.[14]

13. Much of this information on the fourth market is based on research by Allan Young, lecturer at the Baruch School of the City College of the City University of New York and a doctoral student at the Graduate School of Business, Columbia University.

14. Special Study of Securities Markets of the Securities and Exchange Commission, op. cit., Part 2, Chapter VIII, p. 844.

In general, direct trades may be handled on a cash basis or through swapping one security for another. The latter type of transaction, which probably is most directly identified with the fourth market, may arise in various ways. Thus, each of two institutions, heavily concentrated in a single stock, may desire to diversify and therefore work out a direct exchange of one issue for the other. For example, the Ford Foundation, whose portfolio is dominated by the common stock of the Ford Motor Company, and the Rockefeller Foundation, with a portfolio predominantly in the common stock of the Standard Oil Company of New Jersey, have engaged in a number of direct swaps to lighten their single stock concentrations. In the same vein, the Louis W. and Maud Hill Family Foundation has exchanged shares in the Minnesota Mining & Manufacturing Company for stock of the Ford Motor Company, held by the Ford Foundation, and for that of the Standard Oil Company of New Jersey, held by the Rockefeller Foundation. Similarly, an industrial company, often acting for its pension fund, may exchange stock in which it has an important interest, for a heavily held issue of another institution. Or, as we have seen, it is not unusual for one investment company to be selling the stock that another is buying and in certain circumstances direct exchanges may be arranged. Then again, a bank engaged in trust activities may find that the varying objectives of different accounts make it possible to transfer a stock from one to another, or the managers of several mutual funds with differing objectives may be able at times to arrange direct shifts. In another type of transaction, an individual may exchange a portfolio of securities for the shares of a mutual fund, thereby saving commissions and possibly gaining tax benefits.

Rather than confining the notion to swaps, it seems more appropriate to employ the term *fourth market* to describe any direct transaction between institutions or individuals including those in which securities are exchanged for cash. It is not unusual, for example, for the pension fund of an industrial company to buy for cash a large block of stock held by another institution. In 1964, for example, the United States Steel Pension Fund bought 60,000 shares of Hawaiian Electric Company common stock from the Madison Fund, Inc., while during the first nine months of 1965, the Ford Motor Company purchased about one million shares of its stock from the Ford Foundation. In some instances, an investment company that specializes in control situations may find it expedient to engage in direct transactions because of the large number of shares involved relative to the total amount outstanding and because of the possibility of avoiding registration.

By stretching the notion a bit further to include a corporation and its stockholders as the two parties in the direct arrangements, a relatively common transaction may be blanketed within the fourth-market category. This involves the purchase by a corporation of its own stock through tenders for the purpose of reducing its capitalization or its subsequent reissuing of the stock to meet the requirements of stock options, employee stock-savings programs, or mergers and acquisitions. In this broader context, the fourth market simply is a catch-all term to describe all types of direct transactions between buyers and sellers that do not fall within the established channels of the organized exchanges, the traditional over-the-counter market, or the third market—all of which use an intermediary in some form to bring together buyers and sellers, who ordinarily remain anonymous to each other.

SIZE AND IMPLICATIONS

In view of the lack of organized data concerning the fourth market, it is not possible realistically to delineate its dimensions. All that can be done, at present, is to provide fragments of information that in some way reflect upon its size. Thus, individual transactions in this area are known to have been huge, such as the purchase by the Ford Motor Company of over one million shares of its own stock from the Ford Foundation in December, 1961, and the purchase by the Standard Oil Company of New Jersey of one million shares of its stock from the Rockefeller Foundation in the following year. The management of a major group of mutual funds has indicated that it uses the fourth market "a fair amount of the time," and a major commercial bank has referred to the execution in recent years of about one or two fourth-market transactions a month, with the over-all volume representing about 4 per cent of the dollar value and about 1 per cent of the number of its total transactions. These proportions appear high for the fourth market, and in other instances institutions have stated that they either do not participate at all or that they conduct only several such trades a year, amounting to no more than 1 per cent or even less of their total transactions.

As institutions continue to grow and the size of individual commitments increases and knowledge of the feasibility of direct transactions spreads, it is likely that the percentage of business done in this fashion will mount. Thus, among the questions asked of thirty-seven institutions of different size was their expectation regarding the dimensions of the fourth market. Fifteen indicated that they expected further growth, five were not sure, seven provided no relevant information and only ten did not foresee more growth. On the other hand, only four of the thirty-seven respondents thought that the fourth market could ever become a major part of their security transactions. Among the factors suggested that could lead to an increased use of the fourth market were

1. More dealings in large blocks
2. The need to move blocks quickly
3. Greater desire to retain their anonymity
4. Better knowledge of investment intentions of other institutions
5. Determination of a fair way to set prices
6. Thinner exchange markets

Also, should the Government ever restrict the percentage of the outstanding stock of a company that a foundation is permitted to hold, a substantial fillip probably would be given to the process of direct swaps among these institutions.

More information is available on the practice of corporations in buying their own shares of stock. It has been estimated that between 1953 and 1964, there were 355 different companies, out of 651 engaging in this practice, whose own purchases in any single year accounted for 5 per cent or more of total trading volume in their stock on the NYSE. In the aggregate, these active purchasers during the same ten-year period bought back some 103 million shares or over 15 per cent of the total trading in their companies' stock. Of the 103 million shares, some 8 million were acquired through tender offer, thereby short-circuiting to this extent the regular auction process.[15] Use of such tenders,

---

15. Leo A. Guthart, "More Companies Are Buying Back Their Stock," *Harvard Business Review,* March-April, 1965, pp. 50–53; Charles D. Ellis, "Repurchase Stock to Revitalize Equity," *Harvard Business Review,* July-August, 1965, p. 122.

it has been suggested, would be helpful in avoiding any charges of discrimination from shareholders who may feel that they do not receive equal treatment from a policy of open-market purchases. Should corporations actually learn to rely more upon the tender method, a considerable further diversion towards the fourth market could occur because of the extent to which stock-rebuying programs have been going on.

While the fourth market may not present any serious current threat to the organized exchanges, the basis seems present for an extension of direct transactions. In order to appraise the significance of such a development, the need exists to obtain better data concerning these activities. Only then would the SEC be in a position to determine if and to what extent some degree of regulation may be desirable to protect the investor. In any event, to the degree that the direct transactions put pressure upon the organized exchanges and broker-intermediaries to handle large blocks more efficiently and at the best possible prices, the forces of competition are effectively at work.

The Implications of Market Relationships

As the trading markets have evolved in the United States, there has been greater concentration on its individual elements than on the over-all design. The concern of each of the exchanges has been preempted by its own problems, while both the SEC and the NASD have devoted most of their efforts to current judicial and legislative affairs. Yet, any evaluation of the economic role of the trading markets must consider the different parts as an integrated system rather than as a group of relatively separate units.

A PATTERN OF SENSITIVITY

When lines of communication were weak, compartmentalization had some meaning, and the activities of one segment of the market could be largely insulated from the others. Indeed, even at the passage of the Securities Exchange Act, over-the-counter trading was regarded as a mystery, and the nature of its regulation was left to further study. Today the powerful glare of publicity has reduced the number of hidden corners in the securities markets, the different components of which have common participants and are closely intertwined by a complex network of telephone and direct wire facilities.

The interaction of the segments is seen in various ways. Prices of the same security in different markets do not vary from each other because of the activity of arbitragers whose influence is surer than a legal edict. To prevent the SEC's short-selling rule from destroying this influence on prices of arbitragers, an exemption is provided for sales of a security on a national securities exchange that are necessary to equalize its price with the level prevailing on the exchange where the principal market is created.[16]

The absence of block discounts on the NYSE has been an enabling factor in causing institutions to direct orders to regional exchanges to reward nonmembers for services rendered—a flow that might be impaired by the withdrawal of this restriction, with consequent repercussions on the regional exchanges, the nonmembers, and the institutions.

The refusal of the NYSE to provide better rates to nonmember professionals has led member firms to compete for this business through the grant of reciprocal orders to the regional members; should the NYSE change its policy, the pressure to return business to the regionals would be lifted and their volume of activity correspondingly reduced. Any tampering with the minimum commission schedule of the NYSE would have some consequences on the activity of the third market and the ability of small broker-dealers participating in different markets to remain in business. The extension of disclosure requirements to certain over-the-counter companies by the 1964 legislation not only induced a number of large companies to seek listings, with differing effects on the various markets, but also created the possibility of a challenge to the implications of self-regulation, as discussed below.

As a minor offshoot, but of some interest to show the degree of interconnection, another effect of the 1964 legislation was the withdrawal of one part of the SEC rule concerned with unlisted trading. Formerly, a security could have been admitted to un-

---

16. Securities and Exchange Commission, General Rules and Regulations under the Securities Exchange Act of 1964, Rule 10a–1(d)(6).

listed trading on an exchange if there was available reported information concerning it substantially equivalent to that required of listed securities. As a result of the 1964 legislation, such information was created for a large number of over-the-counter securities necessitating the elimination of this provision to prevent a wholesale increase in unlisted trading from this source.

This sensitivity of one part of the trading markets to modifications in another part highlights the importance of adopting a broad point of view towards the markets. This means that changes must be evaluated in the light of over-all market objectives. The propriety of permitting block discounts, for example, is related, at least in part, to a decision concerning the relative desirability of encouraging the third market or increasing the liquidity of the NYSE; the advisability of allowing nonmember commission-splitting might depend to a large extent upon one's attitude towards fostering the regional exchanges; the logic of a uniform minimum commission schedule may rest, to a significant degree, upon the importance to the industry of small as compared with big broker-dealer firms. Establishment of over-all market objectives, in turn, necessitates profounder studies than have yet been undertaken of the characteristics required to permit the market to fulfill its economic functions most effectively.

THE COSTS OF MARKET EFFICIENCY

Pending the completion of studies that permit an objective recitation of standards, certain generalities may be observed. To a large degree, the principles for obtaining disclosure and eliminating manipulation, as presently formulated, were introduced by the securities acts and are generally applicable to all the national exchanges and, now, to much of the over-the-counter market. To the extent that differences exist in this area, they are more in the direction of implementation and of surveillance procedures. On the other hand, the standards formulated to permit liquidity, the structural measures adopted to provide orderliness, and the costs of effectuating transactions are all established more directly at the instance of the individual market places, although they fall within the supervisory province of the SEC. Because of the sensitivity of market interrelationships, as one segment adjusts its activities in these respects, it may influence the position of another segment of the market to fulfill its role. In this give-and-take operation, the NYSE, because of its size and prestige, occupies a strategic position.

The gateway to trading in the organized markets is the requirements that are imposed upon issuers. As the recognized principal exchange, the NYSE can exert a major influence on the securities available for trading in the different markets. Low listing standards may admit to trading issuers whose securities could readily be handled in other markets and at the same time create extra burdens on the trading structure of the NYSE, which must maintain orderly and liquid markets. High standards will expand the roster of securities available to the other markets and ease the structural burden upon the NYSE but will cut down upon its size and importance. The latitude for making decisions in this respect is wide because no quantitative means have yet been devised to ascertain the listing standards necessary to provide orderly and liquid markets with a minimum reliance upon structural props. The basic test for this purpose is the floating supply of a stock, but the criteria of this type thus far imposed have been largely arbitrary. This is particularly true when it is realized, as has been explained previously, that some transactions on the floor of the Exchange may bypass the strict auction process.

The costs incurred by the investor are measured both by the price at which he obtains a stock and the commission or markup he pays. The exact level of execution depends in part upon the market in which the order is placed and the clearest differentiation in this respect at present is probably between the listed and third markets. An important reason for using the third market is, of course, the ability of an institution to obtain a better price (net cost to the institution) compared with the one forthcoming in the NYSE (exchange price plus commission). As orders flow to the third market, therefore, the investor is "protected" in the sense that he may obtain a more favorable price, but, at the same time, the diversion reduces activity on the NYSE. Accordingly, the price tag of possibly lessened liquidity in the exchange market must be measured against the benefit of lower costs. To the extent that the difference in pricing is caused by the greater flexibility available to the market-maker in the third market, compared with the specialist in the NYSE, the decision as to the regulatory changes that may be desirable, in turn, rests with the SEC.

As has been seen, the commission charge established by the NYSE has implications both to structure and level. Because of the structural impediments created, orders may follow a path designed to permit a broker-dealer to meet a business obligation but at the expense of the investor who obtains a less favorable price. A broker-dealer with its own trading department, for example, may direct an order to an over-the-counter dealer simply to satisfy a reciprocal "debt" even though its own trading department may be larger and more efficient. While raising the costs to the investors, these devious flows may benefit both the regional exchanges and nonmember broker-dealers. The issue, therefore, is whether the higher costs to the investor are justified in the light of the benefits accruing to these segments of the market, particularly since this strengthening may be directly advantageous to the investor.

The uniform commission schedule creates still another problem. While the over-all demand for securities is related to a combination of economic, social, and psychological factors, the portion of this over-all demand going to a particular brokerage firm depends upon the price it charges. When these prices are fixed by regulation, their variations are reflected in the differences in the services offered. With respect to the individual firms, the demand for securities is relatively elastic and a cut in prices, measured by the offer of more services, is likely to attract more business. This condition has been reflected in the variety of services offered by the member firms compared with the minimum services provided by the third market dealers who are in a position to compete on the basis of the commission or markup charged. To evaluate the justification of a uniform schedule that does not take into account service differentials, therefore, a determination must be made whether the higher costs incurred by investors for this reason and the hobbles placed on the competing ability of member firms are justified when measured against the conveniences of a uniform schedule. Moreover, if a structural change is permitted so that commission price may be related to service offered, the important question arises as to the basis for establishing this relationship.

Unable to compete on a price basis because of the minimum

commission schedule but provided with a profit differential that otherwise might not be available, large firms, particularly, have developed a variety of investment and other services that they furnish without charge. Customers that do not use these services, in effect, are compelled to pay for them thereby unwillingly contributing to their financing. As a result, the using customers may be able to obtain the services at a lower cost, to the extent that the charge is reflected in the commission rate, than would be the case had the rate been lowered and direct fees imposed. Thus, elimination of the minimum commission schedule might benefit one group of customers but might also result in a less widespread use of investment information.

Similarly, the minimum level of commission rates may provide a protecting umbrella to small broker-dealers, who can now compete with the giant firms that have risen in the industry on a price basis and whose customers are not interested in a wide range of services. Here, the balance may be between the higher costs paid by the investor because of the absence of certain scale-economies, measured against the possible advantages of a broader-based industry. In which direction the balance should be weighted depends upon the conclusions reached regarding the effect of the minimum commission schedule and upon the character of the industry considered most efficient for meeting its economic objectives.

THE IMPORTANCE OF COMPETITION

At one extreme, the question might be raised whether there is any need for more than one centralized market place for securities in the United States. As has been seen, dispersion was essential when means of communication were less advanced in order that local markets could service local financing needs. This viewpoint was expressed by the SEC in one of its few efforts to examine the exchange markets as a whole. In July, 1940, the NYSE announced its intention to enforce a constitutional provision subjecting to proceedings for suspension or expulsion any member of the NYSE acting as an odd-lot dealer or specialist on another exchange or otherwise publicly dealing outside the Exchange in securities dealt in on the Exchange. In analyzing this subject in a proceeding to ascertain the validity of this provision, the Commission determined that enforcement of the rule would have deleterious effects on the regional exchanges and therefore was undesirable because these markets were important to the economy of local regions. More specifically, the Commission stated:

> Local industry, as well as local investors, look to their local financial centers to afford, as they should, a capital market as well as a market in which outstanding securities may be traded under the safeguards which normally attend the functioning of an organized exchange. The regional exchanges have played, and should continue to play, an integral and an essential role in developing and serving industry, the financial community and the investing public within their regions. Therefore, the action of the New York Stock Exchange, even though apparently directed solely to its own members, materially affects inter-exchange competition in a manner harmful to local industry, the general public, and to individual investors.[17]

The ease of modern communications has largely undercut the importance of separate trading markets to local economies, and under present conditions the regional exchanges could not survive if they had to depend upon solely listed stocks.[18] Accordingly, the relative merits of one giant trading market area centralized in the New York area serving the country as compared with some degree of regionalization rest upon other grounds than serving the needs of local communities. Besides this latter justification, probably the strongest argument for maintaining the position of the regional exchanges, and for that matter of the third market, rests upon the competition they offer the NYSE.

In the United States, competition plays a major role in the formulation of business activity. As a matter of public policy, reliance is placed upon the economic rivalry of firms to encourage innovation, to obtain an effective allocation of resources, and to improve the efficiency of operations. Similarly, constraints imposed upon a firm by the competitive practices of rivals serve to

17. "Report to the Commission by the Trading and Exchange Division on the Problem of Multiple Trading on Securities Exchanges," November 22, 1940, as quoted in Securities and Exchange Commission, Seventh Annual Report, Fiscal Year Ended June 30, 1941, p. 134.

18. See, for example, an analysis by the Midwest Stock Exchange pointing to its limited number of new potential listings in the fourteen-state area considered by the Midwest to be its "vicinity." Special Study of Securities Markets of the Securities and Exchange Commission, op. cit., Part 2, Chapter VIII, p. 943.

protect the individual consumer from the danger of exploitation by a single dominant group.

This reliance upon competition does not mean, of course, that there are no imperfections in the system, because pure competition exists principally in the form an economist's theoretical model. More realistically, in most lines of activity, dominant organizations have risen that, by virtue of such advantages as size or control of technical processes, exert special influences on the business practices of the field in which they are engaged. When, in the eyes of the law, these influences reach the stage where they represent an undue restraint of trade, granted that the threshold of distinction is not easy to ascertain, antitrust action has been taken to eliminate the inhibiting frictions. Accordingly, despite the difficulty of describing acceptable conditions, competition remains the cornerstone upon which American business practices rests.

In addition to the allocation efficiency of the securities markets, the operating efficiency of their component institutions may be employed as a gauge of performance. To some extent, operating efficiency, in turn, may be inferred from the presence or absence of competition. While evidence of restrictive practices is not necessarily a proof of inefficiency, it at least suggests that competition cannot be relied on to insure efficient performance.[19] In the securities field, the overshadowing economic power of the NYSE endows that institution with considerable influence and certain of its requirements, as described below, have been the target of antitrust charges. Nevertheless, competition has not been eradicated and may take several forms.

Of importance is the price received by the investor. Generally, the level of price is established by the primary market, but the precise level of execution may vary with the outlet used. While conclusive data were not produced, the evidence uncovered by the Special Study suggested that outside competition had some influence on the exact prices obtained. For one thing, in response

---

19. James S. Duesenberry, "Criteria for Judging the Performance of Capital Markets," *Commission on Money and Credit Memorandum,* April 10, 1960, reprinted in Hsiu-Kwang Wu and Alan J. Zakon, "Elements of Investments, Selected Readings," New York, Holt, Rinehart and Winston, Inc., 1965, pp. 1–2.

to a questionnaire submitted to all members of the Midwest, Pacific Coast, Philadelphia-Baltimore-Washington, and Boston exchanges, a considerable number of dual members gave "better price available" as a major reason for executing transactions in dually traded stocks on the regional exchange. Then again, interviews with officials of the regional exchanges as well as papers in the files of the NYSE suggested that the competition of the regionals exerted pressure on the specialist to carry larger positions and to provide closer quotations.[20] With respect to the third market, it was found that competition of a similar sort was produced. The responses of institutions to a questionnaire confirmed the third market's keen competition in the pricing of transactions, particularly when large amounts are involved. At least one situation was uncovered in which the NYSE put pressure upon a specialist in a listed utility stock, showing substantial off-board trading, to narrow quotations and reduce variations between sales.[21]

Closely related to price is the commission paid. In this area, the minimum schedule of the NYSE has cast long shadows throughout the industry. The inviolability of the schedule has encouraged the growth of the third market, thereby providing nonmember professionals with access to listed stocks while at the same time charging their customers no more than the minimum commission schedule. The ability of institutions to deal in the third market on a net basis also has permitted costs to be shaved with consequent advantages to the investor. A possible influence of this competition, at least to some degree, is seen in the 1965 proposal by the NYSE to allow discounts on blocks of a designated minimum size. Since 1962, relative dollar volume on the regionals has tended to rise, at least in part because of the provisions enabling commission splitting with nonmembers. Despite this trend, the NYSE remained adamant in its refusal to grant any special concessions to nonmembers and, as mentioned previously, its committee investigating commissions had rejected any suggestions along these lines. In the fall of 1965, however, as the list of NYSE firms buying memberships on the regionals grew, it was reported that the committee was reconsidering the proposal, including the possibility of creating

20. Report of Special Study of Securities Markets of the Securities and Exchange Commission, op. cit., Part 2, Chapter VIII, p. 940.
21. Ibid., pp. 904–905.

a new category of associate members who would not own regular seats but could split fees with members.[22]

While the odd-lot differential is not a commission charge, it represents a cost of trading to the small investor. Although the big New York dealers largely control this cost, the potential influence of competition may be detected in their reluctance to change it without accompanying action by the regional exchanges. The idea for the 1951 increase in the differential, for example, arose with the two big New York dealers who found it expedient to work closely with the regional exchanges to bring about a comparable rise, because it was recognized that failure of any regional exchange to follow suit might result in the loss of odd-lot business to that exchange. Indeed, when Boston lagged behind the others in the introduction of the higher differential some rise in odd-lot transactions on that exchange was noticed during this period.

In the realm of operations, the regional exchanges have made some notable contributions. Of considerable importance was the introduction by the Midwest, followed by the Pacific Coast Exchange, of a centralized bookkeeping system which performs a large portion of the back-office work of its participating members, wherever they may be located, at substantial reduction of costs. By this means, individual brokerage firms not in a financial position to automate their operations could obtain such benefits. In August, 1965, the sixth year of rendering computer accounting, the Midwest Stock Exchange Service Corporation, the brokerage accounting subsidiary, expected to handle 13,000 trades a day by the end of the year, an increase of 50 per cent from the 1964 year-end level.[23] Although the NYSE sponsored a member-firm conference on joint bookkeeping operations in January, 1961, and has continued to study the problem, it was not until the summer of 1965 that it announced the formation of a new subsidiary, the Central Computer Accounting Corporation (CCAC), to provide a comprehensive accounting service, initially to subscribing member organizations and eventually to qualifying nonmembers as well. It was expected that the new back-office computer system would be in operation about the middle of 1966.

Other instances of structural innovations by the regionals are

---

22. *The Wall Street Journal*, September 13, 1965; September 22, 1965.
23. *The Wall Street Journal*, August 17, 1965.

the Philadelphia Exchange's establishment of the first stock clearing corporation in 1870, and the Midwest Exchange's adoption of the practices of admitting corporate members and clearing by mail. The Midwest also pioneered in the creation of local transfer offices thereby cutting time and mailing expenses and saving the New York State transfer tax for the benefit of Midwest residents.[24] The suggestion has been made in some quarters that the regional exchanges at least at one time may have excelled the principal exchanges in speed of reporting executions as well as in the reduction of mailing charges on securities and time required for investors to secure stock certificates.[25] On another front, market-makers in the third market have asserted their ability to provide speedier executions, by obviating the necessity of sending an order to the floor, and to provide more flexible arrangements with institutions by working directly with them.[26] Finally, the Pacific Coast Exchange provides trading facilities after the primary markets in New York are closed.

This enumeration of pressures applied by the regionals and the third market on the primary New York exchanges in the areas of pricing, costs, and procedure, has been set forth to indicate their ability to unloose legitimate forces of competition. It is not intended to signify that the New York exchanges have failed to exercise their leadership roles.

In a number of respects the American Stock Exchange has provided innovations that have directly influenced the action of the other exchanges. As interest in the securities markets spread westward following World War II, the American Exchange, for example, recognized the importance of the Western states to the securities markets by lengthening the trading day from 3:00 to 3:30 P.M. while, at the same time, abandoning the traditional half-day Saturday session. These steps were soon followed by the other exchanges. As the nation's largest market for foreign securities, the American Exchange helped to originate the American Depositary Receipt (ADR), to facilitate trading in foreign securities. Through this instrument a United States bank certifies that

---

24. Report of Special Study of Securities Markets of the Securities and Exchange Commission, op. cit., Part 2, Chapter VIII, pp. 946–947.
25. Ibid., p. 939.
26. Ibid., pp. 905–907.

a particular number of shares of a foreign company have been deposited with its overseas office. The American Exchange's category of associate memberships has provided a basis for pointing to the possibility of the NYSE reducing commission fees to non-member professionals. In cooperation with the Teleregister Corporation and its Telecenter in downtown New York, the American Exchange pioneered in introducing its Am-Quote system, the first automatic, electronic voice quotation service in the world.

As the nation's largest organized securities market, the NYSE, in its turn, has set the pace in many areas of operations, thereby raising significantly the standards of the business. It has not been considered necessary to recite these advances in detail because the point is being made that, despite its striking ascendancy, the NYSE is not immune to competitive pressure that serves as a catalytic agent to obtain improved practices in trading markets for the benefit of the investing public.

COMPETITION VS. REGULATION

Throughout the history of the securities acts the SEC, Congress, and the courts have evidenced interest in the preservation of competition. In its 1936 report recommending the continuation of unlisted trading under certain conditions, the Commission expressed its concern that the impairment of the regionals would accelerate concentration in New York City of control over the movement of capital.[27] In following this recommendation, the Senate Committee noted that an amendment providing for three categories of unlisted trading would create "a fair field of competition" in the securities field.[28] As part of its argument for opposing the NYSE multiple ban on trading in 1941, the Commission asserted the possibility that the debilitation of the regional exchanges might leave the investor with the alternative of trading only in the centralized market located in New York or in the over-the-counter market.[29] Later, in the Silver case, where the Supreme Court decided that the NYSE was liable to Silver under the Sherman Act for causing its members to discontinue their wire connections with

---

27. Ibid., pp. 918–919.
28. S. Rept. 1738, 74th Cong., 2d sess., p. 3 (1936).
29. Securities and Exchange Commission, Annual Report for the Fiscal Year Ended June 30, 1944, pp. 283–284.

him, the Court stressed the importance of Commission review, because otherwise there was nothing in the regulatory scheme to prevent an exchange from applying its rules so as "to do injury to competition."[30] This concern with preserving competition in the securities field and, conversely, discouraging the possibility that exchange rules may prove anticompetitive appears repeatedly, almost as a refrain, in the Court's decision.

While competition clearly affords benefits, its attainment may require a price—this time of diminished liquidity and depth in the primary markets. To provide competition means that securities listed in the major exchanges may be executed in other markets thereby affording the participants a choice of alternative trading outlets. So long as this threat exists, pressure is brought upon the primary markets to provide services that will prevent the departure. At the same time, however, to the extent the choice actually is exercised in favor of the other outlets, a reduction occurs in the concentration of trading in the primary markets.

Various factors provide a countervailing influence to the significance of the reduction-of-depth argument. The first is that it is difficult to gauge to what extent this diminution actually occurs. At least a portion of the transactions in NYSE stocks handled by third market firms might not have occurred if they did not have such access to listed stocks, and these firms eventually direct some offsetting business to the floor of the Exchange. Similarly, sole members at the regional exchanges may obtain orders in listed stocks for execution in the NYSE that would not otherwise be forthcoming, thereby bringing business to the NYSE only because of the expectation of some return flow. Also, many of the off-board trades represent the orders of institutions that are executed away from the NYSE simply because of the belief that the facilities of the Exchange could not fully absorb the transaction. In this way, such trades are not much different from the relatively popular secondary distributions of the NYSE, which are also executed off the floor. By diverting a marginal excess of large blocks from the Exchange, the pressure on prices could be alleviated, with consequent benefits to continuity and orderliness. Finally, to the extent that orders flowing from the NYSE might otherwise

30. *Silver* v. *New York Stock Exchange,* 337 U.S. at 358 (1963).

have been completed on the floor by a form of negotiated trans-action, as explained previously, their elimination might have little effect on the basic auction market.

Another consideration is that increased competition alleviates the possibility that the major exchanges will be subject to monop-olistic charges. Competition is a powerful offset to the antitrust threat. To the extent that the public interest is not protected by the forces of competition, the gap must be filled by regulation, if legal action against the various restrictive phases of the business is to be avoided. As has been indicated, anticompetitive measures, such as uniform price schedules, have thus far been condoned primarily on the ground that the investor is accorded sufficient pro-tection through the review exercised by a Governmental agency, in this case, the SEC. In effect, therefore, two opposing alternatives are possible in the securities field, on the one hand, a monolithic structure in which competition is minimized and regulation maxi-mized and, on the other, a structure that provides its legal and economic restraints through competing markets. In between these extremes is the large middle ground, embodying the attempt to create an administered monopoly in which an effective balance is struck between regulation and competition.

THE ANTITRUST THREAT

In the securities field, underlying the principle of self-regula-tion, augmented by suitable doses of competition, is the real threat that if this principle is not suitably observed, the present regulatory pattern could be seriously upset by antitrust action. In the spring of 1965, this threat had taken tangible forms.

Previous to that time, in 1963, the Thill Securities Corporation, a nonmember securities dealer in Elm Grove, Wisconsin, had brought a private antitrust suit in the Federal district court that challenged the right of the NYSE to establish minimum commis-sion rates applicable to all members without permitting them to provide discounts to any outsiders. Following the filing of this suit, it was felt in some quarters that pressure might be exerted on the NYSE to effect a compromise and allow commission-splitting with nonmembers thereby permitting withdrawal of the action.[31] In March, 1965, however, a suit was filed in a Federal

_____

31. *The New York Times,* February 7, 1965.

district court in Chicago on another front. In this case, Harold Z. Kaplan, a stockholder of five investment companies, brought action on behalf of himself, all other stockholders, and the investment companies. The suit charged the NYSE and four major member firms with violating the antitrust laws by setting minimum commission rates on stock purchases. In this suit, it was contended that the dependent funds and the investing public in general "stand to save at least $7 million a year on New York Stock Exchange transactions for each 1 per cent reduction in commission rates."[32] If these suits go to the Supreme Court and are upheld, the result would open the commission business to price competition.

Other legal suits were also possible. Action challenging the right of the NYSE to fix minimum commissions might have followed in the wake of adoption of the proposal to hike NYSE commission charges and to impose a service charge on customers who receive special service. The threat of testing the Exchange's authority in the area of commissions had been raised following the 1958 increase. If the 1965 proposal had been placed into effect, some securities lawyers felt that a court test might have had more chance of success because the planned service charge would have applied to over-the-counter stocks held by member firms, and the right of the Exchange to impose a fee involving securities other than its own was questioned.[33]

Another potential suit would question the validity of Exchange Rule 394, which prohibits member firms from trading listed stocks in the over-the-counter market. The significance of this rule was pushed into the limelight when the Chase Manhattan Bank, in August, 1964, set in motion the procedures to list its stock on the New York Stock Exchange; this move was prompted by the extension of various regulatory requirements to the over-the-counter stocks of large companies by the Securities Acts Amendments of 1964 and by the bank's desire to obtain a broader market for its shares. The Chase shares were actually listed in March, 1965, and represented the first bank stock to be traded on the NYSE since 1954, when the Corn Exchange Bank & Trust Company left the list through merger. It was believed that listing of the Chase shares would be an incentive to other banks to follow

---

32. *The New York Times,* March 25, 1965.
33. *The New York Times,* February 19, 1965.

suit and, if this trend materialized, member firms would be barred
from trading with the nonmember broker-dealers, who formerly
made markets in these issues. To prevent such an eventuality,
a leading bank dealer attempted, apparently with no success, to
persuade the NYSE to exempt bank shares from Rule 394; and
the possibility was raised that he might bring antitrust action on
the ground that the rule unduly restricted trade. He has not taken
any such action, possibly in part because the SEC, at about the
time the Chase stock was listed, made known its intention to investigate Rule 394 of the NYSE and similar rules of other national
securities exchanges. Nevertheless, the dealer continued to raise
questions regarding the implications of the antitrust laws to the
operations of the NYSE, focusing particularly on the application
of Rule 394 to the listing of the stock of the Chase Manhattan
Bank. He argued that the rule injured competition by reducing
the number of market-makers in the stock and barring over-the-
counter dealers and member traders from access with each other.[34]

In February, 1965, the Pacific Coast Stock Exchange, after
a tense period of uncertainty, approved the membership application of the Kansas City Securities Corporation, a newly formed
brokerage subsidiary of Waddell & Reed, Inc., investment manager for United Funds, Inc., the nation's fourth largest mutual
fund organization. Waddell & Reed indicated that it hoped to
lower the cost of doing business through this procedure by cutting the commission charges it pays on the solely and dually listed
stocks of the Pacific Coast Exchange; the Company did not seek
a seat on the NYSE because it is publicly owned, a type of organization that is barred by Exchange rules from obtaining membership. Following this action, a further period of uncertainty
occurred as the giant mutual fund complex, headed by Investors
Diversified, Inc., indicated its interest in listing on the Pacific
Coast Exchange. Eventually, in the summer of 1965, the Pacific
Coast Exchange rescinded the ban on publicly held members and
passed a rule permitting concerns other than specialists or floor

---

34. M. A. Schapiro & Co., Inc., *Bank Stock Quarterly,* "To List or Not
to List," June, 1964, pp. 19–20; Part II, September, 1964, pp. 15–19; Part
III, December, 1964, pp. 17–23; "The SEC and Rule 394," March, 1965,
pp. 14–16; "The Public Investor, The Chase Manhattan Bank, and Rule
394," September, 1965, pp. 6–8.

brokers to be eligible for membership if they and their affiliates are primarily engaged in transacting business directly with the public in the purchase and sale of securities through their own sales representatives. These provisions opened the door to membership to Investors Diversified Services; and a subsidiary, IDS Securities Corporation, purchased a seat on the Pacific Coast Exchange. As a result, any danger of a suit by IDS was eliminated, but should the Pacific Coast policies be construed as discriminatory between institutions, or should other exchanges adopt what is interpreted as discriminatory policies, the possibility exists that antitrust charges will be raised.

The attention of the antitrust division of the Department of Justice had been brought to the practices and policies of the NYSE as a result of the discussion in the report of the Special Study of Securities Markets of the regulatory and competitive aspects of the business. This interest was heightened by the rash of private antitrust suits and threats of suits that subsequently made an appearance. As a result, in the spring of 1965, the antitrust division began its own investigation of the NYSE and other trading markets. It was reported that the division was studying particularly the effects on competition resulting from

1. The NYSE minimum commission schedule.

2. NYSE rules forbidding members from trading most listed stocks in the over-the-counter market.

3. NYSE rules preventing member firms from splitting commissions with nonmembers on business brought to the Exchange by the nonmembers.

4. Allegedly restrictive policies pertaining to membership admission.[35]

The next gambit in the current game to establish more clearly the legal framework within which the NYSE may operate was in the form of a flurry of correspondence between certain members of Congress and Manuel F. Cohen, Chairman of the SEC. On April 29, 1965, Senator A. Willis Robertson, Chairman of the Committee on Banking and Currency, wrote a letter to Cohen inquiring whether or not the Commission had found any problems involving the relationship of the antitrust laws to the securities

---

35. *The Wall Street Journal,* March 26, 1965.

markets that required new legislation or amendments to existing legislation. In response to this inquiry, Cohen wrote a long letter on July 30, in which he pointed out that while the Supreme Court had not provided any final answer in the Silver case regarding the relationship between the Securities Exchange Act and the antitrust laws, it did indicate that outside review was necessary to assure that self-regulatory practices were not inimical to the public interest, and that in the absence of Commission review, the antitrust court was the appropriate forum. Cohen then advanced the Commission's strong view that it was the appropriate agency to achieve a reasonable accommodation between the policies of the securities and the antitrust laws. He then concluded:

> In order to insure that there is adequate Commission review of exchange actions, we believe that specific gaps in the rulemaking, enforcement, and disciplinary areas of exchange activity should be filled by some form of review power and, to that end, we have initiated discussions with the principal exchanges looking toward legislation to be submitted to your committee. The Commission's exercise of such review power would, in turn, be subject to judicial review under Section 25 of the Exchange Act, and consequently, any failure upon the part of the Commission to give proper weight to antitrust considerations could be corrected in that way. It might, therefore, be advisable to provide antitrust immunity in areas subject to this review.[36]

If Cohen's letter was a trial balloon to test the reaction to possible legislation that would provide the exchanges with "antitrust immunity in areas subject to this review," he received a swift and unequivocal answer from at least two sources. On August 17, 1965, Representative Emanuel Celler, Chairman of the House Committee on the Judiciary and of its Antitrust Subcommittee, expressed his views in a letter to Cohen, that "the course of action you are suggesting is contrary to the traditional policies that have been applied by the Government in its supervision of securities markets, and, if adopted, would undermine the basic objective of the Exchange Act to protect investors by prohibiting fraudulent, deceptive, or manipulative practices and to regulate the operation of securities markets in the interest of making them fair, honest and orderly. . . . I shall oppose strongly any legislation that seeks to grant im-

---

36. Congressional Record—Senate, August 2, 1965, p. 18312.

munity from the antitrust laws to the activities of stock exchanges."
On September 2, Senator Philip A. Hart, Chairman of the Senate
antitrust and monopoly investigating subcommittee, echoed these
sentiments in a letter to Cohen, in which he stated, "I would feel
it most regrettable if the Commission were to propose legislation
that would immunize stock exchanges from the unqualified application of established antitrust policies."

The exchange of correspondence continued into the next
month when Cohen forwarded letters to Representative Celler
and Senator Hart seeking to allay their concern by explaining
that the SEC would not seek to change antitrust barriers in "such
traditional areas as mergers, interlocking relationships of stock
exchange members or concentration of economic power." Cohen
explained, however, that in order for the exchanges to carry out
the self-regulating activities imposed by Federal law they and
their members had to act in concert under certain conditions
which raised problems under the antitrust laws. He cited the Silver
case, in which the court implied that, if asked, it would recognize the existence of immunity in those areas of exchange operation that under the law would be specifically subject to SEC
review. In effect, Cohen indicated that he desired for the exchanges the same type of exemptions granted by the 1938 amendments to the securities laws covering the NASD. In that legislation,
Congress granted the SEC review power over NASD actions and
direct authority over NASD rules. Within these safeguards, he
noted, the NASD under the 1938 law was exempted from antitrust laws for actions taken in conformity with the Securities Exchange Act.[37]

At the outset of 1966, it was impossible to determine how far
down the antitrust route any of these actions would be followed.
The Silver case had already demonstrated that the NYSE had no
blanket immunity against an antitrust attack even though such
immunity might apply to actions specifically subject to SEC review. To clarify the status of the stock exchanges, the Commission
was working on new legislation apparently designed to give it
enlarged supervisory authority, but the expressed attitude of two
important Congressional figures suggested that the scope of any

---

37. *The Wall Street Journal,* October 12, 1965.

legislation designed to grant antitrust exemption would be severely limited. To keep the securities business outside the pale of monopolistic charges, therefore, would appear to require not only the rigorous pursuit of its regulatory responsibilities by the SEC, but also a business structure that fostered competition among the markets. Within a strengthened supervisory-competitive framework, it would appear possible for the principle of self-regulation to continue to function effectively.

The Image that Emerges

Experience has taught us several things about the securities business that cannot be overlooked despite its freshened current image. Among the avowed objectives of the NYSE when established in 1792 were the setting up of minimum commission rates and the creation of a preference for members of the Exchange in their dealings with other members. This ability to restrain trade has endowed the Exchange with considerable authority and has permitted it, pacing the rise of New York as the nation's money center, to gain its present ascendancy over the securities business.

The early growth of the NYSE occurred largely in a private-club atmosphere, where the interests of the members took precedence over those of the public. As a result, prices often were divorced from values, considerable investor losses were incurred, and it became increasingly difficult for the markets effectively to perform their functions, even though their role in the economy became more important. In the face of the vital public aspects of the securities markets, Federal control was considered necessary; the form finally selected was self-regulation with the power of the Government held in reserve. In this relationship, there was no intention of providing for a regulatory structure, such as exists in the public utility field, where antitrust immunity follows the grant of exclusive franchises, restraints on entry into the field, and Government regulation of price. It was always recognized, however, that self-regulation involved some degree of impairment of competition and that public control would insure that the kinds and extent of impairment would be no greater than required by the exigencies of regulation.[38] To eliminate uncertainties along these lines, it appears reasonable for the SEC, as it apparently has in mind, to identify those areas where free rein may be given to the role of self-regulation without apprehension of legal reprisals. In these areas, the review power of the Commission would be the proxy for competition. If antitrust immunity is to have any meaning under these conditions, the Commission would have to become a vigilant watchdog, holding its reserve power in check but ready to act if necessary. So long as these areas of liberation from antitrust action are limited, the role of the Commission, although necessarily extended, can remain circumscribed. Any overly comprehensive extension of antitrust immunity, however, might so enlarge the scope of the Commission's responsibilities as to throttle the efficacy of self-regulation. The balance between properly freeing the exchanges from one type of legal liability without excessively imposing another type of legal restraint is a delicate one.

It would appear desirable, however, that immunity should flow as much as possible from the operations of the markets rather than from any defined legal edict. Should legislative enactments grant the exchanges complete freedom from private and Government antitrust suits, the pressure to foster competition as a balancing force in the securities markets would be diminished. With competitive restraints pushed into the background, there would be more freedom for the exchanges unilaterally to adopt measures restricting the actions of members or catering to certain groups of members in a manner antithetical to the best interests of investors. Regardless of how well-meaning administrative bodies may be, the possibility of power cliques obtaining favored treatment would be augmented. The only outside check then would be the supervising authority of the SEC, whose reviewing power over exchanges would presumably be greatly increased. It is highly questionable if the Commission is in a position to assume such responsibility, and if it were, whether its implementation would require such close checks of the exchanges as to destroy the flexibility and freedom for action that make self-regulation peculiarly applicable to the securities markets, where speed of

38. Special Study of Securities Markets of the Securities and Exchange Commission, op. cit., Part 4, Chapter XII, pp. 501–504.

action sets a high premium upon on-the-spot decisions. The dominance of the NYSE does not mean, as has been indicated, that competition has been obliterated but rather that it has been so modified that the constant vigilance of the SEC is necessary to serve as a balancing power—but only to the extent that the securities business does not generate its own checks and balances.

Self-regulation, therefore, has meaning as an effective governing mechanism only when it operates within a framework of competitive restraints augmented by SEC action. In the light of the preceding analysis, this means at least three important things. First, in its supervision of the industry, the SEC cannot relax its responsibilities to evaluate the proposals and actions of the self-regulating agencies; and, when considered desirable, it must require the introduction of measures that are believed essential for the public interest and the protection of investors. Second, the self-regulating agencies must continue to eliminate whatever private-club vestiges remain in their operations by broadening the administrative role played by members who deal with the public, by continuing to adapt their operating procedures to serve the changing needs of the business, and by keeping an alert eye on the means of elevating the "professional" as opposed to the "trade" aspects of the business. Thirdly, both the SEC and the self-regulatory agencies must constantly bear in mind the economic role that the securities field plays in the economy, must define the objectives of the business within the framework of these functions, and must sponsor studies that provide a better understanding of this role and pave the way for measures to strengthen the contributions of the securities markets to the nation's economy.

In erecting the principles of self-regulation on the foundation of competition, encouragement of different markets appears desirable to the extent that they do not erode the effectiveness of the primary exchanges. Some forces in the direction of strengthening competition already have been set in motion. In the face of special plans introduced by the NYSE, the third market has shown considerable viability. The extension of disclosure requirements to the over-the-counter market may stimulate further interest in the desirability of regional listings. The action of the Pacific Coast Stock Exchange in approving the membership of the subsidiaries of Waddell & Reed and Investors Diversified Services will direct more business to that exchange from the transactions of the huge mutual fund groups. Thus, in commenting on the approval, the executive vice-president of Waddell & Reed's brokerage subsidiary stated: "We feel our membership will significantly strengthen the Pacific Coast Exchange and thereby represent a step towards increased competition between exchanges. This competition can benefit the investing public by creating keener and better markets."[39]

It is still too early to assess the full implications of the Pacific Coast's new open-door policy but developments shortly after tended to strengthen its position. A number of NYSE concerns, several of them affiliated with large mutual funds, bought memberships on the Pacific Coast Exchange as well as on several of the other regional exchanges, particularly Detroit. To meet increasing demand for membership, the Cincinnati Stock Exchange, in the fall of 1965, voted a 3-for-1 split of its members, lifting the potential roster to thirty-six members. Purchase of regional memberships by the broker-managers of investment companies, apparently in response to the Waddell & Reed and Investors Diversified Services action, permitted the brokerage concerns to execute the orders of their affiliate firms without the necessity of giving up a portion of their commissions.

The non-affiliated NYSE firms presumably also hoped to use their regional listings to provide their institutional customers with the benefits of broader commission-splitting arrangements. Thus, for some time the Pacific Coast Exchange has permitted its members to give up to 25 per cent of commissions to associate member firms, a status which may be purchased for a modest fee. The Detroit and Cincinnati exchanges have allowed member firms to give up as much as 40 per cent to nonmember broker-dealers that are members of the NASD. Joining the parade, the Boston Stock Exchange, seeking to rebuild its business, amended its rules in the fall of 1965 to permit exchange members to share up to 40 per cent of the full brokerage commission with any other securities firm that is a member of the NASD; the Boston Exchange retained its 50 per cent limit for sharing with members. Shortly after the move by the Boston Exchange, the Philadelphia-Baltimore-

---

39. *The New York Times,* February 19, 1965.

Washington Stock Exchange announced an amendment to its constitution permitting exchange members to share 25 per cent of the commission charge with nonmembers belonging to the NASD. Pointing to the substantial increase in large transactions that had occurred, the Philadelphia-Baltimore-Washington Exchange indicated that its amendment was "aimed at further stimulation of the execution of large block orders on the exchange by mutual funds."[40]

These provisions, as has been explained, enable an institution that has an order consummated through a regional exchange to direct the executing broker to share a portion of the commission with nonmembers that have rendered services to the institution. Expanded interest in the regionals tended to direct more business to them and, in the first eight months of 1965, their percentage of money value of shares sold on all registered exchanges rose to 8.7 per cent, compared to 8.0 per cent in 1964 and 7.3 per cent in 1963.

Despite these trends, special action to facilitate the growth of competing markets may be necessary. Towards this end, the Special Study suggested the possibility of applying distinctions to the regulations applicable to different markets, as it is permitted by the Securities Exchange Act. For example, it mentioned specifically, without necessarily approving, a proposal by the Midwest and Pacific Coast Exchanges to facilitate, on a principal basis, the distribution of solely listed stocks.[41] Similarly, the SEC is confronted with the problem of determining to what extent, if any, there is justification for applying different rules to the organized exchanges and to the trading in the third market.

While such regulatory differences may be desirable, each market segment in the long run must be of sufficient size and stature to handle the increasingly complex demands placed upon its services. In order to provide for bigger and more competitive regional markets, further mergers therefore may be desirable. Perhaps the needs of the country could be better served by having three major market areas—on the East Coast, in the Midwest, and on the

---

40. *The Wall Street Journal,* August 11, 1965; August 13, 1965; September 2, 1965; September 22, 1965; October 28, 1965; *The New York Times,* October 24, 1965; November 3, 1965.

41. Special Study of Securities Markets of the Securities and Exchange Commission, op. cit., Part 2, Chapter VIII, pp. 942–946.

Pacific Coast. In such a context, the surviving exchanges would be the New York and American Stock Exchanges, the Midwest Stock Exchange, and the Pacific Coast Stock Exchange. The extent to which such a development may be desirable or is likely to occur depends to a large degree on how successful the regional exchanges are in their current efforts to raise the effectiveness of their operations. Over-the-counter trading would remain a residual market but, as automation is carried to this area, it may assume increasingly the operating characteristics of the organized market places. The eventual role of the present third market in the system would simply depend upon its competitive ability to survive the extending influence of the organized markets. Through appropriate differences in listing standards, the roles of the different exchanges in meeting the trading requirements of various types of issuers could be satisfied with beneficial effects both to the economy and the competitive aspects of the markets.

The concept of interrelated trading markets, broadly partitioned into three organized exchanges and an over-the-counter segment of changing design, may not be the best answer to the question of providing for an appropriate degree of competition within the framework of the principles of self-regulation. It does suggest, however, the need to visualize the nation's trading markets as an entity and to develop studies in sufficient depth and scope to produce the most effective answers. Such studies and the required action stemming from them are necessary precursors to insure that the securities markets make their optimal contribution to the nation's economy. These studies would constitute a long-range planning program in which the lawyer and economist function as a team. Towards this end, it is important that the SEC and the self-regulating agencies follow the policy of considering specifically the economic implications of all major rules and regulations that may be adopted in carrying out the program.

Bibliography

Altman, Oscar L., "The Integration of European Capital Markets," *The Journal of Finance* (May 1965), pp. 209–221.

Andrews, Victor L., "Pension Funds in the Securities Markets," *Harvard Business Review*, (November-December 1959), pp. 90–102.

Axelrod, Leonard I., "Over-the-Counter Markets: Organization and Problems," *Financial Analysts Journal*, (November-December 1962), pp. 71–73.

Ball, Richard E., ed., *Readings in Investments*, Part IV, "Investment Policy and the Institutional Investor," (Boston: Allyn and Bacon, Inc.), 1965.

Baum, Daniel J. and Ned B. Stiles, *The Silent Partners—Institutional Investors and Corporate Control*, (Syracuse: Syracuse University Press), 1965.

Baumol, William J., *Stock Market and Economic Efficiency*, (New York: Fordham University Press), 1965.

Berman, Alfred, "Regulation of Unlisted Securities, Has Time Come to End the Double Standard?," *Financial Analysts Journal*, (July-August 1961), pp. 45–54.

Bernstein, Marver, H., *Regulating Business by Independent Commission*, (Princeton: Princeton University Press), 1955.

Black, Hillel, *The Watchdogs of Wall Street*, (New York: William Morrow and Company), 1962.

Bogen, Jules I. and Herman E. Krooss, *Security Credit, Its Economic Role and Regulation*, (Englewood Cliffs: Prentice-Hall, Inc.) 1960.

Bratten, Herbert, "Is the CD a Deposit or a Loan?," *Banking*, (March 1964), pp. 46–47.

Brimmer, Andrew F., *Life Insurance Companies in the Capital Markets*, (East Lansing: Michigan State University), 1962.

Brown, E. E., and Douglas Vickers, "Mutual Funds Portfolio Activity, Performance, and Market Impact," *Journal of Finance*, (May 1963), pp. 377–391.

Cary, William L., "A Review of the Work of the Securities and Exchange Commission," *The Record of the Association of the Bar of the City of New York*, (November 1964).

Cary, William L., "Administrative Agencies and the Securities and Exchange Commission," *Law and Contemporary Problems*, (June 1964), pp. 653–662.

Cohen, Manuel F. and Joel J. Rabin, "Broker-Dealer Selling Practice Standards: The Importance of Administrative Adjudication in their Development," *Law and Contemporary Problems*, (June 1964), pp. 694–710.

Cooke, Gilbert W., *The Stock Markets*, (New York: Simmons-Boardman Publishing Corporation), 1964.

Cootner, Paul H., ed., *The Random Character of Stock Market Prices*, (Cambridge: The M.I.T. Press), 1964.

Davis, Shelby Cullom, "How Fire and Casualty Companies Invest," *Financial Analysts Journal*, (November-December 1961), pp. 19–24.

de Bedts, Ralph F., *The New Deal's SEC: The Formative Years*, (New York: Columbia University Press), 1964.

Dougall, Herbert E., *Capital Markets and Institutions*, (Englewood Cliffs: Prentice-Hall, Inc.), 1965.

Duesenberry, James S., "Criteria for Judging the Performance of Capital Markets," in Wu, Hsiu-Kwang, and Alan J. Zakon, *Elements of Investments, Selected Readings*, (New York: Holt, Rinehart and Winston, Inc., 1965), pp. 1–9.

Eiteman, Wilford J. and David K. Eiteman, "Leading World Stock Exchanges," *Michigan International Business Studies, Number 2*, Ann Arbor, 1964.

Ellis, Charles D., "Repurchase Stock to Revitalize Equity," *Harvard Business Review*, (July-August 1965), pp. 119–128.

Fainsod, Merle, Lincoln Gordon and Joseph C. Palamountain, Jr., *Government and the American Economy*, 3rd edition, (New York: W. W. Norton and Co.), 1959, Chapter 14.

Fama, Eugene F., "Random Walks in Stock Market Prices," *Selected Papers No. 16*, Graduate School of Business, University of Chicago, 1965.

Federal Reserve Bank of Chicago, "Bankers' Acceptance Used More Widely," *Business Conditions*, (May 1965), pp. 9–16.

Federal Reserve Bank of Chicago, "Capital Markets—United States and Europe" *Business Conditions*, (September 1964), pp. 9–16.

Federal Reserve Bank of Cleveland, "Trading in Federal Funds," *Monthly Business Review*, (October 1961).

Federal Reserve Bank of New York, "Certificate of Deposits," *Monthly Review*, (June 1963), pp. 82–87.

Ferber, Robert, "Short-Run Effects of Stock Market Services on Stock Prices," *Journal of Finance*, (March, 1958), pp. 80–95.

Friend, Irwin, G., Wright Hoffman, and Willis, J. Winn, *The Over-the-Counter Securities Markets*, (New York: McGraw Hill Book Company), 1958.

Friend, Irwin and Edward F. Herman, "The SEC Through a Glass Darkly," *Journal of Business of The University of Chicago*, (October 1964), pp. 382–403.

Friend, Irwin and Douglas Vickers, "Portfolio Selection and Investment Performance," *The Journal of Finance*, (September 1965), pp. 391–415.

Fuller, John G., *The Money Changers*, (New York: The Dial Press), 1962.

Galbraith, John Kenneth, *The Great Crash*, (Boston: Houghton Mifflin Company), 1955.

Gies, Thomas G., "Portfolio Regulations of Selected Financial Intermediaries: Some Proposals for Change," *The Journal of Finance*, (May 1962), pp. 302–310.

Goldsmith, Raymond William, *Financial Intermediaries in the American Economy since 1900*, (Princeton: Princeton University Press), 1958.

Goldsmith, Raymond William, *The Flow of Capital Funds in the Postwar Economy*, (Princeton: Princeton University Press), 1965.

Guthart, Leo A., "More Companies are Buying Back Their Stock," *Harvard Business Review*, (March-April 1965), pp. 40–53.

Guthmann, Harry G., "The Jenkins Report—English Corporation Law Scrutinized for Reform," in Lerner, Eugenè M., *Readings in Financial Analysis and Investment Management*, (Homewood, Illinois: Richard D. Irwin, Inc., 1963), pp. 193–200.

Hagemann, H. F., "Money Market Forces," *Financial Analysts Journal*, (August-September 1960), pp. 81–84.

Hart, Orson H., "Life Insurance Companies and the Equity Capital Markets," *The Journal of Finance*, (May 1965), pp. 358–367.

Heller, Harry, "Integration of the Dissemination of Information Under the Securities Act of 1933 and the Securities Act of 1934," *Law and Contemporary Problems*, (June 1964), pp. 749–776.

Henshaw, Richard C., Jr., Alden C. Olson, and John L. O'Donnell,

"The Case for Public Regulation of the Securities Markets," *Business Topics*, (Autumn 1964), pp. 69–77.

James, Ralph and Estelle, "Disputed Role of the Stock Exchange Specialists," *Harvard Business Review*, (May-June 1962), pp. 133–146.

Jaretzki, Alfred, Jr., "Duties and Responsibilities of Directors of Mutual Funds," *Law and Contemporary Problems*, (June 1964), pp. 777–794.

Jennings, Richard W., "The New York Stock Exchange and the Commission Rate Struggle," *The Business Lawyer*, (November 1965), pp. 159–183.

Jennings, Richard W., "Self-Regulation in the Securities Industry: The Role of the Securities and Exchange Commission," *Law and Contemporary Problems*, (June 1964), pp. 663–690.

Ketchum, Marshall D. and Leon T. Kendall, ed., *Readings in Financial Institutions*, Parts Four and Six, (Boston: Houghton Mifflin Company), 1965.

Klopstock, Fred M., "The International Money Market," *The Journal of Finance*, (May 1965), pp. 182–208.

Knaus, Robert L., "A Reappraisal of the Role of Disclosure," *Michigan Law Review*, (February 1964), pp. 607–648.

Kuznets, Simon, *Capital in the American Economy: Its Formation and Financing*, Chapters 5, 6, and 8. (Princeton: Princeton University Press), 1961.

Latame, Henry Allan, "Price Changes in Equity Securities," *The Journal of Finance*, (April 1959), pp. 252–264.

Law, Warren A., "New Trend in Finance: The Negotiable C. D.," *Harvard Business Review*, (January-February 1963), pp. 115–126.

Leffler, George L., rev. by Loring C. Farwell, *The Stock Market*, 3rd edition, (New York: The Ronald Press Company), 1963.

Lintner, John, "The Financing of Corporations," in Edward S. Mason, ed., *The Corporation in Modern Society*, (Cambridge: Harvard University Press), 1961, pp. 166–201.

Loll, Leo M. and Julian Buckley, *Over-the-Counter Securities Markets*, (Englewood Cliffs: Prentice-Hall, Inc.), 1961.

Lombourne, Richard W., "Institutional Investing," *Financial Analysts Journal*, (November-December 1961), pp. 61–70.

Loss, Louis, *Securities Regulation*, (Boston: Little, Brown and Company) Volume I-III, 1961.

Ludtke, James B., *The American Financial System: Markets and Institutions*, (Boston: Allyn and Bacon, Inc.), 1961.

Meigs, James A., "The Changing Role of Banks in the Market for Equities," *The Journal of Finance*, (May 1965), pp. 368–378.

von Mehren, Robert B. and John C. McCarroll, "The Proxy Rules: A

Case Study in Administrative Process," *Law and Contemporary Problems*, (June 1964), pp. 728–748.

Miller, Merton R., "Dividend Policy, Growth, and Valuation of Shares," *The Journal of Business of the University of Chicago*, (1961), pp. 411–433.

Mindell, Joseph, "How News Affects Market Trends," *Financial Analysts Journal*, (January-February 1961), pp. 17–22.

Money Market Investments, The Risk and the Return, (New York: Morgan Guaranty Trust Company of New York), 1964.

Mundheim, Robert H., ed., *Conference on Securities Regulation*, (Chicago: Commerce Clearing House, Inc.), 1965.

Mundheim, Robert H. and Gordon D. Henderson, "Applicability of the Federal Securities Laws to Pension and Profit Sharing Plans," *Law and Contemporary Problems*, (June 1964), pp. 795–841.

Murray, Roger F., "Urgent Questions About The Stock Market," *Harvard Business Review*, (September-October 1964), pp. 53–59.

The National Bureau of Economic Research, "Research in the Capital Markets," *The Journal of Finance*, (Supplement: May 1964).

Neill, Humphrey B., *The Inside Story of the Stock Exchange*, (New York: B. C. Forbes & Sons Publishing Co., Inc.), 1950.

New York Stock Exchange, "The Stock Market Under Stress," March 1963. "Institutional Shareownership, a Report on Financial Institutions and the Stock Market," New York, 1964. "Public Transaction Study," March 10, 1965, thirteenth in a continuing series. "Shareownership, U.S.A.," 1965 Census of Shareowners, fifth in a periodic series. "Institutions and the Stock Market," issued quarterly. "The Corporate Director and the Investing Public," November, 1965. "The Corporate Director and the Investing Public," November, 1965. "The Exchange Community in 1975: A Report, its Potential, Problems, and Prospects," December, 1965.

Nichols, Dorothy M., "Trading in Federal Funds," Washington, D.C., *Board of Governors of the Federal Reserve System*, (Washington, D.C.), 1965.

Pecora, Ferdinand, *Wall Street Under Oath*, (New York: Simon and Schuster), 1939.

Rappaport, Louis H., *SEC Accounting Practice and Procedure*, second edition, (New York: The Ronald Press Company), 1963.

Redlich, Fritz, *The Molding of American Banking, Men, and Ideas*, Part II, (New York: Hafner Publishing Company), 1951.

Robbins, Sidney M., and Nester E. Terlechyj, *Money Metropolis*, (Cambridge: Harvard University Press), 1960.

Robbins, Sidney M. and Walter Werner, "Professor Stigler Revisited," *The Journal of Business of the University of Chicago*, (October 1964), pp. 406–413.

Roberts, Edwin A., Jr., *The Stock Market*, (Silver Springs: The National Observer), 1965.

Robinson, Ronald I., *Money and Capital Markets*, (New York: Mcgraw Hill Book Company, Inc.), 1964.

Robinson, Ronald I. and Robert Bartell, Jr., "Uneasy Partnership:
 SEC/NYSE," *Harvard Business Review*, (January-February
 1965), pp. 76–88.

Schneider, Carl W., "SEC Filings—Their Content and Use," *Financial
 Analysts Journal*, (March-April 1965), pp. 42–48.

Schultz, Birl E., *The Securities Market, and How it Works*, rev. ed.,
 (New York: Harper and Row, Publishers), 1963.

Scott, Ira O., Jr., *Government Securities Markets*, (New York: McGraw
 Hill Book Company), 1965.

Selden, Richard T., *Trends and Cycles in the Commercial Paper Market*, (New York: National Bureau of Economic Research), 1963.

Seligman, Daniel and T. A. Wise, "New Forces in the Stock Market,"
 Fortune, (February 1964), pp. 92–95.

Securities and Exchange Commission, "A 25 year Summary of the
 Activities of the Securities and Exchange Commission, 1934–
 1959," (Washington), 1961. "The Work of the Securities and
 Exchange Commsision" *Annual Reports*. (Washington), 1962.

"The SEC Report of the Special Study of Securities Markets and Subse-
 quent Developments." A series of papers and discussion at the
 December 1965 meeting of the American Finance Association,
 Journal of Finance, in press.

Securities Research Unit, Wharton School of Finance and Commerce,
 University of Pennsylvania, in cooperation with the Investment
 Bankers Association, *Banking and the New Issues Market*, a series
 of monographs, in press.

Silberman, Lee, "Critical Examination of SEC Proposals," *Harvard
 Business Review*, (November-December 1964), pp. 121–132.

Silverberg, Stanley, "Bank Trust Investments: Their Size and Significance," *The National Banking Review*, (June 1964), pp. 577–598.

Spray, David E., ed., *The Principal Stock Exchanges of the World—
 Their Operation, Structure and Development*, (Washington, D.C.:
 International Economic Publishers, Inc.), 1964.

Sprinkel, Beryl W., *Money and Stock Prices*, (Homewood, Illinois:
 Richard D. Irwin, Inc.), 1964.

Sobel, Robert, *The Big Board, A History of the New York Stock
 Market*, (New York: The Free Press), 1965.

Stigler, George J., "Public Regulation of the Securities Markets," *The
 Journal of Business of the University of Chicago*, (April 1964),
 pp. 117–142.

Stone, Robert W., "The Changing Structure of the Money Markets,"
 The Journal of Finance, (May 1965), pp. 229–238.

Telser, Lester G., "A Theory of Speculation Relating Profitability and
 Stability," *Review of Economics and Statistics*, (August 1959),
 pp. 295–307.

United States of America vs. Henry S. Morgan, et al., in the *District Court of the United States for the Southern District of New York*, Opinion of Harold R. Medina, n.d.

United States Government, 84th Congress, 1st Session Staff Report to the Committee on Banking and Currency, United States Senate, *Factors Affecting the Stock Market*, (Washington), 1955. 84th Congress, 1st Session, Report together with Individual Views and Minority Views of the Committee on Banking and Currency, United States Senate, *Stock Market Study*, (Washington), 1955. 87th Congress, 2nd Session, House of Representatives, Committee on Interstate and Foreign Commerce, *A Study of Mutual Funds*, (Washington), 1962. 88th Congress, 1st Session, *Report of Special Study of Securities Markets of the Securities and Exchange Commission*, Parts 1–5, (Washington), 1963.

Waterman, Merwin, H., *Investment Banking Functions, Their Evolution and Adaptation to Business Finance*, (Ann Arbor: Bureau of Business Research, School of Business Administration, University of Michigan), 1958.

Weiss, Ezra, *Registration and Regulation of Brokers and Dealers*, (Bureau of Economic Affairs), 1964.

Whitney, Jack M., II, "The SEC and the Financial Analyst," *Financial Analysts Journal*, (July-August 1963), pp. 11–16.

Williams, Charles M., "Senior Securities—Boon for Banks," *Harvard Business Review*, (July-August 1963), pp. 82–94.

Wise, T. A., "Wall Street's Main Event: SEC vs. the Specialist," *Fortune*, (May 1964), pp. 149–152.

Wise, T. A. and the editors of *Fortune*, *The Insiders*, (New York: Doubleday and Company) 1962.

Index

accounting, computerized, 270; *see also* computer
Addressograph-Multigraph Corporation, 134
Administrative Procedure Act, 68, 75
ADR (American Depositary Receipt), 271
after-market redistributions, 88
Albany, N.Y., investment banking in, 167
Allied Crude Vegetable Oil Refining Corporation, 117
Allied Stores Corporation, 18
allocation function, investment banking, 172–176
American Commercial Alcohol Company, 39–40
American Depositary Receipt, 271
American Mind, The (Commager), 78 n.
American Stock Exchange, 21, 26, 74–75, 147–148, 182, 193, 195, 198, 202–203, 251–253, 271, 284; reorganization of, 112

American Telephone and Telegraph Company, 197
Amex, *see* American Stock Exchange
Am-Quote system, 272
antifraud rules, 46, 90–91, 97
antitrust suits, 274–280
artificial market, creation of, 38–44
Atlantic Research Corporation, 93
auction process, 224, 243; *see also* bidding
Austin Nichols & Company, 117
automation, in stock exchange, 190–191, 200, 210–212, 285
Axton-Fisher Tobacco Company, 97

bank commercial paper, 9
banker, investment, *see* investment banking; traditional concept of, 17
bankers' acceptances, 6–7
Banking Act of 1933, 170
Bank of Japan, 141–145
Bankruptcy Act, 60
Bartell, H. Robert, Jr., 161 n., 200 n., 228 n.

bears, versus bulls, 42, 148
Bernstein, Marvin H., 72
bidding, on stock-exchange floor, 22–24
block discounts, 182, 262
block positioning, 224
Blyth & Company, 254
Boeing Company, 134
bond broker, 27; *see also* broker; broker dealer
bonds, Government, *see* Government bonds and securities
bond trading, 27
bookkeeping, joint, 270
Boston Stock Exchange, 247, 250, 269, 283
broker, bond, 27; floor, 23–25; lead, 223; odd-lot, 27; role and operation of, 22
broker-dealer, avoidance of, 227; capital positions of, 143; nonmember, 265; number of, 166; odd-lot business of, 27, 179; quotations by, 207–208; rate schedules for, 177; regulation of loans by, 103–104; self-regulation of, 114; supervision of, 130–131; underwriting of unseasoned issues by, 172; uniform accounting for, 185
Brooks, John, 42 n.
Brown, Russell R., 39–40
Brownian motion, 46
bulls, versus bears, 42, 148
buy-backs, 12

cabinet method, of bond trading, 27
Cady, Roberts & Company, 97
call, meaning of term, 34
call market, 4–5, 23
capital market, 14–29; new-issue market and, 14–20; trading markets and, 20–29
Carlisle & Jacquelin, 27, 188
Cary, William L., 65–67, 71
Case, J. I., Company, 98 n.
Casper, Hugh M., 114 n.
Celler, Emanuel, 278
Census of Shareowners, 137
Center for Research in Security Prices, University of Chicago, 139
Central Certificate System, 25

Central Computer Accounting Corporation, 25, 270
certificates of deposits (CD), 7–8
change, need for, 78
Chase Manhattan Bank, 275
Chase National Bank, 39
Chicago, Burlington & Quincy Railroad Company, 41
Chicago, University of, 139
Chicago Board of Trade, 247
Civil Aeronautics Board, 71
Civil War, 4, 168, 191
Cohen, Manuel F., 71, 277–279
college and university endowments, 221
Commager, Henry Steele, 78
commercial banks, short-term unsecured negotiable notes, 10; stock operations of, 169–170, 217
Commerce Clearing House, Inc., 207
commercial paper, 6
commission rates, 175–188, 264–265, 272; history of, 69; structure and level of, 178–180; theory of, 184–188; underlying issues in, 180–184
Committee on Interstate and Foreign Commerce, 84
Communications Satellite Act of 1962, 15
Communications Satellite Corporation (Comsat), 15, 134
competition, importance of, 266–272; versus negotiation, 16–18; versus regulation, 272–274; reliance on, 268
Comptroller of Currency, 9
computer, use of in stock exchange, 23–24, 143–144, 200–201, 211–212, 270
Continental Air Lines, 134
Continental Can Company, 110
Conway, Carle C., 109
Conway Committee, 110
Cooke, Jay, 168
Cootner, Paul H., 46 n.
Corcoran, Thomas G., 153, 163
Corn Exchange Bank & Trust Company, 275
corporations, licensing and, 86; secrecy of, 49